ITALIAN COLONIALISM IN SOMALIA

ITALIAN COLONIALISM IN SOMALIA

ROBERT L. HESS

THE UNIVERSITY OF CHICAGO PRESS

CHICAGO   LONDON

Library of Congress Catalog Card Number: 66-14115

THE UNIVERSITY OF CHICAGO PRESS, CHICAGO & LONDON
The University of Toronto Press, Toronto 5, Canada

Preface

In the vast literature dealing with European colonialism in Africa attention has focused primarily on the activities of Great Britain and France. For the story of German activity in Africa, Harry Rudin's *Germans in the Cameroons* (New Haven: Yale University Press, 1938) marked a new departure and became a classic of colonial history and of the history of Africa. James Duffy's *Portuguese Africa* (Cambridge, Mass.: Harvard University Press, 1957) accomplished the same task for the oldest colonial power in Africa. And in recent years scholars have turned to the role of Belgium in the unhappy Congo. Yet, other than the vast outpouring of propagandistic materials in the mid-1930's attacking Mussolini's rape of Ethiopia, little has appeared in print about Italian colonialism in Africa.

Sixty years ago Italy was regarded as one of the great powers sharing in the partition of Africa and the scramble for colonies. A relative latecomer, Italy aspired to extend her Eritrean beachhead into the fertile highlands of Ethiopia. During the same period she managed to gain influence over the Somali coast. But destiny seemed to beckon Italy onward to disaster and the ignominy of being the first European power to be defeated by an African state. Fifteen years after the battle of Adowa, in which an Italian army was defeated by the Ethiopian emperor, a resurgent colonialism brought Italy to Libyan shores, and Tripoli, Cyrenaica, and the Fezzan, together with Eritrea and Somalia, became what one Italian historian later aptly termed Mussolini's collection of deserts.

The undisguised imperialism of Fascist Italy in the 1930's, seemingly a throwback to the nineteenth century, again turned Italy's attention to Ethiopia, but Italian colonialism there is more often regarded as an extension of European power politics or as a milestone on the road to Munich than as an example of colonialism per se. Consequently, the work of Italy in Africa is little known. Too many people identify Italian colonialism with Mussolini's blusterings and with his invasion of an apparently innocent Ethiopia. Obviously, there was much more to Italian colonialism than this one episode of aggression. In Somalia, in fact, the history of Italian colonialism is a decidedly different tale of attempts to avoid political commitments and military operations. When the military was employed, the government believed that it was for the purpose of peaceful penetration and for assuring economic development. Only with the advent of Fascism did the colony acquire a militaristic veneer; underneath, the policies of an earlier generation remained unchanged.

It is the purpose of this study to describe the workings of Italian colonialism in Somalia in order to throw additional light on the nature of European imperialism in Africa. In some respects Italian colonial policy paralleled that of other countries; those who are familiar with the colonial history of Africa will find many similarities. But the Italian case also reveals a curious ambivalence toward colonialism and a counter tendency of minimalism that thwarted the expansionists. Italy's two experiments in government by chartered company contribute to an understanding of a trend that brought to the African continent the Royal Niger Company, the British South Africa Company, the Imperial British East Africa Company, the Deutsch-Ostafrikanische Gesellschaft, the Companhia de Moçambique, the Companhia do Nyassa, and the Compagnie du Katanga. The chartered company, neglected except for Heinrich H. Kraft's *Chartergesellschaften als*

Mittel zur Erschliessung kolonialer Gebiete (Hamburg: Friederichsen, De Gruyter & Co., 1943) and M. J. De Kiewiet's doctoral dissertation, "History of the Imperial British East Africa Company, 1876–1895" (University of London, 1956) is worthy of comparative study as one of the main agents for the introduction of colonialism into Africa. Unwittingly, the chartered company often established the basis for official government colonial policy after the termination of administrative concessions.

In an era of emergent African states and strident African nationalism, a study of European colonialism in Africa, especially of a colonialism that ended two decades before the territory's achievement of independence, is almost an anachronism. Yet only through the study of the colonial past, in close conjunction with the reconstruction of an authentic African history, can a better understanding of contemporary Africa be achieved. Colonial history and African history go hand in hand as companion fields.

This study does not purport to be a comprehensive history of the Somali people, although much may be learned about the Somali in scattered sections of the book. On the other hand, it does describe the type of colonial regime to which the Somali were subjected. Moreover, the present Somali Republic, independent since 1960, is the political descendant, not of tribal Somalia, but of the Italian colony of Somalia as well as of its successor governments, the wartime British military administration and the postwar United Nations Trust Territory of Somalia under Italian administration.

The Somali language does not at present have a written form, and there is no generally accepted style of transliterating Somali names into the Latin alphabet. The two most widely used systems call for transliteration into an Italian orthography, as is the practice today in the southern region of the Somali Republic, or into an English orthography, as in the northern region. Since the use of Italian orthography

poses difficulties for the reader who is not familiar with
Italian pronunciation, I have chosen to use a modified English orthography. Thus the Italian "Mogadiscio" has been
rendered for the English-speaking reader's convenience as
the more easily pronounced "Mogadishu." Similarly, "Chisi-
maio" has been rendered as "Kismayu," "Gesira" as "Jesira,"
"Uarsceik" as "Warsheik," "Belet Uen" as "Belet Wen,"
"Mohamed Abdille Hasan" as "Muhammad Abdullah Hassan," "Iusuf Ali" as "Yusuf Ali," "scir" as "shir," and so on.

Lastly, a word about the name of the territory is in order.
Although the British refer to the former Italian colony as
Italian Somaliland, the colony's official name was Somalia
Italiana, and the name "Somalia" was in general use in Ital-
ian, Somali, and Arabic, even as it is today in the Somali
Republic. Throughout this book "Somaliland" is reserved
for reference to the British Somaliland Protectorate and
"Somalia" for reference to the former Italian colony, which
is now the southern region of the Somali Republic.

The major part of the research for this study was conducted
in Rome in the historical archives of the Comitato per la
Documentazione dell'Opera dell'Italia in Africa, successor to
the Colonial Office of the Ministry of Foreign Affairs (1882–
1912), the Ministry of Colonies (1912–37), and the Ministry
of Italian Africa (1937–43). The generous support of the Fulbright program and the co-operation of the Italian authorities
permitted me to be one of the first non-government scholars
to gain entry into these archives, which contain more than
eighty thousand documents on Somalia alone. I wish to express my gratitude to Richard W. Downar, Gabriella Rombo,
and Cipriana Scelba of the American Commission for Cultural Exchange with Italy for their assistance in facilitating
my work in Rome; and to Mario Toscano, historical adviser
to the Italian Ministry of Foreign Affairs, Renato Mori, director of the historical archives of the Ministry of Foreign
Affairs, and Francesco S. Caroselli, last governor of colonial

Somalia, for their assistance in helping me to gain access to the necessary materials. An especial debt of gratitude is owed Mario Gazzini, director of the historical archives of the Comitato per la Documentazione dell'Opera dell'Italia in Africa, who graciously accorded me help and encouragement in my research. I wish also to thank the staffs of the Biblioteca della Camera dei Deputati and the Istituto Italiano per l'Africa.

With the permission of the Fulbright Commission in Rome and the help of Yale University I was able to visit Somalia in the fall of 1957. I am indebted to Ambassador Cristoforo Fracassi of the Direzione Generale della Somalia for his aid in overcoming bureaucratic obstacles and clearing the way for my trip to the horn of Africa. In Mogadishu, Somalia, of great assistance were Sergio Apollonio, head of the Ufficio Studi of the Italian Trusteeship Administration; Alphonso A. Castagno of the African Studies Center, Boston University; Michele Pirone of the Istituto Universitario; and John J. Vianney, editor of the *Somali Chronicle*. Additional thanks for letters of introduction are extended to John Phillips and D. Crena de Iongh of the International Bank in Washington and to Robert S. Lopez of Yale University. Finally, I would like to express my deep appreciation for the inspiration and close personal attention of Harry R. Rudin of Yale University.

Contents

MAPS

Introduction

The Italian Background

Late nineteenth-century Italy was uncertain whether or not to set out upon the road to imperialism. Although political unification had been achieved, true national unity was far off. Regionalism worked against the forces of national unity. The prosperous industrial north and the poverty-stricken agricultural south were continually at odds. The church-state relationship demanded a solution and yet remained unresolved. Rapid economic growth alternated with severe depressions and produced the social conditions for a class struggle that reinforced the lower classes' historic distrust of government.

Italian imperialist thought at the time of the partition of Africa had little connection with the generally accepted ideology of European imperialism. It had no place for theories of social Darwinism, *Realpolitik,* racism, or extreme nationalism. Its main theoretical arguments were drawn either from Risorgimento leaders like Giuseppe Mazzini, Vincenzo Gioberti, and Cesare Balbo or from the commercial expansionists. For the first group, Italy had a mandate to extend its culture comparable to France's *mission civilisatrice.* For the others, economic development and population pressures demanded overseas expansion. Yet from the same background came anti-imperialist arguments. Imperialism was the antithesis of liberal Mazzinian nationalism, which called for the limitation of national power within national boundaries as well as for irredentism. Colonialism would only undermine this kind of nationalism.

Socialists and Catholics also opposed expansionism. Unlike ideological socialists elsewhere, Italian socialists, both Marxists and syndicalists, opposed any policy that drew attention away from the immediate political, social, and economic problems of Italy. Italian missionaries in Africa, like Giuseppe Sapeto in Eritrea and Cardinal Guglielmo Massaia in Ethiopia, occasionally advocated Italian expansionism, but because of the church-state conflict, a sharp distinction was made between the goals of the church in Africa and those of the state it refused to recognize. Italy became the one colonial power in Africa whose goals were not furthered by missionaries.

Of all the devices and rationalizations put forth to convince the nation to undertake a policy of colonialism, those relating to problems of emigration and overpopulation received the most attention. Italian industry was insufficiently developed to absorb the vast number of unemployed workers. The country lacked the raw materials necessary for an industrial civilization, and there was little chance for improvement. By 1870 emigration had become a permanent feature of the national life, and publicists deplored the drain upon the national stock and the government's inertia about finding overseas colonies in which to settle surplus population under the Italian flag.

A second economic argument for colonialism, the search for overseas markets, was advanced when the threat of protectionist policies in England and the United States awakened Italian industrialists to the insecurity of Italy's position in international trade. Industrialists found ready allies in missionaries, explorers, and geographic and colonial societies, all of which had their counterparts in British, French, and German colonialism.

In the second half of the nineteenth century more than seventy Italian expeditions were sent to explore Africa. The emphasis was mostly on northeastern Africa. Italian explorers such as Orazio Antinori, Odoardo Beccari, Pietro Antonelli, Giuseppe Giulietti, and Antonio Cecchi crisscrossed Ethiopia, and many met martyrdom at the hands of hostile tribesmen. Backing the expeditions were geographic and colonial societies such as the Italian Geographic Society, whose bulletin was read throughout Italy; the African Geographic and Commercial Exploration Society, which sent Giulio Adamoli to Morocco, Romolo Gessi and Gaetano Casati to the Sudan, and Pellegrino Matteucci to Ethiopia; and the Italian African Society, which organized the first nationwide colonial conference at Naples in 1885.

A flood of expansionist pamphlets and books appeared as Italian writers awoke to the challenge of the Berlin Conference of 1885. Most of the colonialist writings were characterized by great emotionalism, but they also contained a certain element of caution. Men like Pasquale Turiello and Alfredo Oriani, who advocated the use of force, formed an unimportant minority. In general, the expansionist writers specified the need to avoid power struggles, to co-operate with other powers, and to manipulate alliances in order to obtain overseas benefits. Military conquest was ruled out. If there was to be colonialism, the only possible program would be one calling for peaceful commercial expansion.

In that era the Mediterranean was of prime importance to Italy; it was the focal point of Italian foreign policy and the basis of any colonial policy. For several decades southern Italians had crossed the narrow straits separating Italy from Tunisia. Foreign Minister Emilio Visconti Venosta had even considered partitioning Tunisia between Italy and France in 1864, but the example of France's costly colonial war in Algeria deterred him. Later Benedetto Cairoli, who served as both prime minister and foreign minister, assumed that French and Italian interests in Tunisia could coexist, but he was mistaken. Even if Italian settlers were more numerous, France had far greater investments to defend. When France, in May of 1881, sent troops into Tunisia and forced a protectorate upon the bey, the Italians, unwilling to act and without an ally, were eased out of Tunisia.

For a while, Tripoli was also in the public eye. The geographic societies pointed out the importance of the trade routes south from Tripoli to the Fezzan, Bornu, Wadai, and the western Sudan. Foreign Minister Pasquale Mancini was not averse to occupying Tripolitania in 1883 to forestall a French threat, but on the whole he was more interested in preserving the status quo in North Africa. If necessary, he would do all he could to prevent other countries from expanding in North Africa at the expense of Italy. For this reason he had in 1882 briefly considered joint action with England in Egypt.

Until 1884 Mancini was opposed to action in the Red Sea and the horn of Africa. The Rubattino Steamship Company had been established at Assab on the Red Sea since 1869, but it was not until ten years later that the government took possession of the port. Late in 1884 a new direction in Italian policy became evident. The government began to express political interest in the Red Sea, where formerly its interests had been exclusively defensive and economic and strictly nonpolitical.

Behind this change in outlook lay a changed situation in Africa. With startling thoroughness the Germans had intervened directly in Southwest Africa, Togo, the Cameroons, and Tanganyika. The French, who had been in the Red Sea region since 1862, intensified their activities and caused the Italians to fear that Assab would be outmaneuvered and that their economic interests in the Red Sea would be threatened. Moreover, as a result of the Mahdist uprising in the Sudan, Egypt withdrew its garrisons from Harar, Zeila, Berbera, Beilul, and Massawa. The British, with whom the Italians sought closer relations, were running into difficulties in Africa

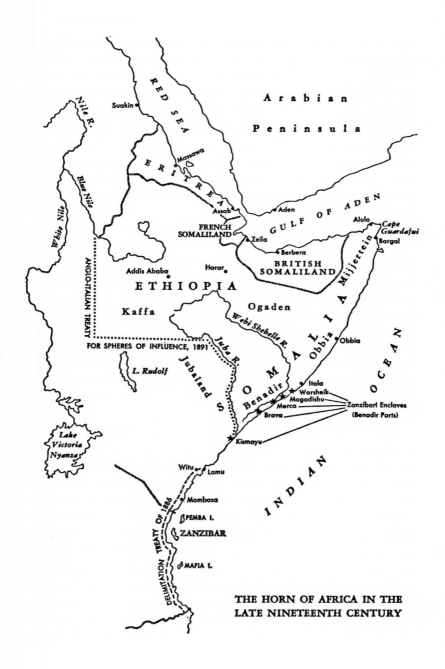

THE HORN OF AFRICA IN THE
LATE NINETEENTH CENTURY

and Asia just as Franco-German relations were seriously de-
teriorating. Against this background, colonialists in the
Italian parliament and throughout the nation demanded vigorous action to defend Italy's international prestige. On the
eve of the Berlin Conference public opinion, such as it was,
opposed the government's colonial policy because it seemed
to be leading Italy into isolation. For the first time, the industrial north, fearful lest Italy be excluded from the conference, became seriously interested in the prospects for colonialism and demanded that the government seek territories
to occupy.

The Somali Background

When the ground rules for the partition of Africa were agreed
upon at the Berlin Conference in 1885, Somalia was open to
penetration by European powers. At that time, the sultan of
Zanzibar exercised a shadowy sovereignty over the Benadir
ports of Kismayu, Brava, Merca, Mogadishu, and Warsheik.
In the north the two sultanates of Obbia and the Mijjertein
fought each other. The intervening lands were regarded as
res nullius, a no man's land occupied largely by nomadic
Somali tribes engaged in an endless quest for adequate pas-
turage and water for their vast herds and flocks.

The Benadir ports were the relics of an earlier age of Arab
city-states stretching from Mogadishu to Mozambique. In the
fourteenth century Ibn Battuta described Mogadishu as the
seat of a rich and powerful sultanate of great commercial
prosperity. Merca and Brava paralleled Mogadishu in their
commercial development. The city-states of Somalia also
traded with the Somali tribesmen of the interior, and the
coastal Arabs gradually intermarried with the Somali. When
the power of the doughty Portuguese extended northward
from the Cape of Good Hope, the coastal towns of Somalia
were of no immediate interest to them, for their sailing routes
from Mombasa and Malindi to Socotra and India bypassed
the Benadir. Nevertheless, the Portuguese made their pres-

ence felt as they disrupted Arab trading routes and caused the decline of Arab trading centers all along the coast of East Africa. On his return from India, Vasco da Gama bombarded Mogadishu. And in 1507, Tristão da Cunha sacked Brava. But the Portuguese left no mark on Somalia, although their incursions hastened the economic decline of the coastal towns. In 1698, when Mogadishu was occupied for a short time by Seif I of Oman during the period the Arabs were reconstituting their trading empire in East Africa, the Omani Arabs discovered that Mogadishu had lost its Arab character. The Benadir ports were now a backwater in the mainstream of East African history.

Mogadishu and the other coastal centers continued their existence as more or less independent political entities as the Somali nomads of the interior spread ever southward and established their own tribal political order. When new centers arose at Bardera and Geledi in the early nineteenth century, the coastal towns became increasingly economically dependent on the interior. In 1823 a squadron of Seyyid Said's ships called at Mogadishu and ordered the city to pay homage to the Omani sultan, who also controlled Zanzibar and much of the coast farther south. Even though Mogadishu was forced to recognize Seyyid Said, it was not until 1842 that the sultan could assert his authority on the Somali coast. Taking advantage of internal dissension, the sultan sent tax collectors to Brava, Merca, and Mogadishu. The military escort of the tax collector at Mogadishu consisted of two soldiers. Thus any authority the sultan of Oman and his successors in Zanzibar (Seyyid Said permanently moved his court from Oman to Zanzibar in 1840) may have had over Mogadishu was more nominal than real. The government of Mogadishu, which in the 1840's had a population of about five thousand, was left entirely to the local chiefs. In the background there loomed the shadow of Mogadishu's real sovereign, the sultan of Geledi. A dispute between two factions of the Shingani quarter of Mogadishu in 1871 gave the Zanzibari sultan an opportunity to establish a military outpost under the first "wali" (governor), Selim Yaqub, who was remarkably successful in winning the townspeople over to a mild form of subservience to their distant ruler. The price was high, however, for Selim Yaqub paid tribute to the sultan of Geledi, Ahmad Yusuf, and promised that his lands on the Webi Shebelle would never be entered.

Two years later, a grandson of Seyyid Said came to Mogadishu from Zanzibar as the second wali. His main achievement was the construction of the fortress known as the Garesa. But despite this very real symbol of his authority, the control of the sultan of Zanzibar over the towns continually diminished under the following nine walis until the system was finally done away with by the Italians in 1905.

Farther north, the Mijjertein region was undergoing a period of internal strife. For several generations the sultans of the Mijjertein had monopolized all maritime trade and run a well-organized industry of salvage operations for the many ships that went aground on the treacherous coast of Cape Guardafui. About 1870, Sultan Osman Mahmud was challenged by Yusuf Ali, a relative who had kept for himself all that had been salvaged from the wreck of a French steamer, the *Mekong*. To punish Yusuf Ali, Osman Mahmud ordered his men to burn several dhows belonging to Yusuf Ali and his followers. The dispute simmered for several years until their kinsmen arranged a temporary settlement. Yusuf Ali was appointed governor of Alula, and, to seal the bargain, Osman married Yusuf's daughter Aisha. In 1878, Yusuf Ali and several dissident chiefs rebelled and founded a sultanate farther south in lands seized from the Hawiya. At Obbia, Yusuf Ali built a fort and declared his independence of Osman Mahmud. In 1884, a peace settlement was again made by the two men, and Osman Mahmud recognized Yusuf Ali as a sultan in his own right. Their rivalry, however, did not end with the peace settlement.

As early as the twelfth century, the Somali tribes of the interior had begun to wrest control of the land from its Bantu and Galla inhabitants. The nomadic Dir, Darod, Ishaak, and Hawiya tribal families occupied northern Somalia, the Ogaden region of Ethiopia, and the North Eastern Region of Kenya. The Rahanwein and the Digil, whom the other groups considered inferior because of intermarriage with the Galla and the Bantu and because of their adoption of a sedentary way of life, moved into the region between the Juba and the Webi Shebelle rivers. All groups proudly trace their genealogies to Muslim Arab antecedents and ultimately to Muhammad. The Hawiya, or a related group, were among the first Somali to move southward from their ancestral home in the region of the Gulf of Aden. In the twelfth century the Ajuran Hawiya crossed the Webi Shebelle into southern Somalia. They had been preceded by the Jiddu Digil, whom they fought against and drove in the direction of Brava. Ajuran tribal traditions recall at least twenty generations in southern Somalia and connections with Mogadishu in the sixteenth century. Pressure from other Hawiya groups in turn forced the Ajuran to move southwest to their present lands on the east bank of the Juba. In general, the Hawiya, and later the Darod, followed an invasion route from the northeast to the southwest.

The Digil and Rahanwein, in contrast, invaded southern Somalia from the Ogaden. They penetrated the plateau region around Baidoa, and early in the seventeenth century, they continued their southward drive as the Galla retreated. Some Digil groups remained in southeastern Ethiopia; the larger number advanced beyond Lugh. In the eighteenth century the Rahanwein fought the Galla and occupied Bur Acaba and the middle Juba valley after a long series of wars. The final great migration came with the occupation of the Jubaland by a section of the Darod who first forced their way between the Ajuran Hawiya and the Karanle Hawiya and crossed the Webi Shebelle. After occupying the plateau north of the Digil tribes, they then entered the Jubaland. Not until the second half of the nineteenth century did they drive the last of the Galla from the area. With the advent of the Europeans, the great migratory movement stopped, although southward pressures continued.

Throughout the nineteenth century European contacts with the Somali coast yielded evidence of nothing but hostility. The coastal tribes generally attacked landing parties in search of water along the barren coast north of the Juba. In 1811, the Bombay government sent Captain T. Smee to East Africa in hope of learning something about Mungo Park's disappearance in the Niger valley six years earlier. It was thought that Park might have crossed the continent from west to east. Smee found the Somali coast bare "of man or beast or plant" until he reached the mouth of the Juba. He dismissed the towns as inconsiderable and found no safe anchorage. His prospecting expedition stirred no interest in the area. By mid-century, as Seyyid Said extended his influence over the coast, the pattern for the rest of the century was fairly well established. Mogadishu, Brava, and Merca, and a small area around each of these once great city-states owed nominal allegiance to Zanzibar. The intervening coastal areas were completely independent of outside influences.

Nevertheless, coastal reconnaissance continued. In 1843, the Englishman William Christopher sailed along the coast, disembarked at Mogadishu, and reached Geledi. From 1846 to 1848, Captain Charles J. Cruttenden, on a commission from the Indian government, explored the northern coast and then, in a feat of daring, penetrated to the interior lands of the Warsangeli Darod. During the same period the French captain Charles Guillain explored the southern coast, made extensive studies of the Benadir, landed at Mogadishu, where he managed to compile the history of that once glorious city, and visited the sultan of Geledi. Guillain's record of the voy-

age of the *Ducouëdic* is one of the major sources of information about Somalia in the past century.

 Exploration of the interior begin with the German explorer Carl von der Decken, who traveled in East Africa
from 1859 until his death near Bardera in 1865. While Von
der Decken traveled up the Juba, the French commander
Vicomte Fleuriot de Langle explored the coast in 1861. Seven
years later, another German explorer, Gottlob Kinzelbach,
stopped at Geledi, his first halt in an effort to reach Bardera. He never continued his journey; his hosts poisoned his
food.

Egyptians made their appearance in the horn of Africa in
1875 in an attempt to gain control of the unknown wealth
of the Ethiopian highlands and the source of the Nile. After
garrisons were established at Tadjoura, Zeila, Harar, and
Berbera, the khedive sent an expedition to the Somali coast.
An Egyptian ship attempted to sail up the Juba, and for a
time the Egyptians challenged the authority of the sultan of
Zanzibar by landing briefly at Kismayu and Brava. The recall of the Juba expedition in 1879 and the withdrawal of
the isolated garrisons in 1884 marked the end of this Egyptian interlude in Somalia.

After the Egyptian invasion, Europeans paid greater attention to the Somali coast. In the early 1880's Antonio Cecchi
published accounts of his travels from Zeila to Kaffa and
staunchly advocated tapping Kaffa's trade through an outlet
on the Indian Ocean. Twenty years earlier, Guglielmo Massaia, apostolic vicar of Gallaland, had tried to interest the
Sardinian government in a similar project. He hinted at
Brava, and hence Somalia, as a southern gateway for commercial and missionary penetration of Ethiopia. The Sardinian premier, Camillo Cavour, however, was occupied
with the more pressing problem of Italian unification. In
1879, the Duke of Genoa inspected the coast from Berbera
to Cape Guardafui. The first major inquiry into the Mijjertein was made from 1878 to 1881 by Georges Révoil, whose

three trips during this period helped fill an important gap in knowledge of Somalia. In 1882, on another journey farther south, Révoil traveled from Mogadishu to Geledi, where he was faced with the familiar Somali hostility and forced to retreat to the coast. Little was yet known of the arid steppes of the interior and its harsh conditions of life. Less was known about its scattered nomadic population. When the Berlin Conference adjourned in February, 1885, Somalia was still a *terra incognita* compared with the rest of the continent.

CHAPTER ONE

The Diplomacy of Imperialism:
Italy, Zanzibar, and Somalia, 1885–93

The first Italian efforts in East Africa and Somalia date from 1885. In the spring of that year Foreign Minister Pasquale Mancini spoke guardedly to a Parliament that reflected the divisions in Italian national life. Anticolonialism, despite the outraged cries of the advocates of overseas expansion, was still very much alive, and Mancini did not dare to speak his piece outright. Rather, he proposed action in Africa on the one basis acceptable to all parties, "the duty to search for outlets for the emigration that has now attained alarming heights." For this reason, he claimed, the popular explorer, Antonio Cecchi, had been sent on a mission to the Juba region in Somalia, and for similar reasons he was also considering an expedition to the Congo under Giacomo Bove.[1] In his speeches there was an optimistic ring: the Cecchi mission and others would surely discover vast fertile areas awaiting peaceful cultivation and commercial penetration.

Mancini's ambitions for Italy had earlier led him to formulate a comprehensive program for expansion into East Africa. His first aim was to punish the Eritrean tribesmen guilty of the massacre of Gustavo Bianchi's exploratory party; to effect this he planned a military expedition to Massawa and Assab. The second step was to be the occupation of the Eritrean coast from Assab to Suakin. After this, he anticipated some com-

[1] *Atti Parlamentari: Camera dei Deputati,* March 17 and May 16, 1885.

mon action with Great Britain in the Sudan. Fourth, Mancini had his eye on the commercial and colonizing possibilities of Harar, then known to Europe through the writings of Richard F. Burton, Arthur Rimbaud, and others as a rich trading city. And last, he aimed at the Juba and Somalia, another link in the long chain of proposals presented to the Chamber of Deputies in May, 1885.[2]

A careful examination of a map of northeastern Africa reveals the true portent of Mancini's program. The essential element of this master plan was the possession of Massawa. Once established in that port, the Italians could bar further French advances along the Red Sea coast and control that Ethiopian outlet to the sea. Occupation of the Eritrean coast would then enable Italy to join with Britain in the troubled Sudan. To the east and south, the occupation of Harar and Somalia would complete a pincer movement that would enclose Ethiopia and permit its peaceful penetration.

The plan was too pat, however. Mancini was ignorant of the actual state of affairs within the eastern horn of Africa and did not properly appreciate the aspirations of Menelik, king of Shoa, who coveted the throne of Ethiopia and lands to the east and south of his kingdom. Furthermore, despite the occupation of Massawa in February, 1885, Parliament failed to support Mancini's full program because of the national preoccupation with internal questions and because Mancini was not forceful enough to push the program through. It will readily be seen, however, that more than one aspect of this program survived in later Italian colonial expansion.

Several weeks after the occupation of Massawa, Antonio Cecchi arrived in East Africa. His orders were to visit Zanzi-

2 Mancini, Rome, to Prime Minister Agostino Depretis, January 22, 1885, Archivio Storico dell'ex Ministero dell'Africa Italiana (hereinafter cited as ASMAI), pos. 2, f. 1; Mancini to Depretis, January 6, 1885, ASMAI, pos. 65, f. 1. [AUTHOR'S NOTE: In references to ASMAI, "pos." = position and "f." = folder.]

bar and its mainland possessions and to explore the Juba
River as a possible commercial highway into the interior.
Cecchi and Commander Matteo Fecarotta of the *Barbarigo*
had the additional task of negotiating a commercial agreement with Sultan Said Bargash. Their major interest, however, was on the mainland, for Mancini had instructed them
to determine whether or not the Juba valley was under Zanzibari sovereignty.[3] No mention was made of the possibility of
white settlement in that area. In this first stage of Italian interest in East Africa, Italy aspired to a leading role as a colonial power equal to Great Britain, Germany, and France.

The choice of Cecchi to head the mission was logical, for he
had been active in the exploration of northeast Africa. In 1876
he had led an expedition from Zeila to the frontiers of Kaffa
in southern Ethiopia. From that time on he was an ardent
partisan of Italian expansion into the horn. Cecchi was probably the first to succeed in directing Italian attention toward
the Somali coast. On the basis of his explorations and his
often unfounded enthusiasm for the area, he insisted on the
importance of the Juba River as the key to a much larger
colonial program:

Once we acquire with certainty the knowledge that the Juba is
navigable . . . then it is certain that it will become the most natural artery for the exportation of the abundant coffee harvest of
Kaffa and the surrounding regions. . . . Now that our Italy has
established itself at Massawa . . . it is possible for Italy to extend
its possessions toward the south. . . . The Juba would thus mark
the extreme southern boundary of our possessions.[4]

On the last day of April Sultan Said Bargash granted the
two Italians an audience. Initially, the sultan was willing to

---

[3] Mancini to Cecchi and Fecarotta, January 4, 1885, *Documenti diplomatici italiani presentati al Parlamento italiano dal Ministro degli Affari Esteri (Blanc): Somalia italiana (1885–1895)* (Rome: Tipografia della Camera dei Deputati, 1895), doc. 1, p. 3 (hereinafter cited as *Libro Verde*). See also Man-cini, Rome, to Cecchi, May 6, 1885, ASMAI, pos. 55/1, f. 1.

[4] Cecchi and Fecarotta, Zanzibar, to Mancini, May 9, 1885, ASMAI, pos. 55/1, f. 2.

negotiate the cession of Kismayu and several other points on the mainland, but events there and at court soon raised some doubts. To Cecchi it seemed that England, France, and Germany were conspiring to embarrass Italy and exclude it from the area. Toward the end of May, he and Fecarotta were convinced that the sultan would not cede any territory.[5] Upon Cecchi's return from a hurried exploration of the coast, the sultan informed him that he no longer wanted to cede Kismayu to Italy. German and Arab interests at court had triumphed. The negotiations for the commercial treaty, on the other hand, progressed rapidly, and on May 28 the treaty was signed. Late in July the *Barbarigo* explored the Somali coast. Because it was the monsoon season, the results of the mission were not nearly so favorable as had been expected. On his return to Italy, however, Cecchi continued to pressure the government to tap the "rich commercial resources" of Somalia.[6]

Despite Mancini's interest in East Africa, Italy had not developed any great commercial interests there. There were only two or three Italians in Zanzibar and its mainland possessions. Almost all the trade between Zanzibar and Italy was handled by Vincenzo Filonardi, who had been active in the clove trade for several years.[7] With the support of the Italian Society for Trade with Africa, Filonardi operated in East Africa in much the same way as other European traders. In 1884, the Bank of Rome and several of his old friends from the Society helped him to form the trading company of V. Filonardi e Compagnia with capital of 180,000 lire. Upon the arrival of Cecchi and Fecarotta, Filonardi, who was probably the most influential Italian in all East Africa, actively collab-

---

[5] Cecchi, Zanzibar, to Mancini, May 16, 1885, and Mancini, Rome, to Cecchi, May 26, 1885, ASMAI, pos. 55/1, f. 1.

[6] Cecchi, Pesaro, to Foreign Minister C. F. Nicolis di Robilant, August 27, 1886, ASMAI, pos. 59/1, f. 1.

[7] Although there is no published work on Filonardi, a short biography may be found in an unpublished collection of biographies of Italians in Africa, galleys 331–32, in ASMAI.

orated with them. At this time his annual trade amounted to approximately 233,000 lire (or about $50,000). Cecchi and Fecarotta realized Filonardi's usefulness and recommended that the foreign ministry appoint him to head the new Italian consulate in Zanzibar.[8]

As Italian consul in Zanzibar, Filonardi frequently reported on the political situation. He found the sultan to be disturbed by a German eruption into East Africa. In August, 1885, five German warships threatened to bombard Zanzibar unless the sultan immediately recognized a German protectorate over five towns on the mainland. Unable to win British support, Said Bargash capitulated to the German demands. Shortly afterward, an Anglo-French-German commission was formed to determine once and for all the extent of the sultan's possessions on the mainland. In their report, the three European commissioners decided arbitrarily which parts of the coast belonged to Zanzibar. In October, Britain and Germany agreed to recognize the sultan's authority only over the islands of Zanzibar, Pemba, Mafia, and Lamu; a coastal strip from the Mninjani River to Kipini to a depth of ten miles inland; and in the north, the Benadir ports of Kismayu, Brava, Merca, and Mogadishu, with their respective hinterlands for a radius of ten miles, and Warsheik for a radius of five miles. The hinterland of the coastal strip was divided into British and German spheres of influence at the Umba River. On December 4, 1886, Said Bargash signed the treaty of delimitation.[9]

While Britain and Germany paved the way for partition, Filonardi observed the sultan's dislike of the Germans. His informants reported that emissaries of the sultan had sailed for the Somali coast to incite the local populations against the

[8] Printed circular on the trade of V. Filonardi e Compagnia, accompanying a letter to prospective stockholders signed by Carlo Filonardi, a nephew of Vincenzo, Rome, March 19, 1888, ASMAI, pos. 55/2, f. 14; Cecchi and Fecarotta to Mancini, No. 1157 (undated, *ca.* June 5, 1885), ASMAI, pos. 55/1, f. 2.

[9] E. Hertslet, *The Map of Africa by Treaty* (3d ed.; London: His Majesty's Stationery Office, 1909), I, 304–8.

Germans. Zanzibari Arabs refused to give news to German landing parties, to sell fresh meat, or even to tell them where there were springs of fresh water. Filonardi wrote that the sultan "hated and feared the Germans. . . . Not only would he be pleased if Italy took possession of the Somali region, but he would support it wholeheartedly." He claimed that the circumstances gave Italy an unforeseen opportunity to acquire the Somali region at small cost.[10]

Filonardi was not mistaken. In September, Said Bargash offered Kismayu to Italy. The offer was similar to the one he had made to Cecchi eighteen months earlier. The plan was the sultan's own; Filonardi's account of the offer stressed Said Bargash's initiative in the matter.[11] His Somali subjects had pleaded with him for assistance against the German ships then off the coast of Somalia. His one hope lay in playing the Europeans off against each other, a hope that was short lived since Filonardi soon advised him that the Italians had no intention of using force to implement their colonial policy. He withdrew the offer, and Zanzibar fell increasingly under the influence of Great Britain and Germany. Italy, the latecomer, had failed to take the opportunity to extend its influence and become the equal of Great Britain and Germany in East African affairs.

From 1887 to 1893, intricate and often discouraging negotiations continued for the cession of Zanzibar's Benadir ports to Italy. Filonardi, who was eager to promote his company's trade with the Somali coast, strove to maintain Italian interest in the area. As chief representative of Italy in Zanzibar, he recommended that Italy act as a third force in East Africa. Failing that, Italy would have no choice but to act in cooperation with either Germany or Great Britain.

On May 15, 1888, after the death of Said Bargash, Filonardi reopened the issue of cession of mainland territory. He wrote to the new sultan, Said Khalifa, to inform him of his inten-

10 Filonardi report, Zanzibar, October 20, 1886, ASMAI, pos. 55/1, f. 4.

11 Crispi, Rome, to Di Robilant, September 10, 1888, ASMAI, pos. 55/1, f. 9.

tion to present him with a personal letter from the king of Italy. Since it was the month of Ramadan, all official business had been suspended for the duration of the fasting period, and Filonardi's letter was not even acknowledged. It is difficult to say whether the slight was intentional. Two weeks later the Italian consul informed the British consul, Charles Euan-Smith, that the sultan had deliberately insulted the king of Italy. He suggested that Said Khalifa apologize by ceding Kismayu to Italy.[12]

Admittedly, Filonardi had his own good reasons for his proposals. In the four years since the formation of his trading company, the volume of business had expanded to approximately 1,000,000 lire. The single most valuable item, cloves, accounted for 87 per cent of the total export trade. Because of its phenomenal success, the company planned to increase its capital to 1,000,000 lire. If Italy were to enter Somalia, Filonardi's company would derive great advantages in all fields of trade.

When Filonardi formally met with the sultan on June 5, he ignored the sultan's protestations that he wished to send to the king a personal message of sorrow at an unintentional slight and demanded the unconditional cession of Kismayu to Italy. Said Khalifa refused to yield to this pressure, and the next morning Filonardi broke off friendly relations with the sultan and lowered the Italian flag at his consulate. In all probability Filonardi hoped that his display of bravado would gain his ends. Only later did he learn that the British agent in Zanzibar had reassured the sultan that he did not stand alone. Moreover, before Filonardi could retract his demands, the incident had international repercussions.

The sultan, it seems, had demanded German intervention to dissuade the Italian government from forceful measures of retaliation. Said Khalifa's actions, naturally, had the stamp of

---

12 Euan-Smith to Lord Salisbury (confidential), June 4, 1888, F.O. 84.1907, No. 125, cited in L. W. Hollingsworth, *Zanzibar under the Foreign Office, 1890–1913* (London: Macmillan, 1953), p. 23.

approval of London, through whose diplomatic channels the German government had been consulted. The Italians quickly learned that forcibly taking Kismayu might be met by the active opposition of England. Further, although Bismarck did not object to a freely offered cession of Kismayu, he felt very differently about the use of force: "Germany would not remain indifferent if that locality were to pass into Italian hands by violent means."[13] Filonardi's tactic, therefore, could not have succeeded, for Zanzibar was in fact, if not in name, under the protection of Germany and Great Britain. If Italy were to participate in the partition of Zanzibar's mainland possessions, it would have to do so under the aegis of one of the great powers. France, whose interest in Zanzibar had declined, was automatically ruled out. German interests in East Africa would not tolerate sharing German lands with Italy. The only hope lay in friendly co-operation with England.

One of several British subjects held in great esteem by the sultan of Zanzibar was William Mackinnon, chairman of the East African Association. In May, 1887, Said Bargash had granted the association a concession for the administration of the mainland coastal strip in what is now Kenya. In return the association was to pay the sultan an annual rent equal to the area's customs receipts for 1887. When Said Khalifa came to the throne, he confirmed these arrangements. The association then enlarged its capital, received a royal charter, and took the name of the Imperial British East Africa Company (IBEA).

While Mackinnon was organizing the IBEA, he was also plotting to thwart his closest rival, the German East Africa Company, by co-operating with Italy. Although the IBEA had a large capital investment, it could not operate a concession equal in area to the Kenya coastal strip, the British sphere of

13 Ambassador Edoardo de Launay, Berlin, to Crispi, June 8, 1888, ASMAI, pos. 55/1, f. 7; Chargé d'affaires Tommaso Catalani, London, to Crispi (confidential), July 3, 1888, ASMAI, pos. 55/1, f. 8.

influence in East Africa, and any proposed additional concessions on the Somali coast. Accordingly, on August 2, 1888,
Mackinnon made a short speech at a banquet of the founders
of the newly formed IBEA in London, in which he manifested
his hope that "in the undertaking to civilise East Africa England would have the co-operation not only of Germany but
also of a young Nation which demonstrates itself to be the
heir to the wisdom and vigour of Rome."[14] The reference to
Italy was received with great applause. Moreover, the Italian
ambassador in London reported that Mackinnon's scheme
had the full approval of the prime minister, Lord Salisbury,
who thought that a better solution could not be hoped for.

In private Mackinnon proposed to the Italian chargé d'affaires, Tommaso Catalani, a plan for the peaceful settlement
of the difficulties between the sultan and Italy. The IBEA
would first obtain a fifty-year concession of the Benadir ports,
with full administrative powers and rights similar to those
granted for the coastal strip. It would then transfer these ports
to an Italian East Africa Company sponsored by the Italian
government. The terms of the Italian company's concession
would be identical to those of the original concession. Kismayu and the Juba River would be under the joint control
and occupation of the two companies. Beyond the ten-mile
radius of the Zanzibari enclave at Kismayu, the Juba was to
be the boundary between British and Italian "spheres of action."[15]

To seek advice on Mackinnon's proposition, Prime Minister Francesco Crispi contacted Cecchi, now Italian consul at
Aden. Cecchi had no great enthusiasm for the British plan.
He distrusted the British because of their insistence on a condominium over Kismayu. Could this mean, he asked, that the
port was quite valuable and hence should belong to Italy

14 Catalani, London, to Crispi, August 3, 1888, ASMAI, pos. 55/1, f. 8.

15 Copy of Mackinnon's proposals of August 2, 1888, enclosed in letter No. 657
    from Catalani, London, to Crispi (secret), August 3, 1888, ASMAI, pos. 55/1,
    f. 8.

alone? After conferring with Filonardi in Zanzibar, Cecchi found more shortcomings in the plan. If an Italian East Africa Company were to assume the concession, then V. Filonardi e Compagnia was naturally the best candidate for the post. But Filonardi was wary of competition with the British company. His capital was inadequate for the venture. He did not shut the door entirely but told Cecchi that if the "difficulty of co-existence" with the British company were removed and if he could raise the necessary additional capital he would accept the concession.[16]

Before the Italians could act, the unstable Said Khalifa announced his refusal to consider further concessions. The hostility of Zanzibari Arab traders to the existing concessions, especially to the unpopular German East Africa Company, stiffened his attitude. In view of the situation, the Italians concluded that the Mackinnon plan would no longer be of use to the British Foreign Office. There was already enough difficulty with the sultan over the issue of the antislavery and anti-arms traffic blockade. They knew that Salisbury did not want to resort to force, particularly after the coastal uprisings against the Germans in mid-August. Crispi had no choice but to instruct the London embassy to wait for a more propitious time to broach the subject again.[17]

In late August Mackinnon renewed his pledge of friendship and co-operation and announced that he had instructed George Mackenzie, a director of the company in Mombasa, to co-operate "at the right time" with Consul-General Euan-Smith.[18] Heartened by this news, Crispi tried to speed things up again. He authorized Catalani to travel to Scotland, where

16 Cecchi, Zanzibar, to Crispi, August 5, 1888, ASMAI, pos. 55/2, f. 15.

17 Copy of confidential memorandum from the Foreign Office consigned to Di Robilant by Sir J. Lister, Undersecretary of State, London, August 31, 1888, ASMAI, pos. 55/1, f. 9. See also Hertslet, *The Map of Africa by Treaty*, II, 695–700; and Crispi, Rome, to Di Robilant, August 15, 1888, ASMAI, pos. 55/1, f. 9.

18 Mackinnon, Balinakill, Clachau, Argyllshire, to Catalani (private and confidential), August 25, 1888, ASMAI, pos. 55/1, f. 9.

Mackinnon was entertaining the Belgian king, in order to offer Mackinnon the title of *marchese*.[19] Mackinnon promised Catalani that he would do all that he could to help the Italians. His one condition was the withdrawal of Cecchi and Italian ships from Zanzibar. The British had taken a dislike to the ambitious Cecchi, whose reports, sometimes exaggerated, sometimes overly enthusiastic, misled his foreign ministry about events in Zanzibar. The Italian government agreed, and Italy resumed friendly relations with Zanzibar.

Mackinnon wanted to act speedily, not because he was seduced by the promise of an Italian title, but because the Italians fitted neatly into his plans. Initially, he had had a vision of a vast East Africa and Zanzibar Company with capital of 50,000,000 pounds sterling. The British government could not support this grandiose plan, and rather than let the Germans gain control of the area, Mackinnon had decided that Italian intervention would help him realize to some extent his original idea. Freed of Cecchi's interference, the IBEA concluded its concession agreement with the sultan on October 9, 1888. The sultan transferred the coastal strip to the chartered company. IBEA had the power to levy taxes, to regulate trade, to appoint administrative officers, and to establish courts of justice. The sole condition was that the administration be conducted in the sultan's name and under his flag.[20] With its own concession assured, the company then negotiated for the Benadir concession. In December it appeared that the sultan would approve the arrangement. In anticipation, on December 8 Catalani signed the preliminary agreement proposed by Mackinnon at the time of the IBEA founding banquet. The document was predated August 1, 1888.[21]

Although the diplomatic groundwork was laid for Anglo-Italian co-operation on the Somali coast, success did not come

[19] Crispi, Rome, to Catalani, September 3, 1888, ASMAI, pos. 55/1, f. 9.

[20] Hertslet, *The Map of Africa by Treaty*, I, 339–45, 350–59.

[21] Catalani, London, to Crispi (confidential), December 9, 1888, ASMAI, pos. 55/1, f. 9.

easily. Early in December Cecchi returned to Zanzibar. He was eager to assert the power of his country on a basis equal to that of England and Germany. A change of orders from the Italian government had sent him on a survey of the coast of East Africa to examine, among other things, alternative plans for a peaceful concession or an occupation by force of Kismayu. The August rebellion on the mainland had spread throughout the entire German coastal strip, and the Italian prime minister no doubt hoped to capitalize on the disturbances should they reach Kismayu. It may have been for this purpose that he ordered an Italian ship to join the Anglo-German blockade of the coast.[22]

Early in January the sultan was on the verge of signing the Benadir agreement with the IBEA. If Cecchi had not committed a grave error of judgment, the Italians might have finally secured the Benadir. On January 4, Said Khalifa called him in to present him with a letter for the king of Italy. In reaction to what he claimed to be the sultan's insolence, Cecchi refused to accept the letter. Crispi later agreed with the British that Cecchi had indeed erred but refused to recognize it as an offense to the sultan. Ironically, the letter that Cecchi rejected contained the sultan's agreement to the concession. Eleven days later Said Khalifa sent a duplicate letter to the British consul-general for transmission to the king of Italy.[23] But Cecchi's action had already done its damage to the cause of Italy. It gave London, which was now disturbed by Italian expansion from Eritrea into the Sudan, an excuse to procrastinate. Salisbury's distaste for Cecchi's behavior prevented the signing of the Benadir agreement between the sultan and the IBEA for another seven months.

The Italians might well have become discouraged in their search for colonies in East Africa had not a sudden impetus

---

22 Minute in Crispi's hand, Rome, December 18, 1888, ASMAI, pos. 55/2, f. 13.

23 Catalani, London, to Crispi (confidential), January 9, 1889, and Crispi, Rome, to London Embassy (confidential), January 11, 1889, ASMAI, pos. 55/1, f. 10; Sultan of Zanzibar to King of Italy, January 15, 1889, ASMAI, pos. 55/1, f. 11.

come from a most unexpected quarter—northeastern Somalia. On December 12, 1888, a delegation from Yusuf Ali, sultan of Obbia, arrived in Zanzibar and requested the protection of Italy. The immediate background of the request was a dispute between Yusuf Ali and the sultan of Zanzibar over the status of the little village of Mruti, not far from the Zanzibari enclave at Warsheik. Filonardi recognized the opportunity for Italy to extend its trade and to obtain a foothold in the supposedly promising Somali area at the spontaneous invitation of one of the local rulers.[24]

Prime Minister Crispi immediately ordered a naval mission "for the purpose of declaring the Italian protectorate, and, according to the circumstances, to proceed to the effective occupation of territory." There was an additional reason for speed: a French squadron was passing through the Suez Canal for an unknown destination. Italian sources in London suggested that the French ships might be heading toward the Somali coast.[25] At the end of January Filonardi left for Obbia to arrange for the protectorate. On February 8, Yusuf Ali placed his sultanate under Italian protection in return for an annual subsidy of 1,200 Maria Theresa thalers.

Filonardi, who was popular among the Somali, remained in Obbia for several days to convince them that their sultan had not sold his lands to Italy. He then sailed for a short visit in Aden, where he consulted Cecchi and the British authorities. Back in Obbia two weeks later, Filonardi discovered that Arab merchants, who resented the Italian protectorate and the loss of their trading monopoly, were stirring the townspeople against their sultan. Yusuf Ali shrewdly perceived the advantages of having Italian strength on his side. In return for Filonardi's support, Yusuf Ali agreed to intervene in be-

---

[24] Filonardi, Zanzibar, to Crispi, December 17, 1888, *Libro Verde*, doc. 2, p. 27.

[25] Instructions to the commander of the *Staffetta*, sent from the naval ministry to the foreign ministry, January 15, 1889, *Libro Verde*, doc. 3, p. 28. The real purpose of the French mission was to survey a Russian expedition disembarking at Tadjoura (Catalani, London, to Crispi, February 10, 1889, ASMAI, pos. 59/1, f. 1).

half of Italy and ask his son-in-law, Sultan Osman Mahmud of the Mijjertein, to accept an Italian protectorate.

Initial attempts at negotiation were unsuccessful. Osman Mahmud was not uninterested, however, and Filonardi's use of Arabic through his clever interpreter, Abu Bakr bin Awod, soon gained the sultan's favor. On April 7 an agreement was reached that was similar in form and simplicity to that signed by Yusuf Ali. There was an increase in the amount of the subsidy to 1,800 thalers, however, which necessitated a revision of the first treaty with Obbia. The Italians notified the signatory powers of the Berlin agreement of the protectorate over Obbia on March 2 and of the protectorate over the Mijjertein on May 16.[26]

The public announcement of the protectorates received scant notice in Italy. *La Nazione* of Florence, an expansionist daily, was content to mention Obbia's possibilities as a coaling station and as a base for blockading slave ships. A word was also said about the increase of Italy's prestige in the area.[27] In Germany, in contrast, the announcement received vivid comments. The *Kreuz Zeitung* of Berlin felt that Italy should compensate Germany in some way for the assumption of a protectorate over Obbia, and the *Kölnische Zeitung* pointed out that Germany had prior claims in the area.[28]

It is true that Germans had been active in Obbia and the Mijjertein before the advent of the Italians. Indeed, Filonardi and Cecchi were well aware of German involvement. But the German newspapers overlooked the fact that the German government had no treaty rights in the area. According to Edoardo de Launay, the Italian ambassador in Berlin, Osman Mahmud had offered to place his sultanate under the protection of Germany on September 6, 1885, but the offer

[26] Treaty for protectorate over the Mijjertein, April 7, 1889, *Libro Verde,* doc. 11, annex I, p. 40.

[27] *La Nazione* (Florence), March 17, 1889.

[28] *Kreuz Zeitung* (Berlin), April 8, 1889; *Kölnische Zeitung,* March 23, 1889.

had not been taken up in Berlin.[29] On November 26, 1885, Yusuf Ali and Claus von Andersen, an agent of the German East Africa Company, had signed a treaty that German journalists considered to have political significance. At the time of the treaty with Italy, however, Yusuf Ali had told the Italians that the German agreement was purely commercial in scope.[30] It appears that Yusuf Ali had used the Germans as a pawn in his dispute with Osman Mahmud. It is significant that as late as the next year, 1890, the German government did not consider the treaty to have political validity and had never notified other nations of a protectorate, as required by Article 35 of the Berlin agreement.[31]

By June, 1889, the extension of protectorates over Obbia, the Mijjertein, and—according to the Italian version of the Treaty of Uccialli—Ethiopia had had some effect in London. Crispi began to raise the question of Ethiopia in connection with that of Kismayu and the Juba, and it soon became imperative that a line be drawn between British and Italian spheres of influence in East Africa. The first step in this direction was taken when Filonardi met with Mackinnon and other officials of the IBEA in London and approved a draft agreement, even though the clause for a condominium over Kismayu remained. The Italians had little choice, for on that the British were adamant. Filonardi was puzzled by the motives of the IBEA and doubted Mackinnon's good faith. Cata-

[29] Launay, Berlin, to Crispi, March 5, 1889, ASMAI, pos. 59/1, f. 8.

[30] Declaration by Yusuf Ali, Alula, April 7, 1889, ASMAI, pos. 59/1, f. 5.

[31] The Italian embassy in Berlin nevertheless strove to ascertain the official German policy on the matter. Germany had never acknowledged receipt of notification of the Italian protectorates in northern Somalia. Evidently, the government did not wish to be embarrassed by recognizing the protectorates and thereby leaving itself open to attack by the active German colonialist party, nor did it wish to create difficulties for the Italians. In an awkward position, the Germans still refused to take formal notice of the Italian protectorates as late as 1895. Launay, Berlin, to Crispi, April 1, 1889, ASMAI, pos. 59/1, f. 2; Graf von Solms, Rome, to Launay (confidential), undated (ca. July 28, 1889), ASMAI, pos. 59/1, f. 8; Launay, Berlin, to Blanc, November 2, 1895, ASMAI, pos. 59/1, f. 12.

lani, however, was convinced that the company was perfectly disinterested and added, as an afterthought, "I strongly doubt that I shall be able to make Mackinnon accept a title."[32]

The negotiations went along smoothly, despite some bad blood between Filonardi and Euan-Smith, who also attended the London meetings. For a short time Crispi insisted on the cession of Kismayu to Italy alone, but to avoid being excluded from the area altogether, which appeared to be the only alternative, he quickly approved the plan as it stood. Finally, Lord Salisbury gave his conditional approval, and the agreement was signed on August 3, 1889 (see Appendix I). In a gesture of friendship and solidarity, the Italian government reimbursed the IBEA for its expenses of 235 pounds spent for telegrams in the period before the signing of the agreement. Four weeks later the sultan of Zanzibar at long last signed the agreement granting the concession of the Benadir ports to the IBEA.[33]

Crispi must certainly have been heartened by the events of 1889. His colonial policy was advancing on several fronts. Unexpectedly, Italy had been able to establish itself in northern Somalia. On May 2 the heralded treaty with Ethiopia was signed at Uccialli. In June General Antonio Baldissera occupied the hinterland of Massawa in Eritrea, and the Italians looked forward to settling a large population of emigrants in the Eritrean highlands. The Benadir concession in southern Somalia seemed to be in the offing. Britain and France were not interested in the Somali coast, and the German government, if not German public opinion, was willing to give Italy a free hand in Somalia. On November 15, Crispi extended an Italian protectorate over

those portions of the east coast of Africa from the northern boundary of the territory of Kismayu to the parallel 2° 30′ of north lati-

32 Catalani, London, to Crispi, July 1, 1889, ASMAI, pos. 55/3, f. 19.

33 Catalani report, London, September 27, 1889, ASMAI, pos. 55/3, f. 19; agreement between His Highness the Sultan of Zanzibar and Gerald Portal, Acting British Consul, Zanzibar, August 31, 1889, ASMAI, pos. 55/2, f. 12.

tude, which lie between the stations recognized in 1886 as belonging to the sultan of Zanzibar.[34]

The northern boundary of the new Italian protectorate coincided with the southern boundary of the sultanate of Obbia. Thus the whole Somali coast from the Juba River to Cape Guardafui was under nominal Italian control, except for the Zanzibari enclaves, which could be blockaded and isolated commercially if the need should arise.

Before the Italians could obtain their concession, the British Parliament had to approve the agreement signed by the IBEA. Lord Salisbury had given the agreement only his conditional approval. When he read the final draft, he knew that there would be difficulty with the fourth clause, which dealt with the Italian and IBEA spheres of influence in East Africa. The next and logical step was to negotiate a treaty defining these spheres. When the deed of transfer for the Benadir concession and the joint occupation of Kismayu was publicly signed in London on November 18, 1889, it was generally assumed that Italian influence began at the Juba and included Ethiopia and the horn, with the exception of the British Somaliland Protectorate. Such was not the assumption at the Foreign Office, and negotiations dragged on until March, 1891, when a protocol for the demarcation of spheres of influence was finally signed at Rome.[35]

The four-year interval between the approval of the IBEA's Benadir concession in August, 1889, and the transfer of the Benadir ports to Italy in July, 1893, must have passed with excruciating slowness for Filonardi, Cecchi, and the other ex-

[34] Crispi to Italian representatives in Berlin, Brussels, Copenhagen, Constantinople, The Hague, Lisbon, London, Madrid, Paris, St. Petersburg, Stockholm, and Vienna, November 19, 1889, *Libro Verde*, doc. 12, p. 45; Catalani, London, to Crispi (confidential), November 15, 1889, ASMAI, pos. 55/3, f. 20. Lord Salisbury had even agreed with Crispi on the formula of notification.

[35] Hertslet, *The Map of Africa by Treaty*, III, 948, 1091–93; *London Post*, November 21, 1889.

pansionists. Changes of regime in both Zanzibar and Italy, as well as protracted negotiations, contributed to their frustration.

Meanwhile, Bismarck and Salisbury had made a final settlement of territorial claims in Africa. On July 1, 1890, an Anglo-German agreement was signed at Berlin. Britain then came to an agreement with France. In compensation for French recognition of a British protectorate over Zanzibar, Britain recognized a French protectorate over Madagascar. Following the proclamation of appropriate antislavery decrees, Zanzibar became a British protectorate on November 4, 1890.[36]

Until the protectorate question was satisfactorily resolved, the British government did not want to proceed with its negotiations with Italy for a spheres-of-influence agreement. Crispi took advantage of the Anglo-German negotiations to use the protectorate issue as an opening to "define the rights of the Italian government to the Benadir ports, as well as the respective spheres of influence in East Africa."[37] The British ambassador at Rome informed Crispi that Italy could count on British support but that Britain must first come to a settlement with Germany.[38] Both sides could afford the delay, for their rights were assured. The new sultan had already written Mackenzie that he had "no objection to any arrangement the Imperial British East Africa Company may make with the Italians."[39]

During the same period, Filonardi completed two missions for the Italian government. Between December, 1889, and May, 1890, he visited the two protected sultans and stopped at the Benadir enclaves. In the north, Filonardi presented Yusuf Ali with rifles, cartridges, and other gifts as a token support

36 Hertslet, The Map of Africa by Treaty, I, 310; II, 738–39; III, 899–906.

37 Crispi, Rome, to Lord Dufferin, June 23, 1890, ASMAI, pos. 55/4, f. 23.

38 Lord Dufferin, Rome, to Crispi, June 26, 1890, ASMAI, pos. 55/4, f. 23.

39 Sultan Said Ali, Zanzibar, to Mackenzie, March 6, 1890, ASMAI, pos. 55/4, f. 23; Euan-Smith and Branchi to Said Ali, undated, ASMAI, pos. 55/4, f. 27.

of the sultan against the anti-Italian party at Obbia.[40] In the south, he tightened existing connections with notables and merchants. At Warsheik, the center of the numerous Abgal tribe, his visit was the first ever made by an Italian ship. Briefly putting ashore at that small town, crew members of the *Volta* were given a hostile reception. Two men lost their lives—the first Italians to suffer death at the hands of the Somali.[41] Seven months later, Filonardi undertook his second mission of preparation for the eventual installation of an Italian administration in the Benadir. First, he took possession of the coastal tract from Warsheik to Obbia and looked for a suitable port. On March 14, 1891, three local chiefs proposed the cession of el-Athaleh, which Filonardi and the naval ministry wrongly considered to be a good port.[42] In honor of his homeland, Filonardi renamed the town "Itala" and, to avoid troubles like those at Warsheik, stationed a garrison of eighty Arab askaris there. Itala thus became the first permanent Italian military establishment on the Somali coast. Filonardi then proceeded to Mogadishu, where he signed treaties of friendship and trade with the local chiefs.

Negotiations for the delimitation of spheres of influence resumed in the last days of 1890. The fall of Crispi's cabinet in February, 1891, caused only a slight interruption. The new prime minister, Antonio di Rudinì, had been antagonistic to Crispi and could certainly not be called a colonialist. His primary concern was the financial and economic condition of the nation. In Parliament he constantly repeated his slogans of "economy" and "stay at home."[43] But at the same time, he did not wish to break off negotiations with Great Britain. He later declared, "I have never been a partisan of the African under-

[40] Filonardi to Foreign Minister, March 2, 1890, *Libro Verde,* doc. 27, pp. 61–62.

[41] Commander of the *Volta,* Aden, to Naval Minister, April 30, 1890, *Libro Verde,* doc. 28, pp. 63–64.

[42] Filonardi-Rosasco report, March 16, 1891, *Libro Verde,* doc. 29, annex II, p. 69.

[43] *Atti Parlamentari: Camera dei Deputati,* February 18, 1891.

taking. I have never regretted this, nor do I regret it now. I do recognize, however, that the sacrifices which were made and the expenses which were incurred have brought some results."[44]

On March 24, 1891, Rudinì and Lord Dufferin signed the protocol delimiting the British and Italian spheres of influence in East Africa. By the terms of the agreement, the dividing line between the two spheres followed the mid-channel of the Juba River from the Indian Ocean to latitude 6° north, then continued along the sixth parallel as far as longitude 35° east, where it turned north, following that meridian to the Blue Nile. Kismayu and its territory remained within the British sphere, with one condition that there was to be equality of treatment of the subjects and protected persons of both countries. On April 15, an additional protocol was signed for the demarcation of Italian and British spheres of influence from Ras Kasar on the Red Sea to the Blue Nile and for the Italian occupation of Kassala in the event of war in the Sudan.[45] The major elements of Mancini's grand plan are clearly evident.

It was now only a matter of time until the Italians took possession of the coast. Four tasks remained: to notify the sultan of Zanzibar of the protocol, to find out more about Somalia, to fix the exact amount of the annual rent, and to form an Italian East Africa Company. The Italians, who may have been ignorant of the sultan's complete dependence on the British, were unsure of the reaction they would get from Sultan Said Ali. They considered his predominant motive to be avarice. After reassurance by Lord Salisbury and the British representative in Zanzibar, Gerald Portal, the Italians notified the sultan of the accord on August 29, 1891. To his surprise, the acting consul found that

His Highness did not make any appreciable observations, for he did not know where the Juba was situated. I had to explain to him

[44] *Atti Parlamentari: Camera dei Deputati,* May 5, 1891.

[45] Hertslet, *The Map of Africa by Treaty,* III, 948–50.

in his language that the Juba is a river located a quarter of an hour's march from Kismayu.[46]

Another mission was sent in the meantime to spread Italian influence on the Somali coast. Commander Giorgio Sorrentino compiled an extensive report on the population, tribes, chiefs, trade, and customs of Brava, Merca, Mogadishu, Itala, Obbia, and Alula. The Somali tribes were ruled by local sultans and tribal chiefs. There was no political unity, "inasmuch as every Somali affects a certain independence of action." Brava was troubled by cattle disease. Merca's trade was stagnant. Mogadishu had been ruled for the past eighteen years by the thirty-three-year-old Suleiman bin Hamed, a relative of the sultan of Zanzibar. Sorrentino regarded him as corrupt but potentially useful and willing to play "two parts in a comedy, to serve well two masters." At Brava, Merca, and Mogadishu, Sorrentino presented the walis, notables, and *cadis* (religious judges) with gifts of turbans, Arab garments, syrups, essences, and Maria Theresa thalers. It was an inexpensive total investment of 296 thalers in gathering friends for Italy.[47]

Although it cost very little to gain the favor of local officials on the Somali coast, Italy could not win the sultan of Zanzibar with such paltry gifts. Said Ali, although he may not have known much about geography, expressed a keen interest in the prospect of receiving a large sum of rental money from Italy for the Benadir concession. Fortunately for the Italians, the IBEA had established a precedent in its contract with the sultan. Thus the annual amount was to be equal to the revenue from customs duties.[48]

The discussions about the annual rental took place in Zanzibar in July, 1892. Portal and Acting Consul Pierre Cottoni

[46] Cottoni, Zanzibar, to Rudinì, September 2, 1891, *Libro Verde*, doc. 47, pp. 90–91.

[47] Report of Commander Sorrentino, Zanzibar, January 22, 1892, ASMAI, pos. 55/5, f. 34. A thaler was then equal to approximately 3 lire or about 65 cents.

[48] Hertslet, *The Map of Africa by Treaty*, I, 355–56.

set about determining what the annual trade of the Benadir was, in order to reach a fair estimate of revenues. Portal produced a document purporting to prove that the government of Zanzibar had received 235,102 rupees for the year ending May 31, 1892. He claimed that that year had been a poor one because of cattle pestilence. On the basis of this figure, Portal at first asked for a rental of 235,000 rupees, or approximately 110,000 thalers, plus 50 per cent of the customs above that net value. Cottoni, readily admitting that he had no qualms about outright bargaining, responded with an offer of 79,000 thalers (about 168,000 rupees). Portal in turn countered with the statement that an Indian merchant, Tarria Toppan, had offered the sultan 200,000 rupees for a customs concession. After much haggling, Portal and Cottoni agreed on a payment of 200,000 rupees for the first year and 160,000 rupees annually afterward. Portal then induced Said Ali to agree to the concession. On August 12, 1892, Portal, representing the government of Zanzibar, and Cottoni signed the agreement granting the concession of the Benadir ports to Italy.[49]

Italy now had clear title to all of Somalia from the Juba River to Cape Guardafui. The government next sought to reach an agreement with Filonardi for the concession of the ports to his company. The new government of Giovanni Giolitti, in power since May, 1892, was not, however, a proponent of an active colonial policy. A depression had hit Italy in the early 1890's, and Giolitti wanted major budgetary reductions, especially in African expenditures. His foreign minister, Benedetto Brin, was in no hurry to implement the Benadir concession. Brin, in fact, tried to postpone parliamentary approval of the concession as long as possible. Cottoni warned the government that if Italy did not act soon, it was quite possible that the British consul might farm out the Benadir customs for a year to a wealthy Indian merchant,

49 Cottoni, Zanzibar, to Brin, July 22, 1892, and Cottoni to Brin, July 30, 1892, ASMAI, pos. 55/5, f. 37; Portal, Zanzibar, to Lord Salisbury, August 11, 1892, F.O. 84.2232, No. 176 (cited in Hollingsworth, *Zanzibar under the Foreign Office*, p. 86); Said Ali to Portal, July 31, 1892, ASMAI, pos. 55/5, f. 38.

Kanji Ranchipur. Brin could only reply vaguely that he favored the status quo.[50]

In December the British agent in Zanzibar lost patience, suggesting sarcastically that perhaps the question should be postponed for several years longer to enable the Italian government to put things in order. Portal urged London to put pressure on Rome. The British ambassador was frank in his note to the Italian government:

> The state of uncertainty . . . has, it appears, brought about an absolute cessation of trade, the loss consequent on which is already severely felt by the Zanzibari Government, and will also ultimately be injurious to Italy, if the King's Government should decide to take up the concession.[51]

Brin finally began to move. He asked the Italian ambassador in London, Giuseppe Tornielli, for advice on the matter. The ambassador responded that he felt that it was impossible to postpone action indefinitely; if an Italian company could not assume the undertaking without a subsidy, perhaps English capital should be invited.[52]

Late in January, 1893, Filonardi made his first overture to the government. If he received a government subsidy, he claimed, the Credito Mobiliare, a bank in Rome, would advance his company 1,500,000 lire. The company would then have capital of 2,500,000 lire. His one request was that the government grant his company an annual subsidy of 300,000 lire for twenty-five years, that is, for the duration of the contract with Zanzibar. These terms were unacceptable to Tornielli, who did not like the idea of a government subsidy; he countered with the example of the non-subsidized British companies. Cecchi, however, in correspondence with the foreign minister, stated his approval of subsidies and government by chartered company and gave an encouraging summary of

[50] Brin, Rome, to Cottoni, November 1, 1892; Cottoni, Zanzibar, to Brin, November 3 and 9, 1892; and Brin to Cottoni, November 11, 1892; in ASMAI, pos. 55/5, f. 39.

[51] Lord Vivian, Rome, to Brin, December 31, 1892, ASMAI, pos. 55/5, f. 39.

[52] Tornielli, London, to Brin, January 23, 1893, ASMAI, pos. 75/1, f .1.

the trade and commercial history of the Benadir and the Ogaden and a glowing description of Somalia's flourishing future. Although there were no new ideas amid all Cecchi's extensive comments, Brin was influenced by his authoritative opinion. On May 15, 1893, Brin and Filonardi signed the contract granting Filonardi the concession of the administration of the Benadir and a government subsidy of 300,000 lire for the Benadir ports and 50,000 lire for Itala.[53] In addition, the Filonardi Company was to deliver the annual subsidy to Yusuf Ali and Osman Mahmud and was to be the intermediary between the Italian government and its two northern protectorates.

Meanwhile Said Ali had died in March. His successor, Said Hamed, was willing to grant the Italians their concession, but in the light of their procrastination in 1892, he insisted that, initially, it be for only a three-year trial period. Accordingly, a supplementary agreement was drafted. The Italian government agreed to pay the sultan 50,000 rupees in the event that Italy abandoned the Benadir concession within or at the conclusion of the term of three years. The indemnity would be increased to 100,000 rupees if any warlike operations should have taken place in Somalia during the three months preceding Italian withdrawal. The annual rent remained the same. This supplementary agreement, signed the same day as the Filonardi contract with the government, was to come into effect on July 16, 1893.[54] With the approval of the Chamber of Deputies in mid-July, Italy made the last preparations for taking possession of the Benadir.

Eight years of diplomacy had come to an end. Marked by delay and disappointment, the period was also one of active

---

[53] Filonardi, Rome, to Brin, January 24, 1893; Tornielli, Rome, to Brin (confidential), February 23, 1893; Cecchi, Aden, to Brin, February 24, 1893; and Filonardi to Brin and Brin to Filonardi, Rome, May 11, 1893; in ASMAI, pos. 75/1, f. 1.

[54] Hertslet, *The Map of Africa by Treaty*, III, 1100–1102.

co-operation between Italy and Great Britain. Although Lord Salisbury may have let the Italians down more than once, he had aided them in the long run. Mackinnon's motives may have been suspected, in particular by Cecchi, but on the whole they proved to be honest. Fortunately for both parties, Italian and British interests in the area, with the significant exception of Kismayu, were complementary.

Proof of the good will of the British, other than in their words, may be found in the actions of one of the local agents of the IBEA. In 1890, Robert T. Simons, IBEA administrator in Kismayu, had the task of concluding treaties with the Somali chiefs in the territory newly acquired by England. Chiefs from the right bank of the Juba gathered in Kismayu to sign treaties on the regular IBEA treaty of protection forms. Some chiefs from the left bank of the Juba were also present. These chiefs were closely related to the others and would have resented not being permitted to sign treaties as their cousins were doing. Aware of the impending agreement on spheres of influence and the Italian Benadir concession, Simons hit upon the rather ingenious idea of signing treaties with the left bank chiefs, too, rather than offend them. Taking the regular IBEA form, he penned in the left margin, "This document to be exchanged later on for one duly signed by Italian authorities." He then filled in the usual blanks for tribal names and locations. Wherever "Imperial British East Africa Company" appeared in the text, Simons neatly substituted "Royal Italian East Africa Company" and initialed all changes with his "RTS." Simons then blithely placed his signature on the treaty "on behalf of the Royal Italian Company, by authority of Sig. Brusuti, Acting Italian Consul at Zanzibar." Such was the name given to Acting Consul Emilio Bencetti by the resourceful Simons, who was more familiar with Arabic and Swahili than Italian.[55]

[55] Treaty of protection between the "Royal Italian East Africa Company" and Somali sheiks of the villages of Haji Ali (Hagiuali) and Lanshunla on the

In his exuberance, Simons signed treaties with more than a dozen chiefs. Although he did not act without Italian knowledge of the matter—he had received permission from the Italian consulate in Zanzibar to go ahead with his plan[56]—it is revealing, nonetheless, to discover the subject of one country concluding treaties of protection for the benefit of another country. Simons received no reward for this gesture of imperialistic neighborly good will.

The "Royal Italian East Africa Company" had been long in coming, but an Italian company finally arrived on the coast. In September, 1893, after the southwest monsoon had blown itself out, Filonardi sailed to take possession of the Benadir. A period of co-operative imperialism ended, and a period of colonial government by chartered company began.

---

left bank of the Juba, Kismayu, May 9, 1890, ASMAI, pos. 55/6, f. 42. Some of these treaties were in English and Arabic, others in English and Swahili.

[56] Lovatelli to Brin, September 2, 1893, ASMAI, pos. 55/6, f. 43. Consul Giovanni Branchi had notified the foreign ministry of this unique arrangement in his report of May 3, 1890.

CHAPTER TWO

The Filonardi Company, 1893–96

The Imperial British East Africa Company, it has been noted, played a significant part in furthering Italian interests in Somalia. The example of its organization was not lost on Filonardi, nor was the obvious advantage of its relatively small cost discounted by the Italian government. Thus the Benadir was handed over to the chartered company organized by Filonardi. The protectorates of northern Somalia were ignored and went their own way most of the time, outside the main stream of Italian colonial development in Somalia.

In June, 1893, Foreign Minister Brin sent instructions to Filonardi. His objective would be to maintain good relations with the sultans and native chiefs of Somalia in order to attract their trade to the Benadir ports. He was to proceed cautiously, for the government did not wish to assume financial or military responsibility for the colony. The government's approval was required for any local treaties the concessionaire might make; and he should keep in mind "that they must not entail any financial burden for the State Exchequer." Whereas Italian law was to be applied to Italian nationals, native law was to be honored for the Somali. In the event of a permanent concession, the government would study the question of native law. For the present Brin's scant instructions were to be closely followed.[1]

---

[1] Brin, Rome, to Filonardi, June 15, 1893, *Documenti diplomatici italiani presentati al Parlamento italiano dal Ministro degli Affari Esteri (Blanc):*

Because Filonardi had been the main source of information about the Benadir, the foreign ministry sought an independent opinion and sent Count Giovanni Lovatelli, a young naval lieutenant, to study local conditions and to advise the government on its Benadir policy.[2] In his initial report Lovatelli condescendingly declared that "the Somali are not men, but children, and it is necessary to treat them as such." He found the coastal populations well disposed toward the Italians. In evaluating the chartered company, he felt that the small scale of its operations would be an advantage. The large European companies in East Africa had met great difficulties because of their size, Lovatelli claimed. The German East Africa Company, for example, whose capital was greater than that of the Italian company, had gone through troublesome times; only after declaring itself bankrupt and reforming itself as a purely commercial company had it become a profitable enterprise. Lovatelli darkly intimated that the capital of the Imperial British East Africa Company was nearly exhausted. As evidence, he mentioned that, for all its strong publicity, IBEA had never paid dividends.[3] Lovatelli summarized his findings with a certain amount of self-deception:

I believe that the best thing the Filonardi Company could do the first year would be to let matters stand as they are, with the exception of Merca. . . . To begin with reforms or change would only

---

Somalia italiana (1885–1895) (Rome, 1895), doc. 71, p. 121 (hereinafter cited as *Libro Verde*).

2 Lovatelli was well qualified for this mission. Earlier the government had assigned him to do liaison work with the British in exploratory expeditions and with the IBEA at Kismayu. It was with the British that the anglophile Lovatelli achieved his greatest success (British Agent Hardinge, Zanzibar, to Blanc, December 10, 1894, Archivio Storico dell'ex Ministero dell'Africa Italiana (hereinafter cited as ASMAI), pos. 55/6, f. 45). In February, 1893, Lovatelli saved the life of British Consul Todd in a combat with hostile Somali at the Kismayu IBEA trading station (Rennell Rodd, Zanzibar, to Secretary of State for Foreign Affairs, February 10, 1893, *Libro Verde,* doc. 78, pp. 155–56).

3 Lovatelli report, Brava, May 27, 1893, ASMAI, pos. 55/6, f. 41.

arouse the distrust of the natives. . . . With the exception of the Arabs of Merca, all these peoples ardently desire Italian occupation.

This happy disposition of the Benadir peoples toward Italy, wrote Lovatelli, would facilitate the work of the company, which despite its meager finances could transform the colony into a permanent and profitable possession of Italy within a few years.

While Filonardi remained in Zanzibar and prepared for the trip to Mogadishu after the change of monsoons, Lovatelli continued his investigations. In mid-July he reported his progress to Brin. One disturbing note was contained in his letter: Faki Addu, a local Somali sheik, had warned Filonardi about his employment of Abu Bakr bin Awod, an Arab interpreter familiar with the Somali coast. Abu Bakr had contacts among the Arabs of Merca, who were hostile to the dominant Bimal Somali. Faki Addu advised the Italians that if they did not watch their step they would become involved in Arab-Somali hostilities. Abu Bakr, he claimed, was intriguing against the Somali, who offered their friendship to the Italians to counter the Arab bid for local dominance. Despite the warning from Faki Addu, Filonardi made no attempt to discharge Abu Bakr, who remained in his service for the duration of the concession.[4]

Filonardi was more concerned with a Somali uprising at British Kismayu. If the British took strong action against the Somali rebels in their sphere of influence, there was a strong possibility that British Somali would cross the Juba. The Italians could not prevent the passage of any Somali groups into their sphere of influence, but if they failed to maintain existing tribal boundaries, their prestige among the Italian Somali would be endangered. To remedy the situation, Filonardi proposed that the Italian government help his company estab-

---

[4] Lovatelli letter, Gobwen, July 13, 1893, and Sheik Faki Addu of Narwen to Filonardi, undated, ASMAI, pos. 55/6, f. 42.

lish a garrison at Jumbo, strategically located on the left bank of the Juba a few kilometers from Kismayu.[5]

As Filonardi continued his preparations to take possession of the Benadir, he consulted the foreign ministry and Edoardo Incoronato, the commander of the *Staffetta,* which was then stationed off the Somali coast. Inasmuch as a question of change of authority was involved, Filonardi proposed that the sultan of Zanzibar summon the wali of Mogadishu, Suleiman bin Hamed, and other elders to Zanzibar to inform them of the change. Then, after a ceremony of investiture, Filonardi and the Somali leaders would return to the Benadir.[6] On September 21 the wali of Brava and twelve Somali chiefs from the various Benadir ports arrived at Zanzibar. After a brief delay caused by the illness of the British agent, the sultan received the notables according to plan on September 26.[7] Thus Filonardi paved the way for a smooth transfer of authority.

Before the arrival of the Somali leaders, Filonardi drafted a provisional ordinance for the administration of the Benadir ports and for the protected territory lying between the ports. He covered a multitude of subjects. All uncultivated lands, unless their owners were properly ascertained, were to become the property of the Italian government.[8] The government was to have the exclusive privilege of exploiting, or granting concessions to exploit, minerals or deposits of any sort of metals, minerals, mineral oils, and precious stones. Special permission would be required to cut wood from the forests along the lower courses of the Juba and Webi Shebelle

---

5 Filonardi telegram, Zanzibar, August 22, 1893, ASMAI, pos. 55/6, f. 42; Filonardi report, No. 134, Zanzibar, September 1, 1893, and report of Commander Incoronato, Zanzibar, September 1, 1893, ASMAI, pos. 55/6, f. 43.

6 Filonardi, Zanzibar, to Foreign Minister, September 2, 1893, *Libro Verde,* doc. 79, pp. 167–69.

7 Filonardi, Zanzibar, to Foreign Minister, October 1, 1893, *Libro Verde,* doc. 80, pp. 170–71.

8 Usually the phrase "unoccupied land" is employed in such decrees. The Italian text, however, describes *terre incolte,* literally "uncultivated lands."

—Somalia's sole source of wood. The slave trade was prohibited, and the gradual abolition of slavery was promised. Additional clauses dealt with the regulation of justice and commerce.[9]

To convince the local population of his good intentions, Filonardi, who was usually on excellent terms with his Muslim "subjects," clarified the position of native law. Article VI of the provisional ordinance stated that "the law will be applied according to the standards of the Muslim Shariʿa." In October he issued another ordinance spelling out how justice would be administered by company-appointed cadis, or judges. Only sentences passed by cadis who represented the Filonardi Company would be recognized as legitimate. Registers were to be kept as a type of court record. Court costs amounted to either one-half or a full Maria Theresa thaler, depending on the nature of the dispute.[10] Receipts were to be divided among the company (75 per cent), the wali (10 per cent), and the cadis (15 per cent).[11]

Given a more or less free hand by the government, Filonardi drew up a set of customs and tariff regulations for the Benadir ports. Faithful to Article VIII of the Brussels Act of 1890, he prohibited the importation and sale of firearms and ammunition. All ships had to receive a certificate of permission before unloading; in this way, the company could inspect cargoes for contraband. By means of a low import tariff and a scale of high export taxes, Filonardi sought to set his company on a profitable course in the Benadir. All imported goods were

9 Provisional Ordinance for the Government and Administration of Territory under the Protection of Italy, annexed to Filonardi report, No. 171, September 16, 1894, ASMAI, pos. 75/1, f. 3.

10 The Maria Theresa or Levantine thaler is a coin of high silver content (.833 fine) issued for trade purposes since 1780. Originally an Austrian coin, the thaler had no fixed relation to any other currency. It varied in value from approximately 45 to 65 cents.

11 Ordinance for the application of the Muslim Shariʿa, signed by Filonardi, October 24, 1893, Historical-Documentary Collection of the Garesa at Mogadishu, item 33.

subject to a 5 per cent ad valorem import tariff, with the exception of transit goods, coal, naval equipment, provisions, and machinery and equipment for agriculture and for construction of roads and transportation facilities. Spirits and alcoholic liquors were taxed a high 25 per cent ad valorem for import, although beers and wines of less than 20 per cent alcoholic content by volume were taxed the regular 5 per cent. High tariffs were imposed upon the exportation of such valued items as tobacco (25 per cent ad valorem); ivory, copal, and rubber (15 per cent); and cloves (30 per cent). Special consideration was given to Zanzibari goods, lest they be charged a double tariff; technically, the Benadir was still under the Zanzibari flag.[12]

Thus before arriving on the Benadir coast in his official capacity on October 5, 1893, Filonardi had undertaken the administrative ordering of his company's concession. Filonardi's policies sometimes entailed indirect rule, as in the use of the walis and cadis. At other times his administration was nothing more than an outright beneficent and paternal rule by decree. When needed, force was applied. There was no over-all plan of unity. In fact, none was needed, for Filonardi meant to keep the administrative process as simple and as inexpensive as possible.

From the very beginning of the concession, Filonardi had few illusions about the ease with which his company could be established. He was taking a chance, a businessman's calculated risk, that depended on the peace and prosperity of the area in which he hoped to trade. For this reason he was deeply concerned about the Somali uprising at Kismayu and Lovatelli's participation in aid of the British.[13] It was with

12 Customs Ordinance for the Benadir Ports, signed by Filonardi, September 20, 1893, ASMAI, pos. 75/1, f. 3.

13 "Affairs at Kismayu," *Gazette for Zanzibar and East Africa* (September 6, 1893), pp. 1–2. For his heroism at Kismayu in February, 1893, Queen Victoria granted Lovatelli the title of Honorary Companion of the Order of Saints Michael and George (Tornielli, London, to Foreign Minister, November 29, 1893, ASMAI, pos. 55/6, f. 43).

some relief that he learned at Brava, his first stop on Somali shores, that the Somali of that town were well disposed toward the new regime. The next day Filonardi and his party disembarked at Mogadishu, having also visited Merca and its aged wali Sheik Salih bin Muksim.[14]

The *Staffetta,* on which Filonardi had been traveling, continued its voyage up and down the coast, familiarizing the coastal populations with the symbol of Italian might. Again at Brava on the seventh of October, Commander Incoronato sent ashore a landing party. Captain Ugo Ferrandi, an Italian commercial explorer familiar with the Somali region, led the party, which consisted of Lieutenant Maurizio Talmone (the ship's doctor), a member of the crew, thirty askaris supplied by the wali of Brava, and two men from each of Brava's five tribes. The route taken was the main road to Bardera. In the course of a ten-hour march, the Italians learned much that did not bode well for the future of the concession. Because of intertribal warfare, which was a daily condition of life in Somalia, the agriculture of Brava's hinterland was stagnant, and the Webi Gof, an irrigation channel deriving from the Webi Shebelle, had been blocked during the hostilities. Nevertheless, the party was of the opinion that with kindness and a conciliatory attitude, the apparently friendly native populations could be won over. Talmone's report was illustrative of the general optimism of the Italians:

Even if our Benadir establishments should not produce immediate results, despite the riches of which I believe them capable . . . it will not have been unpleasant for us to have been among the pioneers who prepared for future generations of Italians a convenient outlet for the overflow of our people and our products.[15]

Talmone's hopes for a peaceful penetration of Somalia were short lived; within forty-eight hours of the completion

[14] Filonardi, Mogadishu, to Foreign Minister, November 10, 1893, *Libro Verde,* doc. 81, p. 177.

[15] Lieutenant Maurizio Talmone, Brava, to Commander of the *Staffetta,* October 9, 1893, *Libro Verde,* doc. 81, annex, pp. 178–80.

of his report he was mortally wounded, the victim of a Somali fanatic at Merca on October 11, 1893. A spear had struck him as his launch approached the beach through the surf. An askari immediately shot down the Somali. Filonardi subsequently learned that the murderer regarded his act as a gesture of Somali superiority over the Italians. As punishment, the dead murderer's hand was cut off, the aged wali was replaced, the city was shelled, and the population was compelled to surrender all its firearms.[16] The Filonardi Company thereafter maintained a garrison of two hundred eighty Arab askaris at Merca, under the command of the new wali, Suleiman bin Hamed, and eight Arab mercenary captains.[17] The Merca incident was a rude awakening for the Italians. Filonardi, whose health had gravely suffered from intestinal disturbances, fever, and jaundice during September, became depressed at the unpleasant prospect of difficult times ahead.[18] After the bombardment of Merca, the Bimal tribesmen of the interior no longer brought their goods to the city, which suffered from a food shortage and high prices. To ease the situation, Filonardi sent grain to the boycotted city, but Merca remained a problem for some time to come.

The Benadir ports had been subjected to Italian control, and complete satisfaction had been obtained for the death of Talmone; but the price for the pacification of the Benadir

16 Ironically, at the end of September, 1893, the wali of Merca had remarked to Commander Incoronato that he had heard a rumor to the effect that the purpose of the *Staffetta*'s mission was to bombard Merca. Incoronato reported that the *Staffetta*'s cannons would sound only in salute or in proclamation of a holiday, "which closed the incident with great hilarity on the part of everyone" (Incoronato report, No. 75, Zanzibar, September 28, 1893, ASMAI, pos. 75/1, f. 3).

17 Filonardi, Mogadishu, to Foreign Minister, November 10, 1893, *Libro Verde*, doc. 81, p. 177.

18 Filonardi, Mogadishu, to Foreign Minister, November 10, 1893, ASMAI, pos. 75/1, f. 3. In this thirty-six-page report, Filonardi wrote, "I do not have the strength to stay up all night to organize my notes and send, as is my desire, a detailed report to Your Excellency; I limit myself to writing a few explanatory lines."

was beginning to rise. Filonardi was determined that his company remain a purely commercial-administrative organization; to make it a paramilitary organization would prove its financial ruin. Yet, for the sake of the company's prestige, Filonardi knew that he could no longer proceed gradually but had to speed up construction of walls and garrisons. Here he found himself in a dilemma. If he did nothing to raise the company's prestige, he would be inviting disparaging actions and words from the Arabs of the coastal towns, who regarded the Benadir as their exclusive trading area, and from the Somali of the hinterland, who would expand the range of their traditional raids to the coastal region. A third danger, barely visible over the horizon, lay in the menace of Ethiopian expansionism. Yet, to undertake a minimal program of fortifications and garrisons would require an initial expense far beyond the company's means, in view of the impermanent nature of the concession. Filonardi estimated the cost of defense fortifications at 25,000 thalers, a sizable investment of doubtful value. If the concession had not been temporary, the amortization of such a sum normally could have been carried over a period of fifty years.[19] Because this method of raising money was not possible, Filonardi had to inform the government of the company's straitened position. As consul-general at Zanzibar, he requested that the government give the company an advance of 150,000 lire, that is, half of the next subsidy.[20]

The government now showed signs of concern for its Benadir possession. Commander Incoronato had warned the government of obstacles to the development of the colony. He found the Somali to be "untamable and lazy . . . preferring to live by war and rapine." Pessimistically, he reviewed one of the basic facts of the Benadir's geography, "the absolute lack of, I shall not say ports, but of havens for ships . . .

[19] Filonardi, Mogadishu, to Foreign Minister, November 10, 1893, ASMAI, pos. 75/1, f. 3.

[20] Filonardi report, No. 90, Zanzibar, December 31, 1893, ASMAI, pos. 75/1, f. 3.

a fact *without remedy*." And he reminded the government
that because of tribal hostility and the company's relative
isolation and limited means, they should not forget that one
day they might "be obliged to intervene."[21]

It could hardly be said that Incoronato shared Cecchi's
glowing reports of the trade potential of the horn of Africa;
in fact, he even doubted that the Benadir ports were or could
ever be outlets for southern Ethiopia and the Kaffa region.
He came to five other conclusions:

Somalia is fertile in the river regions, but the population is more
concerned with internal disputes; this situation could work to our
advantage.

Somalia is not a good country for emigration; Europeans could
only be supervisors, not workers.

Cotton, though of poor quality, might provide a good export
crop; meat and grain might also be exported to Eritrea.

The so-called port of Itala is useless.

Not much can be expected from the company, inasmuch as it lacks
serious guaranties and the act of concession is such that no one
would want to expend large sums. Yet there is promise of trade
with the interior, especially if a station were set up at Lugh on the
Juba.[22]

Incoronato then pointed out that Italy was morally and materially committed to the Benadir and could not back down
on its commitments. Somewhat ominously, he wrote, "The
government ought to think of taking the company's place."

The government had already taken action, although of only
a limited kind. The naval ministry had sent the gunboat
Volturno on another exploratory mission to the Benadir, but
its commander's report was as discouraging as Incoronato's
had been. Commander Edoardo Ruelle spoke no more highly
of the Somali or of the Benadir ports. Yet he came to the

---

21 Incoronato report, No. 90, Zanzibar, December 3, 1893, ASMAI, pos. 75/1, f. 3.

22 Incoronato's final report to Naval Minister, Port Said, January 10, 1894,
Libro Verde, doc. 82, pp. 181–83.

conclusion that "it is indispensable that above all else the company establish itself securely and not require the government to intervene at any time to put down revolts, avenge insults, or subjugate rebels."[23] Convinced of the importance of strengthening the Filonardi Company, Ruelle argued that its three-year contract was too vague. Early in December Foreign Minister Brin pursued the problem further. Count Lovatelli, who had advised the government on its policy six months earlier, was instructed to "inspect and supervise the operations of the Filonardi Company . . . and to suggest possibilities for the definitive solution of the Benadir question."[24]

For several months Filonardi continued to manage his company's affairs and to administer the Benadir ports as best he could. Certainly, he was a man of broad and earnest views and great energy. Few people were as well acquainted with the Somali coast as he. Having travelled frequently up and down the coast of East Africa both as trader and as consul-general at Zanzibar, he knew the Benadir and its peoples. But however great were the efforts and abilities of Filonardi and his hard-working agents to better the conditions of local commerce and of customs revenues, they were not enough to cover the expenses of administration. The Filonardi Company was a financial failure.

Desperately, Filonardi appealed to the foreign ministry to renegotiate the government's convention with the sultan of Zanzibar and lower the annual rental payment for the Benadir ports. The rental, it appeared, constituted some 60 per cent of the company's budget.[25] But the foreign ministry was no longer so sympathetically inclined toward the Benadir venture. The Giolitti government had fallen over the question of agrarian unrest in Sicily and had been replaced by a

[23] Ruelle report to Naval Minister, Zanzibar, December 1, 1893, *Libro Verde,* doc. 83, pp. 187–88.

[24] Brin, Rome, to Lovatelli, December 4, 1893, ASMAI, pos. 55/6, f. 44.

[25] Filonardi report, No. 221, Zanzibar, December 31, 1893, ASMAI, pos. 75/1, f. 3.

new Crispi ministry. Baron Alberto Blanc had assumed control of foreign affairs and was less than cordial to Filonardi. In reply to Filonardi's demands for changes in the terms of concession, he brusquely telegraphed: "You can make no modifications in the contract with the sultan of Zanzibar. That is the Royal Government's concern. Please send me your resignation as consul."[26] Filonardi had no choice but to resign, leaving the government free to appoint as consul at Zanzibar someone who could watch over the operations of the Filonardi Company.

Relieved of his consular position, Filonardi devoted himself even more seriously to company affairs. He frequently requested the government to cancel the contract because his company could no longer fulfil its obligations. Bitterly, he wrote that although the company was doing its best the government had left it "without means of defense and contributed directly to destroying its credit, its morale, and its prestige among the natives."[27] These harsh words did not deter Blanc from his course of action. Rather, the government was swayed by reports from another quarter. Word came from London that the British government, as protector of the sultanate of Zanzibar, wished to inquire "whether the Italian Government are contemplating withdrawing from the Ports of the Benadir. . . . It is quite possible that Filonardi & Co. have discovered by experience that they have let themselves in for a bad thing and are consequently desirous of getting out of it!"[28] The Italian government could not withdraw gracefully now, for Italian prestige in Europe was at stake.

Within a fortnight of receiving the British note, Blanc appointed Antonio Cecchi as consul in Zanzibar. Cecchi was ordered to investigate the Filonardi Company, and Lovatelli,

---

26 Blanc, Rome, to Filonardi, March 17, 1894, ASMAI, pos. 75/1, f. 5.

27 Filonardi, Zanzibar, to Foreign Minister (confidential), April 2, 1894, ASMAI, pos. 75/1, f. 5.

28 British Ambassador F. C. Ford, Rome, to Blanc, March 11, 1894, ASMAI, pos. 75/1, f. 5.

who had barely arrived at Aden on the mission assigned to him by Blanc's predecessor, was given new instructions. He was to accompany a hunting expedition organized by William Astor Chanler as special government delegate empowered to make treaties of protection with chiefs resident in the Italian sphere of influence.[29] Cecchi was not content with his appointment as consul in Zanzibar and, in a series of letters and telegrams, revealed an unpleasant side of his character: he was jealous of those who might appear as rivals for the attention of his superiors. Cecchi could not understand why Lovatelli was also present in East Africa. "It is neither necessary nor convenient," he wrote, "to hold two distinct functionaries here. . . . Frankly, I know of no reason why I should tolerate this situation."[30] From then on there was a running dispute between the two men until Cecchi persuaded Blanc to recall Lovatelli in the spring of 1895. In the meantime, ironically, Lovatelli served as acting consul in Zanzibar during the absences of Cecchi on the Benadir coast.

By June, 1894, Cecchi had collected the first results of his inquiry on the Benadir. In typical fashion he prefaced his report with remarks of an incisive nature. He was determined to put the Filonardi Company in a bad light. He found the company to be "simply a name, or very little more." Abu Bakr bin Awod, the company's interpreter, he found to be astute and greedy. Distrusting Filonardi's statistics, Cecchi audited the company's books, which he described as in chaotic disorder. He claimed that the company's income for the year 1893–94 amounted to 461,000 lire, including government subsidies of 300,000 lire for the administration of the Benadir and 50,000 lire for the occupation of Itala. Administrative expenses amounted to 376,554 lire, including the rental of 256,000 lire paid the sultan of Zanzibar. Thus, according to Cecchi's figures, the Filonardi Company made a profit of

[29] Blanc, Rome, to Cecchi, May 19, 1894, and Blanc, Rome, to Lovatelli (confidential), May 21, 1894, ASMAI, pos. 55/6, f. 44.

[30] Cecchi, Zanzibar, to Blanc, May 6, 1894, ASMAI, pos. 55/6, f. 44.

almost 85,000 lire.[31] A later government inquiry, however, ascertained the company's income for the period under study to have been 463,076 lire, including subsidies, and its expenses to have amounted to 493,934 lire, including the rental. According to these figures, then, the company had a deficit of 30,858 lire.[32] (See Appendix II.)

Cecchi's recommendations were neither new nor refreshing. First, he proposed that at the end of the Filonardi concession the government request the sultan of Zanzibar to reduce the yearly rental. The IBEA, Cecchi claimed, paid only 240,600 lire for its concession on the Kenya coast, and its port of Mombasa alone provided an income equal to 560,000 lire. Second, Cecchi advised that, inasmuch as the Filonardi Company had too small a capital for the venture and could not fulfil its obligations, the government should cancel the concession and assume direct administration of the Benadir. In the event of direct government administration, Cecchi continued, the support of a warship would be required. Last, he suggested that the government negotiate for the cession of Kismayu, recently abandoned by the IBEA, as it was doubtless the only adequate port on the whole Somali coast.[33] His first point was one that Filonardi had made in his correspondence with Foreign Minister Blanc in December, 1893. And the second point was not unfamiliar to Filonardi. The final suggestion—about Kismayu—was almost an *idée fixe* of Cecchi, but it was one with which the naval ministry strongly sympathized.

The government's response to the Cecchi report was to criticize Cecchi, whose enthusiasm for imperialistic ventures

---

[31] Results of the Cecchi inquest into the Filonardi Company, Zanzibar, June 10, 1894, ASMAI, pos. 75/1, f. 5.

[32] Quirighetti report (1896), ASMAI, pos. 75/4, f. 34; see also Appendix II for figures derived from the Quirighetti and other reports. Filonardi denied that Cecchi's data were accurate (Filonardi, Rome, to Blanc, July 15, 1895, ASMAI, pos. 75/1, f. 9).

[33] Results of Cecchi inquest, June 10, 1894, ASMAI, pos. 75/1, f. 5.

it did not share. Blanc sharply warned Cecchi that the cancellation of the Filonardi Company's contract was out of the question. If he thought government administration less costly, let the expenses of the Eritrean experience prove otherwise. Blanc instructed Cecchi to come to terms with the company and authorized him to offer Filonardi an annual stipend of 30,000 lire if he would consent to the reorganization of his administration by Cecchi. As an alternative plan, Blanc proposed a twenty-five-year concession of the Benadir, provided that the Filonardi Company raise capital of at least 2,000,000 lire exclusively from Italian sources.[34]

Throughout the balance of 1894, while Filonardi and his company continued to trade on the Benadir, Cecchi shuttled back and forth between Zanzibar and Mogadishu. Following Cecchi's advice, Filonardi instituted some misguided economies: the chartered weekly steamship service was discontinued; company warehouses and installations in Zanzibar were closed; and the garrisons at Merca and Brava were reduced by thirty and sixty men respectively as the immediate danger of tribal uprisings subsided. The total savings amounted to approximately 36,000 lire. A shift in the lira-rupee exchange rate enabled the company to make a 47,000 lire profit on the government subsidy. But although the company's finances were ordered to Cecchi's satisfaction, he still found the company's attitude to be negative. Filonardi refused to accept the government offer of a stipend until the government reimbursed his company for repairing the city walls of Mogadishu.[35] Undaunted, Cecchi continued to demand that the government take positive action. "What we need in the Benadir is precisely a COLONY. . . . [The Filonardi Company is] in itself an eloquent document of in-

[34] Blanc, Rome, to Cecchi, September 21, 1894, ASMAI, pos. 75/1, f. 6.

[35] Filonardi, Mogadishu, to Cecchi, November 27, 1894, ASMAI, pos. 75/1, f. 6. Filonardi claimed a reimbursement of 300,000 lire for work Cecchi said should not have cost more than 12,000 lire.

capacity. . . . We need instead valid political organization."[36]

During this period when the government showed no particular haste in reaching a definitive solution to the Benadir question, Filonardi continued to stabilize his company's position on the Somali coast, and Cecchi, for his part, continued to submit report after report on the organization of the Benadir concession. The matter seemed to have reached an impasse, when Giorgio Mylius, a wealthy Milanese industrialist, arrived at Zanzibar early in January, 1895, to "gain impressions" of the Benadir coast. Mylius' impressions of the Benadir were "not among the most favorable." Lack of capital and of good ports north of the Juba were, of course, mentioned. But most interesting are Mylius' comments on the concessionary company: "The company does not really exist except in the person of Signor Filonardi. He, on his part, is under the absolute control of the Arab Abu Bakr, his alter ego and a man who inspires little trust."[37]

A connection between Mylius and Cecchi was not long in becoming apparent. The industrialist was particularly interested in the possibility of growing cotton in Somalia, and perhaps of equal importance, he was Cecchi's nephew.[38] Cecchi was determined to let the Filonardi Company's concession expire at the end of its three-year term and to replace it with a chartered company more to his liking. Early in March, Blanc too came to this conclusion, but unwilling to commit himself further, he suggested only that Cecchi visit Eritrea to exchange ideas with the governor of that Red Sea colony.[39] By May, when he had concluded his mission to

36 Cecchi report, Zanzibar, December 24, 1894, ASMAI, pos. 75/1, f. 6.

37 Mylius, Zanzibar, to Cecchi, February 6, 1895, ASMAI, pos. 75/3, f. 24.

38 A. Ribera, *Vita di Antonio Cecchi* (Florence: Vallecchi, 1940), p. 235.

39 Blanc, Rome, to Cecchi, March 2, 1895, *Libro Verde*, doc. 87, p. 212. At this time the government was still unsure of its solution for the Benadir. Blanc relied heavily on the advice of G. Silvestrelli, chargé d'affaires at the London embassy, who opposed the principle of concessions on the ground that the aims of concessionaire and government would always differ and that foreign capital, so badly needed in colonial enterprises, would end up

Eritrea, Cecchi was convinced that the ailing Filonardi, in whom he found a certain patriotism, would abide by any decision the government might make. Filonardi wanted only to know the exact date the government wished to abrogate the accord. Cecchi busied himself with making substitute arrangements and advised the government to continue the concessionary agreement for its full term, that is, until July, 1896.[40]

In the summer of 1895 both Filonardi and Mylius put pressure on the government to reach a solution. The Milanese industrialist was confident that a well-directed new company with agricultural as well as commercial interests was the key to the situation.[41] The Roman trader was more concerned that the government come to a fair settlement of debts due his company.[42] Filonardi traveled to Rome and bitterly assailed the government for trying to avoid full payment of its debts. His trip's sole accomplishment was to confirm the government in its desire to rid itself of V. Filonardi e Compagnia.

Cecchi now undertook a full and open espousal of the cause of Mylius and his partners. In November, the government ordered him to return to Italy for consultations on the Benadir. Cecchi first journeyed to Milan to stimulate interest among manufacturers and industrialists in the "great commercial advantages" of the Benadir.[43] Always conscious of an imperial strategy and fearful of trouble with Ethiopia, Cecchi frequently mentioned the strategic importance of Somalia

---

in control of the colonies (Silvestrelli memorandum, Rome, April 10, 1895, ASMAI, pos. 75/1, f. 7).

[40] Cecchi to Blanc, May 3, 1895, ASMAI, pos. 75/1, f. 7.

[41] Mylius, Rome, to Blanc, July 10, 1895, ASMAI, pos. 75/3, f. 24.

[42] Filonardi, Rome, to Blanc, July 15, 1895, ASMAI, pos. 75/1, f. 9.

[43] "For Commercial Speculation in the Benadir," *Il Commercio* (Milan), November 17, 1895, p. 1.

in his conferences and in newspaper interviews.[44] While the public was reading of this renewed interest in East Africa, Cecchi and Mylius, in collaboration with eight prominent Milanese, quickly drew up the constitution for a new company to take over the Benadir concession. Upon hearing of this move, Prime Minister Crispi notified the founders of the new company of his "extreme delight to see them participating in . . . and promoting this noble undertaking."[45] Within a short time the new company had approved a concessionary scheme drafted by Mylius; Blanc responded by promising the new company the government's full moral support.[46]

Cecchi's allusions to difficulties with Ethiopia came at a critical moment. For years the disputed frontier between Eritrea, the Sudan, and Ethiopia had been the scene of skirmishes with the Mahdists and the untamed border tribes. When General Oreste Baratieri, military governor of the colony, returned to Eritrea in January, 1895, after consultations in Rome, he decided upon a policy of force to secure the Italian position in Eritrea. Soon Italian forces occupied part of the Tigrean region of northern Ethiopia and drove Ras Mangasha of Tigre into closer alliance with Menelik, the emperor of Ethiopia. At the same time Italian relations with Menelik continued to deteriorate. Menelik refused to recognize the validity of the Italian text of the Treaty of Uccialli, by which Europeans regarded Ethiopia as an Italian protectorate. Instead, he had expansionist ideas of his own, not only in the direction of the Red Sea, but also into the lowlands of Somalia.

The foreign ministry was aware of the Ethiopian threat

[44] "Italy in the Benadir: An Interview with Captain Cecchi," *Corriere della Sera* (Milan), November 22, 1895, pp. 1–2.

[45] Crispi to Prefect of Milan, November 21, 1895, ASMAI, pos. 75/3, f. 24. The founders of the company included Duke Visconti di Modrone, Count Alberto Amman, Ettore Ponti, Luigi Erba, Silvio Crespi, Felice Schreibler, Ferdinando Bocconi, and Count Emilo Turati, all of prominent Milanese families.

[46] Blanc, Rome, to Mylius, Crespi, and Carminati, December 7, 1895, ASMAI, pos. 75/3, f. 24.

and took tentative measures to secure the hinterland of the Benadir, whose boundary with Ethiopia was also undefined. On May 3, 1895, Foreign Minister Blanc concluded an agreement with the Italian Geographic Society to send Vittorio Bòttego on an East African expedition for purposes not purely geographical. Bòttego, who had explored the upper courses of the Juba for the society in 1892 and 1893, was instructed "to see to the establishment of a commercial station at Lugh" and to study localities where the Italians might eventually conclude "political and commercial agreements . . . in order to tie the trade of those areas to the Lugh station and to the ports of the Benadir."[47] Thus the Italians sought to establish their control over the vast hinterland of the Benadir. The Bòttego expedition was organized in August, 1895, on the eve of the Italian invasion of Tigre.

After taking on a company of two hundred fifty men and a large quantity of ammunition at Massawa, the Bòttego party disembarked at Brava in mid-September. News soon reached Bòttego of the temporary occupation of Lugh by a column of some two thousand Ethiopians. Judging the situation precarious, he pressed inland and reached Lugh on November 18. The Ethiopians were nowhere to be seen, and Bòttego arranged to leave Captain Ugo Ferrandi and forty-five askaris in Lugh to set up a trading station, to establish friendly relations with the Somali tribes, and to pacify and arbitrate intertribal disputes. On November 21, 1895, he concluded a treaty of protection and friendship with the sultan of Lugh. Five weeks later, assuming everything to be under control, Bòttego and his expedition continued inland.

What Bòttego did not know was that relations between Ethiopia and Italy had deteriorated even further during the course of his expedition. On December 7 the Italian forces in Eritrea had suffered a setback at Amba Alagi; Menelik had

---

[47] Enrico De Leone, *Le prime ricerche di una colonia e la esplorazione geografica, politica ed economica* (Vol. II of *L'Italia in Africa;* Rome: Istituto Poligrafico dello Stato, 1955), p. 339.

finally intervened, destroying an Italian detachment and surrounding the fortress of Makalle by vastly superior forces.
Bòttego continued his explorations in complete ignorance of
these events, peacefully penetrating deep into southwestern
Ethiopia by the end of February. Nor was the Italian expedition aware of Menelik's decisive defeat of the Italian army at
Adowa on March 1, 1896. Ten days later the imperialistic
Crispi government fell. Not for months did Bòttego learn of
this disaster to the cause of Italian expansionism.

The defeat at Adowa had a great effect on the development
of Italian colonialism in Somalia. Cecchi, who was in Rome
when the Crispi government fell, quickly penned a letter to
Onorato Caetani, the new foreign minister. The indomitable
Cecchi politely reminded the new minister that before the
new concession could take effect it would be necessary to
make arrangements for the disposition of the old concession
before its expiration on July 16, 1896. It followed, said Cecchi,
that he should return to the Benadir as soon as possible to
make such arrangements before the advent of the southwest
monsoon in mid-May.[48] In the meantime, Cecchi presided
over the negotiations between the government and the new
company. On April 15, 1896, a convention was signed by
Prime Minister Rudinì and other members of the cabinet
and the officers of the Società Anonima Commerciale Italiana
del Benadir, more commonly known as the Società del Benadir (or "Benadir Company").

The convention, subject to approval by the Italian Parliament, called for the "peaceful management" of the Benadir
coast and towns and of the hinterland described in the Anglo-
Italian protocols of 1891 and 1894.[49] The company was to
concern itself with the commercial and administrative development of the land. The government reserved the right to

[48] Cecchi, Rome, to Foreign Minister, March 11, 1896, ASMAI, pos. 55/6, f. 46.

[49] Original text of the convention between the government and the Società
Anonima Commerciale Italiana del Benadir, April 15, 1896, ASMAI, pos. 75/3,
f. 26.

inspect and "watch over" the operations of the company but did not contract "any obligation to defend the colony from external attacks, reserving to itself full liberty of action to take such steps as it may consider necessary in the public interest." In return for its efforts, the Benadir Company was to receive an annual subsidy of 400,000 gold francs, or about 50,000 lire more than the Filonardi Company had received.[50] The increase in subsidy was to cover the operation of trading stations at Jumbo, Bardera, Lugh, and perhaps elsewhere. After twelve years, the subsidy was to be reduced to 300,000 gold francs.

The company was to have full control over customs and taxes, mining rights, and domain lands. Products of Somalia were to receive the same preferential treatment in Italy as those of the Eritrean colony. The company was to fly the Italian flag, pay the sultan's rent, administer the subsidies to the sultans of Obbia and the Mijjertein, maintain the buildings received from the government, operate a postal service, respect existing laws and treaties, and apply the general acts of Berlin and of Brussels regarding slavery, alcohol, and trade in firearms.

The company undertook a guaranty that two-thirds of its shares would always remain in Italian hands and that its board of directors would comprise only Italians resident in Italy, Eritrea, or the Benadir. The government absolved itself of responsibility of any sort for "any credit operations made by the company, even in the interest of the colony, and the company in such operations [could] offer as guaranties only its own private property and its private credit." For purposes of defense, the company was entitled to withdraw arms and munitions from the military depot at Massawa at cost price; the government also agreed to station a warship in East African waters. To ensure the company's long-term investment, the convention was of fifty years' duration beginning July 16,

50 The gold franc and the lira were almost on a par at this time.

1896. The government was permitted to cancel the contract after twenty-five years with two years' notice of such intention; the company could cancel after twelve years with one year's notice.

This in broad outline was the plan of the convention signed by government and company officials. In an attempt to profit by the experience of the Filonardi Company, the two parties to the contract had expanded their respective commitments. In essence, however, the agreement was similar to that made with Filonardi. The government meant to keep its colonial commitments in the Benadir at a minimum and delegated as much responsibility as possible to the chartered company. Some of the pitfalls encountered by Filonardi were avoided by the sounder financing of the Benadir Company and the guaranty of a term of at least twenty-five years in which to make a profitable investment in Benadir commerce and agriculture. But before the new company could assume full administrative responsibility for the concession, the convention had to be approved by Parliament, an unlikely prospect after Adowa had made colonialism unpopular.

Early in May Cecchi returned to Mogadishu with an official letter informing Filonardi of the government's intentions in the Benadir. Somewhat irritated and displeased by the trend of events, Filonardi nevertheless agreed to the detailed plan for the change of administration. On July 15, 1896, he transferred the administration of the concession to a representative of the Benadir Company, remaining, however, until the September monsoons as acting royal commissioner for the Benadir in order to maintain order and security.[51] This temporary administration was, of course, under the direct control of Antonio Cecchi, consul at Zanzibar.

Of immediate importance for the safe functioning of the chartered company was the preservation of peace among the various tribes in Somalia. Because of his close personal ties with many of the Somali chiefs and elders, Filonardi had

51 Cecchi, Zanzibar, to Foreign Minister, May 26, 1896, ASMAI, pos. 75/2, f. 15.

achieved a *modus vivendi* whereby real trouble with the Somali was, if not permanently resolved, at least postponed. Confident of a turn for the better now that the Filonardi Company was being replaced by one more to his liking, Cecchi now described the tribesmen as rather well disposed toward the Italians; the mutually hostile Bimal and Abgal tribesmen around Merca, in particular, had apparently ended their grievances amicably upon the death of the unpopular wali of Merca.[52] How long the tribesmen of the interior would remain at peace was unknown; this was an issue which Cecchi preferred not to face.

In the months of July and August Cecchi concerned himself with the task of approaching the sultan of Zanzibar for a reduction of the annual rental. Letters and telegrams passed back and forth between London and Rome and Zanzibar until the Italian and British authorities agreed among themselves that the rental could safely be reduced by some 40,000 rupees to 120,000 rupees (192,000 lire) per annum. When the behind-the-scenes bargaining was finished, Cecchi contacted the acting British agent-general, Lloyd Mathews, to discuss "the advisability of coming to some sort of friendly understanding by which we could reduce the annuity to a more moderate amount."[53] By the first of September agreement had been reached, greatly facilitated by the succession to the throne of Seyyid Hamoud bin Muhammad, a ruler completely dependent on British support. Cecchi thus helped the new company to achieve at least the prospect of a balanced budget.[54]

On September 12, Cecchi left Zanzibar for Mogadishu, where he found evidence of discontent with the policies established by the Filonardi Company. A group of Indian merchants had petitioned him to redress their grievances. The

[52] Cecchi, Zanzibar, to Foreign Minister, May 30, 1896, ASMAI, pos. 75/2, f. 15.

[53] Cecchi, Zanzibar, to Mathews, August 12, 1896, ASMAI, pos. 55/7, f. 49.

[54] Cecchi report, No. 141, Zanzibar, September 2, 1896, ASMAI, pos. 55/7, f. 49.

merchants, who had been settled in Mogadishu for several decades, claimed that the Filonardi Company had monopolized all trade in Itala, Warsheik, and other coastal villages. They also alleged that Abu Bakr bin Awod, whom they hated, had been using his position in the company for his own personal advantage and to their detriment. At one and the same time the Indians found him to be imperious, haughty, and fanatically devoted to his employer, "Mr. Felunardy the Consul."[55] In the light of later events, the position of Abu Bakr bin Awod constituted a threat—unrecognized by Cecchi—to those who sought to displace Filonardi.

Late in September Filonardi left Mogadishu. The departure of the well-liked Filonardi placed Cecchi and the new administration in a difficult position. Despite the fact that Abu Bakr and other pro-Filonardi Arabs and Somali were muttering about an uprising that might take place after Filonardi's departure, Cecchi reported "a state of tranquillity and security" in the Benadir.[56] This time of relative peace was not to last long. Although Italy and Ethiopia had come to terms in the Treaty of Addis Ababa (October 26, 1896), the frontier between Somalia and Ethiopia remained undefined, having been left open to further negotiation.[57] The state of war between the two countries had been ended, however, and the Treaty of Uccialli officially abrogated. What the Italians could not know at the time was that Menelik, with whom they had signed the new treaty, had little control over his vassals on the fringes of his empire.

In 1887 Menelik had first entered the Ogaden, a region bordering Somalia; at the present time, Menelik's local commanders looked to another renewal of the centuries-old rivalry with the Somali in the hope of extending Ethiopian ter-

---

[55] English translation of letter in Arabic from nine Indian traders, Mogadishu, to Cecchi, July 29, 1896, appended to letter from Cecchi, Zanzibar, to Foreign Minister (confidential), September 4, 1896, ASMAI, pos. 75/1, f. 11.

[56] Cecchi report, No. 179, Zanzibar, November 6, 1896, ASMAI, pos. 75/2, f. 17.

[57] E. Hertslet, *The Map of Africa by Treaty* (3d ed.; London: His Majesty's Stationery Office, 1909), II, 458–59.

ritory to the shores of the Indian Ocean.[58] On November 13, 1896, a column of about one thousand Ethiopians once more threatened the town of Lugh on the Juba. Under the command of Dedjazmatch Wolde Gabre and other chiefs, the Ethiopians demanded the evacuation of the Italian garrison. Captain Ugo Ferrandi, however, held fast and rejected their demands, whereupon the invaders moved eastward into the plateau region around Baidoa, flanking the Italian coastal possessions. Faced with an imminent Ethiopian invasion, against which he had so often warned, Cecchi decided to make an alliance with the strategically located sultan of Geledi on the Webi Shebelle River. Such a tie would also serve to expand trade relations with the tribes of the interior, especially those between the Webi Shebelle and Mogadishu.[59]

With government approval, Cecchi prepared for an expedition into the interior. By November 25, he was ready to move; his caravan consisted of seventy askaris, Commander Ferdinando Maffei of the *Staffetta,* Commander Francesco Mongiardini of the *Volturno,* and fourteen other Italians, for the most part members of the crews of the two ships. That very night their encampment at Lafolè, some twelve miles inland, was attacked. Unsure whether the surprise attackers were Ethiopians or Somali, Cecchi hesitated until it was too late. He had moved too impetuously into the unknown interior. In the early morning hours, as the caravan once more got under way, it was attacked again. Within a matter of minutes, the hired askaris abandoned the Italians to their fate; by eight-thirty in the morning of November 26, all but three sailors were dead or dying. First Adowa, then Lafolè; the future of Italian colonialism in the horn of Africa looked very unpromising at the end of 1896.

[58] See E. S. Pankhurst, *Ex-Italian Somaliland* (London: Watts, 1951), pp. 13–14, and the map on p. 22.

[59] Foreign Minister Visconti Venosta, Rome, to Cecchi, December 2, 1896, *Documenti diplomatici italiani, terza serie: 1896–1907* (Rome: Libreria dello Stato, 1953), I, 217.

CHAPTER THREE

The Benadir Company, 1896–1905

After news of the death of Cecchi and his party reached Rome, the foreign minister appointed Commander Giorgio Sorrentino as royal commissioner extraordinary for the Benadir. Sorrentino was instructed "above all to provide for the security and tranquillity of the region." After a complete investigation of the causes of the attack at Lafolè, he was to take whatever steps should appear "indispensable for our dignity and for the security of the colony."[1] Above all, he was to assume no commitments other than those that "have the certainty of a successful outcome . . . within the limits of a clearly defined budget."[2] Once again the government took a firm stand against financial commitments and ex-panded political action in Somalia.

By the end of December, 1896, word began to reach Rome of the background of the Lafolè massacre. Emilio Dulio, the Benadir Company's commissioner, reported that the Ethiopians had been besieging Lugh since late November and that their onslaught had at first posed a threat to the trade routes leading to Brava on the coast. But the Ethiopians had

[1] Visconti Venosta, Rome, to Sorrentino (confidential), December 23, 1896, *Documenti diplomatici italiani, terza serie: 1896–1907* (Rome: Libreria dello Stato, 1953), I, 233–35.

[2] Brin, Rome, to Sorrentino (confidential), December 15, 1896, Archivio Storico dell'ex Ministero dell'Africa Italiana (hereinafter cited as ASMAI), pos. 75/2, f. 17.

retreated after losses suffered in an encounter with Rahanwein tribesmen; it was thought that they were also fearful that Italian reinforcements would be sent to Lugh.[3] There was no apparent connection with the incident at Lafolè. On January 26, 1897, Sorrentino landed in Mogadishu and immediately began his investigation. Within ten days he had determined that Lafolè was neither the precursor of a general uprising against the Italians nor an Ethiopian ambush but an isolated case of action by Wadan tribesmen and the tribes of Geledi, who had been spurred to the act by two Arabs from Mogadishu. Upon closer inspection Dulio and Sorrentino discovered that Abu Bakr bin Awod, Filonardi's interpreter, and a certain Islam bin Muhammad were the two Arabs responsible for instigating the massacre. Their motive had been fear of losing the profitable position they held under the Filonardi administration.[4] Abu Bakr was arrested and transported to Massawa, where he languished in prison without benefit of trial or lawyer until his death several years later.[5]

Sorrentino soon unearthed a new problem for the Italian administration: slavery and a form of domestic servitude were both recognized institutions on the Benadir coast. In fact, Cecchi himself had owned a fifteen-year old Galla servant girl. Under the circumstances—the already difficult relations with the interior tribes—neither Dulio nor Sorrentino could act immediately against slavery. Such action would have committed the Italians to a costly undertaking of doubtful outcome, a risk that Sorrentino had been ordered not to take. Instead, Sorrentino and Dulio had to content themselves

---

[3] Dulio, Mogadishu, to Foreign Minister, December 31, 1896, ASMAI, pos. 55/7, f. 50; Acting Consul Marvasi, Zanzibar, to Foreign Minister, January 4, 1897, *Documenti diplomatici italiani, terza serie: 1896–1907*, I, 239–40.

[4] Giorgio Sorrentino, *Ricordi del Benadir* (Naples: Trani, 1912), pp. 27–28.

[5] Dulio, Mogadishu, to Foreign Minister (confidential), March 20, 1898, and Foreign Minister, Rome, to Keeper of the Seals (highly confidential), April 4, 1899, ASMAI, pos. 55/7, f. 50.

with a punitive expedition against Geledi. This pleased Sorrentino, who found the Somali to be liars, thieves, and murderers. "We've got a nasty cat to skin!" he wrote. "May God protect us!"[6]

Meanwhile, trade with the interior was at a standstill. "Here in the Benadir," wrote Sorrentino in his diary for April 6, "everything must be rebuilt. We need time and patience to cut out the rot and raise a life worthy of humanity."[7] When reinforcements of two companies of Eritrean askaris finally arrived in March, the Italians completed their plans for the punitive expedition against the Wadan and Geledi. On April 20, Sorrentino led his expedition inland and burned Lafolè and several other villages. The encounter with the Italians subdued the sultan of Geledi, who quickly signed a treaty of peace and pledged obedience to the Italian government.[8] At the same time Sorrentino acted upon the advice of Ferrandi, who was in command of the station at Lugh, and arrested and deported a certain Hussein Dera of Mogadishu and other Somali for collaboration with the Ethiopians and instigation of Somali attacks on trading caravans between Lugh and the coastal towns.[9] With Abu Bakr arrested, the Ethiopians in voluntary retreat, Lafolè avenged, and leaders of Somali opposition deported, Sorrentino had virtually accomplished his mission by the end of April. The way again seemed open for the full entry of the Benadir Company into Somalia now that a peace of sorts had been restored.

The company was in an anomalous position, however, for Parliament had not yet ratified its convention with the government. Between 1896 and 1898, in fact, the Rudinì cabinet attempted to abandon Crispi's African policies. Adowa had marked a great moral defeat for the cause of colonialism, and

6 Sorrentino, *Ricordi del Benadir*, p. 51.

7 *Ibid.*, p. 183.

8 G. Pesenti, *Le Guerre coloniali* (Bologna: Zanichelli, 1947), p. 239.

9 Sorrentino, Mogadishu, to Foreign Minister, April 2, 1897, ASMAI, pos. 75/2, f. 21.

355,000,000 lire had been spent in Africa in exchange for bitterness and disillusion.[10] Minister of the Treasury Luigi Luzzatti was fearful that ratification of the Benadir convention would entail "new and useless expenses harmful to the budget. . . . The funds available to the Treasury could be better applied to internal affairs."[11] It was also difficult to settle accounts with Filonardi, and out of necessity, Foreign Minister Visconti Venosta had to use funds taken from the budget voted for Eritrea to liquidate the government's obligations.[12] To persuade Parliament to ratify the Benadir convention and its large annual subsidy proved to be an even greater problem for the cabinet.

While the government continued to move slowly, news arrived about the fate of the expedition led by Vittorio Bòttego. Lost in the shuffle of Adowa, the fall of Crispi's ministry, and Rudinì's advent to power, this expedition had dropped out of public notice. Not only was Italy ignorant of the Bòttego expedition, but the explorers were completely unaware of the unsuccessful Italian campaign against Ethiopia. On March 17, 1897, the expedition came upon an unaccountably hostile group of Ethiopians some one hundred miles west of Addis Ababa. Bòttego fell, and all but two members of the expedition were slain, martyrs for the country that neglected them.

In the meantime the handful of Italians stagnating in the Benadir on government service could only watch and wait for the government to act. The months passed, and the pro-

---

10 Direzione Centrale degli Uffici Coloniali, *L'Africa italiana al Parlamento nazionale, 1882–1905* (Rome: Tipografia Unione Cooperativa Editrice, 1907), p. 541.

11 Luzzatti, Rome, to Foreign Minister, August 10, 1897, ASMAI, pos. 75/1, f. 12.

12 Authentic copy of transaction between the government of Italy and the Società V. Filonardi e Compagnia, notarized in Rome, June 13, 1896, ASMAI, pos. 75/1, f. 14. Filonardi claimed that the government owed his company 273,000 lire for construction expenses in fortifying Mogadishu and other towns. The final settlement amounted to 149,870 lire. For its notorious parsimony, Rudinì's cabinet was known as the "Compagnia della lessina," or Misers' Club.

visional government administration continued. Sorrentino ruled in a paternal way and for the most part followed the spirit of the administrative ordinances decreed by Filonardi in 1893. Steps were taken to promote the security of the Italian holdings; in July, 1897, Ferrandi established a new trading station at Jesira, some thirteen miles southwest of Mogadishu on the coast, in order to keep open land communications between Mogadishu and Merca.[13]

Sorrentino considered as possible threats to the colony the Ethiopians, hostile Somali tribesmen, and the restless Arab askaris stationed at Itala, Warsheik, Mogadishu, Jesira, Brava, Merca, and Lugh. Fortunately for the Italians, Somali resistance to the Ethiopians reduced the danger of Ethiopian inroads in the hinterland of the Benadir; moreover, Ferrandi had been able to hold fast at Lugh. Although some Somali tribes were hostile to the Italians, the likelihood of a coalition of all tribes to rid themselves of Italian domination was small; despite the common bond of an occasionally fanatic religion, intertribal rivalries worked against Somali unity. To obviate this danger entirely, Sorrentino advocated military establishments, or presidios, especially north of Mogadishu, where the Italians possessed only Itala and Warsheik. To avoid the possibility of a revolt among the Arab mercenaries stationed at the presidios, he maintained garrisons of mutually hostile Muscat and Hadramaut Arabs.[14] By these and other means, Sorrentino did what he could to prepare the ground for another experiment in government by chartered company.

In Rome the Rudinì government was confronted by domestic crises. Rudinì was aware that unless Parliament ratified the proposed convention with the Benadir Company before July 1, 1898, it would become, by virtue of its prefatory protocol, null and void. But Parliament proved obstinate.

---

13 In December, 1897, Dulio and Sorrentino reported that in their opinion the untrustworthy Wadan were only temporarily at peace with the Italians (Sorrentino report, December 11, 1897, ASMAI, pos. 75/2, f. 20).

14 Sorrentino report, Zanzibar, October 25, 1897, ASMAI, pos. 66/3, f. 32.

Upon the advice of the head of the Colonial Office, a newly created section of the Ministry of Foreign Affairs, the government granted the Benadir Company *provisional* administration of the Benadir within the terms of the earlier agreement (see Appendix III). The provisional administration, beginning May 1, 1898, was to last only until December 31, 1898. This strategy would enable the Benadir Company to enter Somalia without awaiting the outcome of parliamentary debate and, the foreign ministry hoped, would also force the Chamber of Deputies to act. In the interim, Somalia became the Benadir Company's problem and not the government's.[15]

In June, Rudinì's cabinet fell. His successor, General Luigi Pelloux, continued to press Rudinì's plan for the Benadir. The Benadir, however, was kept in the background by a serious economic depression in Italy, rioting in the streets of Rome and Florence, and the ensuing domestic political crisis commanding national attention. On November 21, Pelloux and his foreign minister finally managed to present the proposed law for ratifying the convention with the Benadir Company.[16] Time was running out for the company's provisional administration, but Parliament still refused to vote the necessary subsidy; the anticolonialists once again successfully pleaded their case before receptive deputies. The government had no choice but to extend the provisional arrangement with the Benadir Company for a year.

Needless to say, the directors, the stockholders, and the colonial employees of the chartered company were greatly disturbed by the difficulties the Benadir bill had encountered. In Somalia, the company's hands were tied. Dulio refused to investigate the possibility of an irrigation scheme in the area between Brava and the Webi Shebelle because of the

---

15 Convention between the government and the Benadir Company, May 25, 1898, ASMAI, pos. 75/4, f. 30; memorandum to Foreign Minister from the Colonial Office, unsigned, July 5, 1898, ASMAI, pos. 75/4, f. 31. See also Appendix III.

16 *L'Africa italiana al Parlamento nazionale, 1882–1905*, pp. 591–92.

uncertainty as to the concessionary company's future in East Africa; nor did he wish to establish an Italian garrison at Bardera, where, on the opposite bank of the Juba, the English had set up a rival trading station.[17] At a stockholders' meeting in Milan a resolution was passed "that the present state of affairs should not continue" beyond December 31, 1899.[18]

The government again brought the Benadir law up for discussion in the Chamber of Deputies on November 28, 1899. The opponents of any sort of African policy, with Adowa still fresh in their minds, raised again the basic issues of former debates: colonial subsidies, the financial burdens of the state, and relations with Ethiopia. The alternative of direct government rule was less appealing, however, than the prospect of subsidizing the Benadir Company, and on the next day the bill passed the Chamber 173 to 151. One week later, Foreign Minister Visconti Venosta presented the same concession agreement to the Senate, whose members opposed the idea of politico-military colonies but eventually decided that a purely commercial colony administered by a subsidized chartered company was not completely repulsive to them. On December 19, the bill passed the Senate 66 to 10.[19] When King Umberto approved the convention with the Benadir Company on Christmas Eve, 1899, there was little elation over this anticlimactic victory among those affiliated with the demoralized company. Angelo Carminati, secretary of the company's board of directors, declared in January that "for the present the company's activity cannot assume either brilliant or impressive forms in any way whatsoever." On the market Benadir Company shares dropped in value as the company paid very small dividends; the largest shareholder from southern Italy had sold his stock "as quickly as he could . . . and others who have not had the patience and the

17 Pestalozza, Zanzibar, to Foreign Minister, May 6, 1899, ASMAI, pos. 75/5, f. 42.

18 Alfonso Sanseverino Vimercati of the Benadir Company, Milan, to Foreign Minister, September 30, 1899, ASMAI, pos. 75/5, f. 41.

19 L'Africa italiana al Parlamento nazionale, 1882–1905, pp. 616–21, 624–26.

courage to wait have done the same." Carminati lamented, "As you see, our hands are tied and we can only hope that fortune will help us."[20]

The Benadir Company's first governor, Emilio Dulio, ruled southern Somalia from December 25, 1899, to October 5, 1903, after nearly three and one-half years of biding his time at Mogadishu as provisional royal commissioner. Dulio was well acquainted with East African affairs and had been on exploratory expeditions in Ethiopia. He had served as a newspaper correspondent in Eritrea and had participated in the inquiry into the massacre of Cecchi's party at Lafolè.[21] He was also a member of the Benadir Company's board of directors. An ambitious man, Dulio had high hopes for the colony and aspirations that differed sharply from the very modest proposals of the other directors of the company.[22] His plans did not call for much in the way of changing existing lines of administrative policy. In fact, a direct line of development may be traced from the days of the Filonardi Company through the provisional government administration to the years of rule by the Benadir Company.

The Benadir administration was composed of the governor, a group of local administrators on loan from the navy, and a group of civil employees. As governor, Dulio had powers similar to those granted Filonardi; in the Benadir his word was almost absolute. The local administrators were an outgrowth of Filonardi's method of administration; agents of the Filonardi Company at the small trading stations at Merca and Brava had also functioned as government agents, informing the local population of governmental decrees and collecting customs revenues. Filonardi had had only one European on his civilian staff; Abu Bakr and other Arabs served

[20] Carminati, Milan, to Agnesa of the Colonial Office, January 30, 1900, ASMAI, pos. 75/5, f. 42.

[21] Unpublished biographies of Italians in Africa, galleys 513–14, ASMAI.

[22] Carminati, Milan, to Dulio, December 28, 1900, ASMAI, pos. 75/5, f. 42.

his purposes just as well and less expensively. After Lafolè, Sorrentino had recommended an expansion of this form of local rule by agents into residencies. Residents, at first located only at Merca and Brava, were not only to trade for the company but also to moderate tribal differences upon appeal from the decisions of the cadis and the walis. In practice, the resident ruled his administrative area paternally, in a manner similar to that of the district officer of British Africa. The position of vice-resident was later added at Merca and Jumbo. The civil employees included a physician who also served as sanitation officer, an accountant in charge of the budget and treasury of the colony, and customs officials at Mogadishu and Merca.[23]

In the isolated towns that made up the colony, which had communication with Zanzibar only twice monthly from September to May, morale among the personnel was very low. Dulio was accused of favoring some officials over others, and personal disputes were rife. In February, 1903, a report to the naval ministry confirmed the suspicions of the government: "There is nothing that could possibly justify the present dissension—only little frictions, poorly worded and badly interpreted phrases, little lapses of proper form and tact increased by isolation."[24]

When Dulio returned to Mogadishu in December, 1902, after a home leave, he found great discontent among the personnel. His administrative staff had divided into two hostile camps, one loyal to him, the other led by Igino Badolo, the resident at Merca. An inquiry into the situation was conducted by the Italian consul at Zanzibar, Giulio Pestalozza, who found ample evidence of poor morale. Badolo had once nurtured the hope of becoming governor but had fallen out of Dulio's favor after embroiling the company in legal pro-

---

[23] List of Italian personnel resident in the Benadir, annex to Carminati letter to Foreign Minister, November 13, 1900, ASMAI, pos. 75/5, f. 44.

[24] Report of Captain O. Di Monale of the *Volturno* (highly confidential), Zanzibar, February 8, 1903, ASMAI, pos. 75/5, f. 50.

ceedings over the cost of constructing in Italy in 1899 a river-boat that proved to be too large for the Webi Shebelle. Now he risked a charge of insubordination rather than co-operate with a man he personally disliked. The accountant Guido Mazzucchelli was in ill health. Doctor Carlo Mucciarelli, who had once hoped to become resident of Brava, was apathetic and unenthusiastic about his duties. The engineer Sala whom Dulio had brought to Somalia in April, 1902, had little work to do and brooded over an insult from Dulio, who had called him an unstable drifter.[25] A further source of discontent may well have been the great difference in salaries between the governor and the other officials; Dulio earned 30,000 lire an-nually, compared with 12,000 lire for Badolo, 6,000 lire for Eugenio Cappello, the resident at Brava, 5,000 lire for Doctor Mucciarelli, 4,200 lire for the accountant Mazzucchelli, 3,650 lire for the vice-resident at Jumbo, and 2,400 lire for the cus-toms officers at Mogadishu and Merca.[26] This demoralization of the administration was to play a singular role in precip-itating a crisis for the Benadir and for the chartered company.

Also potentially dangerous was the fact that Dulio regarded himself as independent of control by either the Benadir Com-pany or the Italian government. The board of directors had more than once taken Dulio to task for his "too high aspirations." Consul Pestalozza, under government orders to watch over the Benadir administration, also found Dulio diffi-cult and requested the foreign minister to remind the gov-ernor of his obligation "to deal with [the consul at Zanzibar] for urgent affairs and for affairs of a political nature."[27] Now the charge was brought forward that some of Dulio's actions verged on irregularity; before going on home leave in 1902,

[25] Pestalozza, Zanzibar, to Foreign Minister, February 8, 1903, ASMAI, pos. 75/5, f. 50.

[26] Carminati, Milan, to Foreign Minister, December 5, 1900, ASMAI, pos. 75/5, f. 44.

[27] Visconti Venosta, Rome, to Dulio, November 15, 1900, ASMAI, pos. 75/5, f. 43.

he had left instructions that disputes between Europeans and natives be judged by the cadis according to Muslim law. Moreover, the residents claimed that they had received "no standard for the administration of justice, so that in the various stations justice is administered according to each resident's individual criteria." If everything appeared to be going well in the Benadir, it was only because "everything is hushed up. . . . In substance there is no organization of justice, no military organization, no guaranty of trade and communications, no internal or external security."[28] With these basic administrative difficulties and personality conflicts, it was small wonder that the Benadir Company found it difficult to function well.

In its early years, the Benadir Company had great hopes for the economic development of its concession. Beyond the revenue from the customs taxes on imports and exports, the directors of the company looked to profitable agricultural investment in the Benadir. But the company soon discovered that agriculture on a small, private scale could not be profitably promoted in Somalia:

It would be a major woe for the colony to repeat the error committed in Eritrea by the Hon. [Leopoldo] Franchetti, who transported Italian pauperism into a region ill-adapted to European cultivation. . . . [More feasible would be] the emigration of proprietors who could go to Brava with adequate means and devote themselves to cultivation of the local products, cotton included.[29]

In order for agriculture to succeed in Somalia the company would have to attract heavy investors. Efforts to do so met with failure, and the company's source of income was limited

[28] Eduardo Cappa, Brava, to Elia Raicevich, Inspector of the Benadir Company, March 11, 1903, ASMAI, pos. 75/6, f. 60.

[29] Enrico Alamanni, agent of the Italian trading syndicate in Zanzibar, to Carminati, December 30, 1898, ASMAI, pos. 75/4, f. 32. See also Carlo Rossetto, "La Colonizzazione italiana agricola del Benadir," *L'Italia coloniale,* I (December, 1900).

to the government subsidy and customs revenues (see Appendix IV).

Over the years the Benadir Company did make a respectable profit in Somalia. And the criticism was raised that the company merely pocketed the difference between the government's annual subsidy of 400,000 lire and the rental due the sultan of approximately 192,000 lire.[30] From time to time Carminati presented the Colonial Office with elaborate programs calling for the extension of communications services, the construction of bridges over the Webi Shebelle, the opening of roads between Mogadishu and Geledi and from Brava to Bardera and Lugh, the excavation of irrigation canals, the construction of port facilities and markets, and the promotion of an animal husbandry program.[31] Yet for all this, and although the company remained in the black, the Benadir did not experience a period of great prosperity. For the greater part of the population, life continued in the unchanged pattern of centuries. In practice, the jurisdiction and trading range of the Benadir Company were limited to the few towns in which there were residents; Lugh, although valued as an important trading station for the commercial penetration of Ethiopia, remained an isolated and neglected outpost.[32] For the most part, stagnation was to be found in commerce as in administration.

Even if the company had been able to interest investors in the unproven agricultural potentialities of the Benadir, it is unlikely that such endeavors could have prospered, given the insecurity of the colony's position. From the north came the constant threat of intertribal warfare and Ethiopian intervention. The still undefined border between Menelik's empire and Somalia intensified Italian preoccupation with "the feared occupation of the station at Lugh or of the Rahanwein

30 *L'Economista italiano*, VII (April 30, 1903), 6–7.

31 Carminati, Milan, to Agnesa, January 8, 1902, ASMAI, pos. 75/5, f. 45.

32 Carminati, Milan, to Foreign Minister, March 27, 1902, ASMAI, pos. 75/5, f. 46.

plateau [between the Juba and the Webi Shebelle] by the Amhara, whose raids could cut off Lugh from all assistance . . . and would thus completely prejudice the future peaceful development of the colony."[33] Certain tribes, like the Tuni of Brava, preferred Italian rule, but the Italians did not attempt to pacify other, hostile tribes of the interior. "We make no expeditions against tribes guilty [of hostilities] but arrest individuals of that tribe who happen to be in town; [this policy] has persuaded the Bimal and the Somali of Mogadishu that we are not strong." The impression made by the punitive expedition after Lafolè could hardly have been called lasting. For defense, there was the same military organization of askaris as in the days of Zanzibari rule; the whole system lacked discipline and order.

It is not rare to find old askaris who shoot without aiming, for the only thing they know [about guns] is how to pull the trigger. By initiative of some residents, rifle ranges were set up, but these were suspended some years ago for reasons of economy, by order of the governor.[34]

If the state of military organization was merely shocking, social conditions were appalling and scandalous. It was on the question of slavery that all the other issues in the Benadir converged. Filonardi had recognized the existence of slavery in the Benadir but had limited his actions to suppression of the slave trade on the high seas.[35] In September, 1902, chafing under the Dulio administration, the resident at Merca, Igino Badolo, requested Dulio's recall to Italy and leveled accusation after accusation against his hated superior: "In a word,

---

[33] Carminati, Milan, to Foreign Minister, November 16, 1901, ASMAI, pos. 75/5, f. 47.

[34] Lieutenant Gaetano Bossi, "Notes on the Benadir Colony," Rome, December 3, 1902, ASMAI, pos. 75/4, f. 35.

[35] According to his convention with the government, Filonardi was responsible for suppressing the slave trade on land and on sea. There is indirect evidence in ASMAI that Filonardi purposely did not suppress the slave trade in the Benadir, in order to keep peace with the Somali.

nothing is being done here, and no one wants to do anything. Slavery is still at its zenith; Lugh and Bardera are two veritable slave markets."[36] Three months later, Gaetano Bossi, a naval lieutenant sent on a government mission of preliminary investigation, confirmed the grave accusation: "Slavery does exist in Italian Somalia, and it is impossible to abolish it without the effective occupation of the country by the Italian government, as in the Benadir towns."[37] The Dulio administration had done nothing but see that slaves were not mistreated, wrote Bossi, although admitting that in some instances, as at Brava and Jumbo, slavery was merely a form of domestic servitude.

It is quite possible that the government would still not have acted had not Bossi and Luigi Robecchi Bricchetti, a well-known explorer, initiated a newspaper campaign against conditions in the Benadir. Robecchi Bricchetti had been the first European to travel by land from Obbia to Alula in northern Somalia in 1890. The following year he journeyed from Obbia to Berbera on an exploratory mission for the Italian Geographic Society. After a secret mission to Tripolitania in 1895, he returned to Italy, where he helped to promote interest in the new Benadir Company. On December 18 and 19, 1902, Bossi and Robecchi Bricchetti published in the Milanese newspaper *Il Secolo* a series of articles exposing Governor Dulio and his acquiescence in the existence of slavery.[38] Within a month the antislavery campaign spread to the ranks of the Benadir Company itself. At a stockholders' meeting, Robecchi Bricchetti followed through with a sharp attack on the administration of the colony.[39] The repercussions of these accusations spread far and wide.

[36] Badolo, Brava, to Foreign Minister, September 20, 1902, ASMAI, pos. 75/6, f. 54.

[37] Bossi memorandum on slavery, December 2, 1902, ASMAI, pos. 75/6, f. 54.

[38] Carminati, Milan, to Agnesa, December 17, 1902, ASMAI, pos. 75/6, f. 55.

[39] "L'Assemblea della Società italiana per il Benadir," *La Perseveranza* (Milan), January 18, 1903, p. 2.

Early in 1903 the government ordered another preliminary investigation to determine whether slaves were still entering the Benadir, whether slaves were bought and sold with the sanction of local authorities dependent on the Benadir Company, whether their condition was one of domestic servitude or of true slavery, and what the company was doing to abolish the two institutions. The conclusions reached by Commander Onorato Di Monale, who conducted the inquiry, were damning:

[The chiefs and notables of Brava] affirmed that not only did slaves enter the Benadir ports, but that the last slaves to enter the town date back only to last December. . . . Slaves are bought and sold in the Benadir towns, not only under the eyes of Italian authorities dependent on the company, but according to the registers of the cadis of Mogadishu . . . with the sanction of those authorities. On this issue there was a REAL NEGLECT on the part of all the functionaries of the colony. . . .

In the Benadir a slave can be bought, sold, imprisoned, inherited, given as a gift, exploited, and, rarely, liberated. A slave can be freed by the spontaneous action of his owner, by purchasing his liberty for a price determined by his owner, and finally by act of a government official. . . . Cases of slaves purchasing their own freedom are extremely rare. . . . The residents or Italian employees sometimes buy and liberate women whose "services" they then utilize. The governor has proclaimed the freedom of many slaves and each act has been recorded in the cadis' registers, but these slaves . . . came from the interior, fugitives from enemy tribes. I have heard it said that fugitive slaves from friendly tribes are arrested and returned at the request of the tribe. . . .

Far from taking steps toward the gradual disappearance of domestic servitude, the company is perpetuating it and aggravating the condition. . . . There has been only a general warning by Governor Dulio last September prohibiting the slave trade. . . . This belated measure, which took place only after word reached Italy about slavery in the Benadir colony, had neither a follow-up nor an application. There is then no norm, no rule, to guide the Benadir officials in cases of slavery; at Kismayu the vice-resident of

Jumbo told me that he had NO INSTRUCTIONS relative to slaves and slavery.[40]

It was no surprise to the government when on March 2, 1903, an inquiry was made in the Chamber of Deputies about "the grave question recently brought up by the press."[41] Although Dulio had denied the earlier charges made in *Il Secolo*, it is evident from the archival records that on that very day of his denial he had issued in Mogadishu a belated notice to all chiefs prohibiting the purchase, sale, or pawning of slaves.[42] This notice had provided that all slaves wishing to purchase their freedom were entitled to do so at a just price determined by the local resident; the earnings and possessions of a slave were guaranteed as his absolute property; and all slaves owned by a slave who purchased his own freedom were declared *ipso facto* free.[43] On April 20, not long after the question had been raised in Parliament, Dulio published an ordinance establishing tribunals in all the Benadir stations to handle questions arising over slaves, "no longer according to the norms of the Shariᶜa, but according to the decrees and ordinances passed by the sultan of Zanzibar for the application of the General Act of Brussels."[44] Two days later in Rome the sixteen-year-old Anti-Slavery Society of Italy opportunely convened its first congress. (It was this society that had sent Robecchi Bricchetti to the Benadir in March to investigate slavery.) The congress, dominated by churchmen and by women of the nobility, called further attention to an issue that could no longer be ignored.[45]

[40] Di Monale report, February 8, 1903, ASMAI, pos. 75/6, f. 56.

[41] Summary account of discussion in the Chamber of Deputies, March 2, 1903, ASMAI, pos. 75/6, f. 55.

[42] Dulio, Mogadishu, to Foreign Minister, February 14, 1903, ASMAI, pos. 75/6, f. 55.

[43] Notice to all chiefs in Mogadishu, signed by Dulio, March 2, 1903, ASMAI, pos. 75/6, f. 57.

[44] Governor's Ordinance, No. 1737, Mogadishu, April 20, 1903, ASMAI, pos. 75/6, f. 57.

[45] *Atti del Primo Congresso Antischiavista Italiano* (Rome: Polo, 1903), p. 16.

The Benadir Company had no choice but to take the initiative before the matter got completely out of hand. Even before Dulio's decrees and before the Anti-Slavery Congress, the company's board of directors formally requested that the government conduct an inquiry into the state of affairs in the Benadir. In an effort at explanation, Carminati, Mylius, and S. B. Crespi reminded the government that company administration of the Benadir had not really begun until January, 1900, and that the company had been troubled by conditions to the north of the Benadir. But, aware of the true state of affairs, the three directors cautiously added that should the investigation indicate that the situation was bad beyond a doubt "the government of the colony ought to pass into other hands."[46] Early in April, the company informed the government of a change in personnel in the residencies; at the same time, the Benadir Company began its own inquiry into the affairs of the colony.[47]

The man who conducted the government's investigation was the new consul-general at Zanzibar, Luigi Mercatelli. The purpose of his mission was twofold: he was to supervise the company's own investigation, and he was to inform the government what had been done and what remained to be done. Under no circumstances was Mercatelli to indicate to anyone connected with the company that the government would assume the company's responsibilities.[48] Not too long afterward, the Benadir Company's commission of inquiry, composed of Gustavo Chiesi and Ernesto Travelli, arrived in the Benadir to conduct its investigation. Within a short time, the worst had been confirmed: the company could no longer hope that the crisis would blow over and permit a return to normalcy

46 Carminati, Mylius, and Crespi, Milan, to Foreign Minister, March 20, 1903, ASMAI, pos. 75/6, f. 56.

47 Carminati, Milan, to Foreign Minister, April 11, 1903, ASMAI, pos. 75/6, f. 56.

48 Foreign Minister, Rome, to Mercatelli, May 17, 1903, ASMAI, pos. 75/5, f. 49.

and a resumption of trading after some mild corrective measures.

After questioning Badolo, Bossi, Sala, and Mazzucchelli in Milan, Chiesi and Travelli consulted with Dulio, Mercatelli, local company officials, and cadis in the Benadir. Within a matter of months, they had concluded their report and had determined the responsibility of colonial officials, of the Benadir Company, and of the government. The two investigators blamed Dulio for never having revealed to the government the actual state of affairs regarding slavery. They accused him of remaining silent in order not to create difficulties for himself in the enjoyment of his important and profitable charge. In sum, the investigators found him guilty of tolerating and concealing from the homeland the existence of slavery.[49] Dulio soon sensed that things were not going his way; Mercatelli, in a letter to the foreign minister, hinted that the governor, badly shaken by the investigation, feared that he would be arrested.[50] Instead, on October 5, 1903, the company relieved Dulio as governor of the Benadir. Eugenio Cappello, the resident at Brava, served as acting governor until Alessandro Sapelli was appointed provisional governor on December 9, 1903. The commission of inquiry also found fault with several other company officials for neglect and incompetence. In particular, Badolo was blamed for having ordered a steamship for use on the Webi Shebelle without first having made any attempt to determine the navigability of the river. His incompetence in the matter, the commission reported, had resulted in a law suit, impairment of the company's reputation, and material damage. The commission was also aware that Badolo had conspired for the removal of Dulio in hopes of succeeding to the governorship himself, and that

[49] Chiesi and Travelli report, ASMAI, pos. 75/7, f. 68; later published as *Le Questioni del Benadir* (Milan: Bellini, 1904).

[50] Mercatelli, Zanzibar, to Foreign Minister, November 2, 1903, ASMAI, pos. 75/5, f. 49.

he had made no effort to notify the company of the existence of slavery. The commissioners concluded,

The company was betrayed in the colony by its two chief officials, Dulio and Badolo; and it has been badly served by the other personnel, the responsibility of whom, however, is attenuated by the extremely grave and undeniable responsibility of the two who had the fate of the colony in their hands.[51]

The commissioners then fixed the responsibility of the Benadir Company. With the perception of hindsight, Chiesi and Travelli reported that the company's board of directors should have sent one or two of its members to inspect the colony annually and to supervise or control the officials, from the governor down. They found unworkable a situation in which the governor was also a member of the board of directors. The company's second error was its failure to recognize its moral obligations "to the government, the country, and the civilized world." And third, it was at last admitted that the Benadir Company had assumed the concession with a disproportionately small amount of capital. This chain of errors had been compounded, according to Chiesi and Travelli, by the company's failure to investigate for itself conditions in Somalia before assuming responsibility for the Benadir.

In the present conditions of disfavor in public opinion, of government hostility, and of slender means, we believe that the Benadir Company cannot continue in the enterprise without meeting up with new failures, without incurring greater responsibilities which could have incalculable consequences for the colony and the country. . . .

Two questions demand solution: the question of slavery and that of opening up the bush country as far as the Webi Shebelle. The solution of these two questions calls for all types of sacrifices . . . without which our permanence in the Benadir is vain, our civi-

51 Chiesi and Travelli, *Le Questioni del Benadir*, p. 379.

lizing mission is illusory, our protectorate over southern Somalia is useless.[52]

After calling for the revision of the convention between the Benadir Company and the government, Chiesi and Travelli proceeded to establish the responsibility of the government in the crisis. They claimed that the government had political and moral responsibilities in the Benadir. Completely refuting the basis of Italian colonialism in Somalia, they asked how a nation could want or attempt to create colonies without a political directive. They accused the government of proclaiming to the world its interest in the Benadir but of doing little else to sustain that interest. "It is our understanding, however, that once you enter in the European colonial movement, for better or worse, on the African continent you have to have some kind of political directive."[53]

The days of government by chartered company were now numbered. When the foreign ministry's budget for 1903–4 was discussed in the Senate on December 21, 1903, Senator Francesco Vitelleschi inquired what the government intended to do with the Benadir. To entrust the administration of the colony to a chartered company, he declared, was equivalent to abandoning it altogether. Vitelleschi had raised a question that was to be echoed throughout the halls of Parliament. On February 20, 1904, Foreign Minister Tommaso Tittoni replied that the government had begun negotiations with the sultan of Zanzibar and with Great Britain for purchase of the Benadir ports and, hence, for the acquisition of full Italian sovereignty over southern Somalia; while the government carried on its negotiations for purchase of the Benadir ports, the Benadir Company would administer southern Somalia in a caretaker capacity. On March 14, another attack on government policy was initiated in the Chamber of Deputies by Gustavo Chiesi, who, as a member of the Benadir Com-

[52] *Ibid.*, pp. 380–81.   [53] *Ibid.*, pp. 382–83.

pany's commission of inquiry, had much influence among his fellow deputies; Tittoni gave a similar reply to him.[54] On May 18, 1904, Tittoni informed the Chamber of Deputies that the government had finally decided to assume the direct administration of the Benadir and that the company would be transformed into an agricultural and commercial enterprise devoid of political responsibilities.[55]

Thus the period of government by chartered company drew to an ignominious close. For twelve years, including the brief period of direct governmental administration from 1896 to 1900, the government had ignored its responsibilities in the Benadir and had tried to avoid increasing its commitments. It had attempted to do so by delegating its administrative powers first to the Filonardi Company and then to the Benadir Company. Yet commitments and responsibility were exactly what the government could not avoid in a colonial undertaking. Government freedom from responsibility had led to irresponsibility on the part of company administrators and a full-blown scandal over slavery.

A change in administration, it had been decided, would take place; but the basic problems of a colonial power in Somalia were still present—low morale, little security, slavery, and native hostility. In January, 1906, Alessandro Sapelli, the company's provisional governor following the slavery scandal, returned to the Benadir as vice-commissioner in the government service. Italian sentiment could perhaps be summed up by the greeting he received from his lieutenant upon disembarking at Mogadishu: "How sad I am that you too have come to die here. . . ."[56]

[54] L'Africa italiana al Parlamento nazionale, 1882–1905, pp. 728, 735, 741.

[55] Tittoni memorandum on government's decision to assume administration of the Benadir, May 18, 1904, ASMAI, pos. 75/9, f. 100.

[56] A. Sapelli, Memorie d'Africa, 1883–1906 (Bologna: Zanichelli, 1935), p. 215.

CHAPTER FOUR

The Slavery Question and
the Occupation of Southern Somalia

Since 1893 the Benadir had been administered by chartered company in an arrangement that was never completely satisfactory for either government or company. Only when a slavery scandal embarrassed the government and tarnished the name of Italy did the cabinet decide that the government had to take over the direct administration of southern Somalia.

Complicating the government's position were two factors: the anomalous position of the Benadir ports, which were still technically the property of the sultan of Zanzibar, and the control of Kismayu, which attracted much of the Somali trade into the British sphere of influence. The British government, protector of Zanzibar, was pleased with the existing arrangements whereby the Zanzibari government could anticipate an annual rent of 8,000 pounds for the next thirty-five years.[1] The experience of the two chartered companies, on the other hand, had demonstrated that in the uncertain economic conditions of southern Somalia the annual rent was a heavy burden for the colonial economy. As early as 1901 an official of the Colonial Office had proposed that Italy purchase the Benadir and acquire at least trading rights at Kismayu.[2] In 1904,

[1] British Ambassador, Rome, to Foreign Minister, February 11, 1903, Archivio Storico dell'ex Ministero dell'Africa Italiana (hereinafter cited as ASMAI), pos. 55/8, f. 59.

[2] Unsigned memorandum, Colonial Office, Rome, 1901, ASMAI, pos. 55/8, f. 59.

when Foreign Minister Tittoni began to consider taking over the Benadir, he discovered that the British government was anxious to reduce as much as possible the bothersome privileges and immunities enjoyed in Zanzibar by the subjects of numerous foreign powers. In return for the abrogation of Italian treaty rights in Zanzibar, the British government was willing to negotiate the sale of the Benadir but not of Kismayu.

In general, the members of the cabinet were content with this proposition, with the exception of Luigi Luzzatti, minister of the Treasury. Luzzatti made the protest against colonies that had always come from the Treasury:

It has not been demonstrated to me . . . that, after renouncing her privileged position and assuming the definitive sovereignty of the Benadir, Italy is not making a bad bargain and will not be facing vast expenses, new sacrifices of every kind, and new delusions.[3]

Although Tittoni assured Luzzatti that the deal could be financed by the use of existing funds for the Benadir, economies on Eritrean military expenditures, and a loan from the Treasury, Luzzatti was far from satisfied. He responded in a prophetic vein:

The future interest of Italy will never be in Eritrea or in the Benadir, which will not become colonies for settlement, but are destined to represent a perennial economic delusion and consequently a political weakness.[4]

Despite Luzzatti's well-based opposition, Tittoni's colonial program carried the day. On January 13, 1905, Italy purchased the Benadir ports for 144,000 pounds, or 3,600,000 lire, and acquired the right to maintain commercial installations at Kismayu in British Jubaland.[5] The government and the Benadir Company dissolved their relationship, and the com-

3 Luzzatti, Rome, to Tittoni, August 17, 1904, ASMAI, pos. 55/8, f. 59.

4 *Ibid.*

5 E. Hertslet, *The Map of Africa by Treaty* (3d ed.; London: His Majesty's Stationery Office, 1909), III, 954–60.

pany was transformed into a purely commercial enterprise. On March 15, 1905, the colony was consigned to the government, whose official rule began on May 1. The government immediately became heir to all the problems of the chartered company, the most urgent of which were the suppression of slavery and the threat of a Somali uprising that would involve vast military expenditures.

The first governor of the new colony of Southern Italian Somalia was Luigi Mercatelli, who had conducted the government's inquiry into the Benadir Company's affairs and at the height of the slavery scandal had taken measures to combat slavery. In May, 1904, he and Alessandro Sapelli, the company's last governor, had promulgated an ordinance outlawing the slave trade and permitting the emancipation of slaves. Mercatelli had explained the ordinance to the most important chiefs of the interior, who allegedly had given no protests worthy of note.[6] Within a short time, however, Mercatelli realized how wrong he had been to expect an antislavery ordinance to root out a centuries-old institution. By August, the Bimal tribes southwest of Mogadishu were openly hostile to the colonial government. Slaves were necessary for their way of life. Settled in the area between the Webi Shebelle and the Indian Ocean and commanding the hinterland of Merca and Brava, the warlike Bimal tended their flocks and raided their neighbors while Bantu slaves cultivated their fields. The basis of Bimal prosperity was the grain raised by slaves, which they traded with the townspeople of Merca in exchange for imported cloth and hardware. Without their labor force, the Bimal, who had the nomadic Somali's traditional disdain for agriculture, would be reduced to a bare subsistence economy.

The Bimal revolt began on October 27, 1905, when rebel forces attacked Jilib, a coastal village six miles northeast of Merca. Merca was surrounded and land communications with Mogadishu were disrupted. Whether the Italian government liked it or not, only military action would quell the revolt in

[6] Mercatelli, Brava, to Foreign Minister, May 2, 1904, ASMAI, pos. 75/6, f. 64.

Somalia. To complicate the situation, the fiery dervish leader Muhammad Abdullah Hassan and his Bah Geri allies on the upper Webi Shebelle gave aid and encouragement to the Bimal. Nevertheless, the liberation of slaves continued. The quarterly reports of this period from the residents at Mogadishu, Merca, and Brava reveal that approximately 1,300 slaves were given their freedom in Mogadishu, 850 in Merca, and 150 in Brava.[7]

The revolt brought home to the government the nature of the responsibilities it had assumed along with direct administration of the colony. If the colony were to be exploited commercially, or even if it were only to pay its own way, it had to have a healthy economy. Yet the main component of the labor force in the agricultural areas was Bantu slavery. The government was committed to mitigate the evils of slavery and ultimately to eliminate it. To do away with slavery, however, meant to antagonize those Somali tribes who, like the Bimal and the Wadan, were dependent on slavery for their own welfare. To meet hostility and tribal opposition military action was required, but both the Eritrean and the Ethiopian experiences warned against the use of force. Finally, there was the all important tradition of maintaining as small a colonial budget as possible.

For more than three years, the intransigent Bimal endangered the position of Merca and disrupted land communications. The prestige of the new colonial administration was in the balance until February, 1907, when Captain Gherardo Pàntano, commander of the presidio at Merca, organized a column of five hundred askaris from both Mogadishu and Merca and marched against the Bimal. After burning several villages, the column encamped on the sand dunes overlooking the fishing village of Danane, midway between Merca and Mogadishu. On the night of February 9, three thousand Bimal launched several attacks on the encampment under

---

[7] List of slaves freed by the residents at Mogadishu, Merca, and Brava, July, 1905, to November, 1908, ASMAI, pos. 75/6, f. 58.

cover of darkness. Bimal ardor cooled as each successive attack failed. The Italian-trained askaris had learned a measure of discipline, and by dawn the Bimal were in retreat.[8] Although Bimal power was considerably weakened by the defeat at Danane, the war was not over. At the end of March, the colonial government sent a strong detachment to Jilib to assure the loyalty of that village and to watch over the Bimal, who continued to present a threat to the peace.[9]

Acting Governor Giovanni Cerrina Feroni had warned the government early in 1906 that the only solution to the problems of slavery and pacification of the interior was military occupation of the home country of the Bimal and of the Wadan, as far as the Webi Shebelle.[10] Not until four months after the battle of Danane did Foreign Minister Tittoni decide on the general outlines of such a positive program for the Benadir. To the new governor, Tommaso Carletti, he wrote:

In order to administer the Benadir colony with the aim of realizing its fullest potential in agriculture and commerce, it is necessary for the government to assert itself materially and morally over the populations surrounding the Benadir stations. To do this we must organize ourselves strongly on the coast and then gradually undertake the peaceful penetration of the interior and extend our direct administration to the line of the Webi Shebelle. Only then can we guarantee the trade routes of the interior and make the commercial and agricultural development of the colony possible. This action must be simultaneous with another political and commercial action . . . which will radiate into the southern provinces of Ethiopia via Lugh.[11]

Tittoni's "peaceful penetration," of course, meant nothing less than military conquest. It is significant to note, too, that

[8] Pesenti, *Le Guerre coloniali* (Bologna: Zanichelli, 1947), pp. 240–42. In 1907, Pesenti was a lieutenant at Danane.

[9] Cerrina Feroni, Mogadishu, to Foreign Minister (confidential), March 28, 1907, ASMAI, pos. 75/9, f. 105.

[10] Cerrina Feroni, Mogadishu, to Foreign Minister (confidential), February 26, 1906, ASMAI, pos. 75/9, f. 105.

[11] Tittoni, Rome, to Carletti, May 1, 1907, ASMAI, pos. 75/9, f. 108.

Tittoni considered Ethiopia to be a target for Italian expansionism after the achievement of a cautious, effective occupation of southern Somalia.

After several months in the colony, Carletti was ready to implement Tittoni's plan. Relations between the sultan of Geledi and the Italians were particularly good, and Carletti convinced the sultan that his alignment with the Italians against the Bimal and the Wadan was to the advantage of them both.[12] For the time being Carletti was content just to keep communications open between Mogadishu and Merca, which were constantly threatened by the two hostile tribes. His dealings with the Somali had convinced him that the occupation of the interior could take place only when the time was right. After increased contacts with the Italians on the coast, the populations of the interior, he believed, would invite the Italians to establish themselves on the river.[13] Until then, gradualism would be the order of the day. *Festina lente.*

By the deployment of sixteen hundred askaris in presidios at Merca, Jilib, Danane, Jesira, and Mogadishu, the Italians secured the whole coast from Merca to Mogadishu. The situation was well in hand by March, 1908, although the Italians were still unable to protect friendly tribes against Bimal and dervish raids.[14] Throughout April of that year the appeal of Muhammad Abdullah Hassan's dervish movement was strong among the youth, but the sultan of Geledi effectively stemmed that tide by deriving adequate proof from the Koran that an epidemic among the new dervish recruits was a punishment inflicted by Allah.[15] Chiefs of the Shidle, Hawadleh, and Mobilen Somali began to swear allegiance to the colonial power. After the submission of these chiefs and of several Wadan chiefs, the Somali enemies of the Bimal and the re-

[12] Sultan of Geledi to Carletti, October 14, 1907, ASMAI, pos. 75/9, f. 109.

[13] Carletti report, No. 99 (confidential), Jumbo, July 30, 1907, ASMAI, pos. 75/9, f. 109.

[14] Carletti report, No. 260, Mogadishu, March 30, 1908, ASMAI, pos. 75/9, f. 100.

[15] Carletti report, No. 395, Mogadishu, April 27, 1908, ASMAI, pos. 75/9, f. 110.

maining Wadan tribes petitioned Carletti to move Italian forces inland, as Carletti had predicted. The governor reported to the foreign minister:

With naïve guile they seek to prick my *amour propre* to make me move without delay. I have a sheaf of letters in which they do nothing but repeat: Why don't you come? You have rifles, you have cannons, what do you fear? You ought to know that the Wadan, the Hintere, the Bimal say that you are afraid, that you will never come into the interior, that Muhammad Abdullah has forbidden you to move.[16]

The gradualism of Carletti and Tittoni looked more like inaction to their Somali allies, who began to doubt that the Italians had serious intentions of reaching the river and putting down the rebels once and for all.

Never before had Carletti found the situation so favorable. On June 24, 1908, he requested full powers to effect the military occupation of the interior with the forces under his command.[17] At this time the Italians had 2,600 men stationed in the Benadir presidios, including a colonial force of 1,000 rifles and 4 pieces of artillery and four companies of Eritrean askaris (600 rifles) under the command of Major Antonio Di Giorgio. After a series of sharp encounters with the Bimal, Di Giorgio and his forces occupied the four major fords of the middle Webi Shebelle: Mallable, Audegle, Barire, and Afgoi. By September the Italians had full control of the region between the Indian Ocean and the river.[18] Bimal power was completely broken. Meanwhile, Di Giorgio was informed of the advance of dervish forces to the vicinity of Balad, thirty miles upriver from Afgoi. Impetuously, and without authority from the governor, he secretly led his Eritreans across the river on rafts and marched up the right bank of the Webi Shebelle, the deepest penetration ever made by the Italians into

[16] Carletti report, No. 475, Mogadishu, June 2, 1908, ASMAI, pos. 75/9, f. 110.

[17] Carletti report, No. 524, Mogadishu, June 24, 1908, ASMAI, pos. 75/9, f. 110.

[18] Carletti, "Report on Southern Italian Somalia for the year 1907–1908," Mogadishu, November 30, 1908, ASMAI, pos. 75/12, f. 129.

the hinterland from Mogadishu—twenty-five miles. The dervish forces attempted to surround the colonial troops on September 24, but the tide of battle turned against them and Di Giorgio energetically occupied Balad.[19] Thus the Italians finally occupied a very small part of the vast hinterland of the Benadir coast, some fifteen years after Vincenzo Filonardi had first landed at Mogadishu to assume administration of the Benadir.

Throughout 1909 the pacification of the Somali tribes continued with apparent success. In April the Matan tribes submitted after government forces seized their herds. A road was cut through to Balad; and chiefs of the Hillivi, Daud, Mobilen, and some additional Bimal tribes indicated a willingness to negotiate with the government for their submission.[20] By October, 1910, the new governor, Giacomo De Martino, could look with satisfaction on the progress of pacification of the lands along the middle Webi Shebelle and cast his eyes on the lands beyond the river, toward the Juba and the confines of Ethiopia.[21]

De Martino's expansionist ideas reflected a larger movement in Italy. In the first decade of the twentieth century, Italy experienced a wave of chauvinism similar to that in Germany, the United States, and England. This new mood found its expression in many forms, some reflecting the Darwinian and Nietzschean thought of the time, others harking back to the once glorious past. Italy, like other European powers, wanted a strong army and navy; irredentism, which had been dormant for some decades, revived and advocates began to call for the "return" of the Alto Adige-Südtirol, Trieste, Nice, Corsica, and Malta. Discontented with liberalism, many men turned to the right. In art the futurists ex-

[19] Pesenti, *Le Guerre coloniali*, pp. 244–45.

[20] Gino Macchioro report, No. 408, Mogadishu, May 4, 1909, ASMAI, pos. 75/10, f. 112.

[21] De Martino, "Report to H. E. the Foreign Minister: The Present and the Future of the Colony," Mogadishu, October 10, 1910, ASMAI, pos. 75/12, f. 131.

tolled conquest and the virtue of force in a reaction against rationalism and moral idealism. Extreme nationalists called for another age of Italian expansionism. In 1910, men like Enrico Corradini and Luigi Federzoni founded a new Nationalist party and unabashedly claimed to be the heirs to Crispi's imperialism. The public was whipped into a frenzy over Tripoli and Cyrenaica, and war loomed with Turkey for the possession of Libya. Against this background, De Martino called successfully for new military operations in Somalia.

While the war with Turkey was at its peak, De Martino moved in Somalia. His plans called for the occupation of the territory between the existing line of deepest penetration at the Webi Shebelle and an advance line stretching from Lugh to Bur Acaba and Mahaddei Wen, lands inhabited for the most part by the peaceful and poorly armed Rahanwein, Eile, and Shidle. The Shidle and Eile tribesmen around Mahaddei Wen and Bur Acaba had, in fact, already manifested sympathy for the Italians and welcomed their intervention, for they stood to gain most in intertribal disputes with their hostile nomadic neighbors. Both the Shidle and the Eile were Bantu agriculturalists, whom the Somali tribes regarded as inferior and by nature slaves. Italian occupation of the region meant additional security and protection for the Bantu against the incursions of the Galjal Somali.[22] To assure the peaceful penetration of the region, De Martino convoked a great *shir* ("assembly") of the trans-Webi Shebelle tribesmen at Afgoi on December 12, 1911, in which twelve thousand Mobilen, Shidle, Dafet, Gerra, Galjal, Hillivi, Murosade, and Daud participated. At first De Martino felt some uneasiness over Muslim fanaticism and possible pro-Turkish feelings, but he was soon relieved of fear of a jihad, or holy war. The government's program was explained and was well received.[23]

The new campaign began on February 27, 1912, with a

[22] *Ibid.*

[23] De Martino, *La Somalia italiana nei tre anni del mio governo* (Rome: Tipografia della Camera dei Deputati, 1912), pp. 15–16; *Bollettino Ufficiale della Somalia Italiana* (December 31, 1911), p. 30.

force increased to some four thousand colonial troops and aided by Somali irregulars. Moving from Balad, the Italians raised their flag over Mahaddei Wen on March 1. At a huge *shir* of twenty thousand tribesmen, the governor proclaimed the region to be directly subject to the colonial government. The colonial forces then occupied without resistance the villages of Wanle Wen, Bio Addo, and Afgoi Addo. In this stage of operations approximately 9,000 square miles were added to the area under effective Italian administration. The next stage of operations, completed in 1913, saw the occupation of Bur Acaba (June 13) and of the important wells at Baidoa (June 25). Concurrently, other forces pressed up the Webi Shebelle and occupied Bulo Burti.

With the occupation of the plateau region between the Juba and the Webi Shebelle, an additional 22,000 square miles came under the Italian flag.[24] At the close of military operations in February, 1914, the Italians were in possession of territory from the coast to a line from Lugh to Baidoa to Bulo Burti, which was defensible against possible inroads by both dervishes and Ethiopians. The occupation met little serious resistance and with its successful outcome the colonial government felt itself ready to derive great benefits from a pacified Somalia.[25]

As the colonial government completed its occupation of southern Somalia, the slavery question was slowly being resolved. Not all of the administrators of the colonial government shared the aversion to slavery so widely expressed by the Anti-Slavery Society of Italy. Few Italians in Somalia indulged themselves in the luxury of denouncing the institution outright. For them, more was at stake than ridding the colony of a recognized evil. To the government official in Somalia, slavery was a special problem in a particular social, political,

24 Unsigned memorandum on Acts of Government in Somalia (*ca.* 1913), ASMAI, pos. 151/1, f. 3.

25 De Martino, *La Somalia italiana* . . . , pp. 31–32.

ITALIAN OCCUPATION
OF SOUTHERN SOMALIA

1905–8

1908–14

★ Residencies before 1905

⊙ Later Residencies

SOMALI TRIBES
BANTU TRIBES

0   50   100

MILES

and economic environment.[26] As such, it could not be abolished without consideration of the grave political consequences.

The Italian press was especially impatient with the government. When the slavery scandal first broke in 1903, the press reacted immediately with accusations that the colonial government was not moving fast enough. Yet the hands of the colonial government were tied. Before the effective occupation of the hinterland, slavery could be abolished in name only. Nor could the government afford to buy the freedom of each slave who presented himself before a resident.[27] In some cases, the Anti-Slavery Society provided the necessary ransom, but their funds were limited.

The slavery issue became prominent again when the first governor of Southern Italian Somalia, Luigi Mercatelli, became the center of a new controversy. Mercatelli was a rigid and conscientious administrator, somewhat authoritarian and completely intolerant of the press. Hardly had he assumed office than a journalistic campaign was begun against him. Prominent among the charges was the accusation that Mercatelli had purchased a young slave girl for immoral purposes.[28] The government, unwilling to have the question of slavery in the Benadir forever on the front pages of the newspapers, recalled Mercatelli to Italy in January, 1906. It is highly doubtful that Mercatelli was lax in combating slavery. He had been in the colony since June, 1903, and it was he who had led the government investigation of slavery.

---

26 Giovanni Cerrina Feroni estimated that the total number of slaves and serfs in southern Somalia was 25,000 to 30,000 in a population of approximately 300,000 (Cerrina Feroni, *Benadir* [Rome: Tipografia del Ministero degli Affari Esteri, 1911], p. 124).

27 President Filippo Tolli of the Anti-Slavery Society of Italy, Rome, to Foreign Minister Guicciardini, March 6, 1906; Guicciardini, Rome, to Tolli, March 26, 1906; and Cerrina Feroni, Mogadishu, to Guicciardini, June 11, 1906; in ASMAI, pos. 75/6, f. 64.

28 "La Stampa e le accuse contro Mercatelli" (1905–6), ASMAI, pos. 75/8, ff. 86–91.

Moreover, the Bimal uprising was the direct result of his promulgation of an antislavery ordinance.

In Mercatelli's absence Alessandro Sapelli, the last Benadir Company governor, served as acting governor. Sapelli approached the abolition of slavery with a policy of gradualism. He was bitter that the "theorizing elements" of the Italian Parliament had placed so much pressure on the government to abolish slavery at once. He knew that such a policy could not succeed. Instead, together with Mercatelli, he had prepared an ordinance designed to mitigate slavery gradually by converting it into a form of domestic servitude and then, eventually, by converting domestic servitude into a system of wage labor. Sapelli was of the opinion that the slaves of the Benadir were not in dire straits, and he found little evidence of cruelty. Indicative of his attitude is an anecdote he told of two slaves from the interior, a man and a girl, who had presented themselves before the local Italian authorities for liberation. The Italians, in accordance with the Brussels Convention, gave the man two sets of liberation papers. The man, somewhat confused, asked for an explanation. After the Italian authorities had explained the procedure, he replied, "Ah, no! *My* papers are all right, but the girl is *my slave!*"[29]

Giovanni Cerrina Feroni, who succeeded Sapelli as acting governor, was convinced that the stories of cruelty to slaves, widespread in the homeland, were greatly exaggerated. Cruelty did exist, he admitted, but self-interest militated against abuse of the worker who was a source of income for his master. In his experience, Cerrina Feroni said, ardent abolitionism had proved to be harmful to the slaves in that they were now more frequently enchained by their masters. In a matter-of-fact way, he related that irons were used only for punishment and as a precaution against attempts at escape. His attitude seemed to imply that more could not be expected of a people

[29] A. Sapelli, *Memorie d'Africa, 1883–1906* (Bologna: Zanichelli, 1935), pp. 235–37.

whom he considered barbaric; besides, he declared, the slaves
had an extraordinary tendency toward vice and theft.[30]

Cerrina Feroni concluded that antislavery laws had to be
applied with tact and prudence. The policy he followed was
to suppress slavery by prohibiting the sale, transfer, or pawning of slaves; declaring free all those born after a certain
date; granting freedom in cases of maltreatment; freeing,
with payment, those slaves who no longer wanted to remain
with their masters; and, when possible, freeing the concu-
bines and children of liberated slaves. But local officials were
also instructed to keep in mind that payment was to be
avoided as an unnecessary expense and that an attempt should
be made to reconcile master and domestic servant whenever
possible.[31]

The next governor, Tommaso Carletti, applied the same
gradualism in his slavery policy that he was putting to such
good use in the occupation of the lands along the Webi
Shebelle. Carletti regarded the slavery issue as an aspect of the
economic question; the Bimal revolt confirmed him in this
opinion. Going one step further, Carletti declared with more
firmness than truth:

There are races (I am saddened to find myself in agreement with
old Aristotle) that, either by innate intellectual inferiority, or because of historical development, appear destined to be servants,
or at least are not capable of unconditional freedom.[32]

Despite Carletti's use of this specious argument that smacks
of the "white man's burden" attitude, he did believe that
slaves could be "morally elevated" by evolving through domestic servitude to salaried employment. He suggested that
freed slaves be organized into villages that would offer a ready

---

[30] Cerrina Feroni, *Benadir*, p. 124.

[31] Cerrina Feroni, Mogadishu, to Baldassare Pedrazzini, new resident at Itala,
April 5, 1906, ASMAI, pos. 75/9, f. 105.

[32] Carletti, Brava, to Foreign Minister (confidential), July 19, 1907, ASMAI,
pos. 75/6, f. 64.

labor supply for the day when the agricultural development of Somalia could begin in earnest.

In the course of the Carletti administration, a carefully supervised domestic servitude replaced slavery in the coastal towns of the Benadir and along the Juba River. In the area between the coast and the Webi Shebelle, slavery continued unabated until the Bimal uprising was put down. Villages of slaves were organized under their own chiefs in areas occupied by the Italians, and Italian officials warned masters against mistreating their slaves. For the most part, the Italians sought to arbitrate differences between master and slave rather than outlaw the institution and precipitate a conflict with the Somali tribes of the interior. In the area beyond the Webi Shebelle—before the Italian occupation—the colonial government could only recommend that masters treat their slaves humanely. Among the Bantu Shidle and the Mobilen Hawiya, slaves were harshly treated, often kept in irons, overworked, and underfed, contrary to the claims of Cerrina Feroni for other Somali tribes. Near the presidios, the Italians frequently freed such slaves without payment to their owners. Where Italian authority meant little, however, the government was powerless to act. "Our error derives from not willing to consider that it took 2,000 years of Christianity and civilization before every trace of slavery disappeared from among civilized peoples," Carletti declared, as he admonished those who wished to act hastily. "Can we really hope to abolish slavery in East Africa in one fell swoop by the stroke of a pen and by a decree?"[33]

As the Italians extended their influence and authority inland, the condition of slaves improved. By 1914, when other problems occupied both colonial and metropolitan governments, the worst evils of slavery had been mitigated. Among the nomadic tribes beyond the Webi Shebelle, there were

[33] Carletti, "Report on Southern Italian Somalia for the year 1907–1908," Mogadishu, November 30, 1908, ASMAI, pos. 75/12, f. 129.

but few slaves. Only those tribes that based a part of their welfare on agriculture in addition to stock-raising had possessed large numbers of slaves. With the submission of the hostile Bimal and Wadan, the centers of resistance to Italian policy were broken, and slavery was gradually converted into domestic servitude, to the evident satisfaction of master, slave, and government.[34] In time the domestic servant would be able to buy himself out of bondage and would supply a ready source of labor for future agricultural enterprises.

It is difficult to estimate the total number of slaves freed in Somalia, for the records are often incomplete. If, as Cerrina Feroni claimed, there were 25,000 to 30,000 slaves and domestic servants in the colony, the record of emancipation is not very spectacular. From 1900 to 1914, only about 4,300 slaves were liberated by Italian authorities.[35] Many ex-slaves remained with their masters as bond servants, preferring a life of security and tribute-payments to one of freedom and economic uncertainty. Thus a kind of serfdom succeeded slavery, but the worst excesses were eliminated in a part of the world where slavery continued to exist until comparatively recent times.

34 De Martino, *La Somalia italiana* . . . , p. 32.

35 Lists of slaves freed by the residents at Afgoi, Audegle, Baidoa, Balad, Bardera, Barire, Brava, Itala, Jelib, Jumbo, Lugh, Mahaddei Wen, Margherita, Merca, Mereg, Mogadishu, Wanle Wen, and Warsheik, July, 1905, through October, 1914, ASMAI, pos. 74/1, ff. 1, 3–5; pos. 75/6, f. 58; pos. 75/11, ff. 124–28.

CHAPTER FIVE

Creating a Colony, 1905–23

When the Italian government assumed direct administration of southern Somalia in 1905 after years of drifting, vacillation, and avoidance of responsibility, it faced the task of creating a colony out of the wreckage of two experiments in government by chartered company. By the outbreak of World War I, the Italians had evolved a system of administration and a native policy which they could extend readily into newly occupied territory.

The administrative system was not entirely new. Of necessity much of it was an outgrowth of the system employed by the chartered companies. The first set of administrative regulations, introduced by Governor Mercatelli in 1905, gave the governor a free hand in legislating for the colony, and the residents of the six administrative subdivisions of Brava, Merca, Lugh, Itala, Bardera, and Jumbo, all of whom were professional military men, considerable freedom in the exercise of their executive powers as well. In addition, the ordinance established permanent offices for the sanitary services, postal service, customs, and accounting.[1] Until the metropolitan government drafted a basic law for the colony, the regulations, extremely simple in their form and substance, served as a guide to "simple administration . . . for the main-

[1] Schedule of administrative posts in the Benadir, Mogadishu (1905), Archivio Storico dell'ex Ministero dell'Africa Italiana (hereinafter cited as ASMAI), pos. 75/9, f. 105.

tenance of order" within the limits of the territory already occupied.[2]

The Mercatelli regulations found a fuller development in the basic law of April 5, 1908, which united all the areas of southern Somalia into a single administration under the name *Somalia Italiana*. By virtue of this law, the supreme legal power was divided among the Parliament, the metropolitan government, and the colonial government. The government and the administration of the colony remained in essence unchanged. The powers of the colonial government were broadly defined. The civil governor controlled export droits, regulated the rate of exchange, could raise or lower native taxes by one-third in any one year, and administered all civil services and matters relating to hunting, fishing, and conservation. The governor was directly in charge of the colony's police force. He nominated local residents and proposed military arrangements to the metropolitan government; his requests for troops, however, were reviewed each year. Last, the governor prepared the annual colonial budget.[3] In brief, the law provided for an authoritarian regime that would have been tolerated in few European countries of that time.

These very broad powers were the embodiment of proposals suggested to Foreign Minister Tittoni by Governor Carletti.[4] The governor had consulted the administrative laws of Eritrea, but he had altered the Eritrean model in one significant way: he did not provide for an officer in command of colonial troops. In effect, Carletti made certain of his own absolute rule over all aspects of administration in Somalia,

[2] Résumé of instructions to Acting Governor Cerrina Feroni (urgent), Rome, April 21, 1906, ASMAI, pos. 75/9, f. 105.

[3] Gennaro Mondaini, *La Legislazione coloniale italiana nel suo sviluppo storico e nel suo stato attuale (1881–1940)* (Milan: Istituto per gli Studi di Politica Internazionale, 1941), I, 253–55.

[4] Carletti report (confidential), Mogadishu, October 15, 1908, ASMAI, pos. 75/10, f. 118.

including the military. It was not long before the military, straining at the restrictions imposed by a policy of gradual peaceful penetration, overstepped its bounds. The occupation of Balad by Major Antonio Di Giorgio without orders from the governor is a case in point, the climax in a two-year dispute between civil and military leaders.

Carletti had already refused to accept a commanding officer in charge of troops, even though Major Gennaro Mozzoni had been assigned to Mogadishu before the enactment of the basic law. Carletti agreed to entrust Mozzoni with military instruction and discipline, on the condition that all correspondence between the military and local civil authorities pass through his office in Mogadishu. This arrangement worked against both discipline and morale. An askari of the Brava presidio, in custody for a minor infraction of the rules, spent forty-five days in detention until his sentence of fifteen days' arrest was approved by Mogadishu. Major Mozzoni finally resigned when a captain, Simone Buongiovanni, was appointed acting governor during the governor's absence in 1907; the unfortunate Mozzoni could not tolerate a situation in which his military inferior was at the same time his civil superior, an unhappy position for any military man to be in.[5]

When Carletti urged the military occupation of the Webi Shebelle in February, 1908, the foreign ministry appointed Major Antonio Di Giorgio to command the colonial troops in the Benadir and to serve as military consultant and director of military services.[6] From the beginning, Carletti's insistence on his prerogatives as governor made Di Giorgio's position difficult, and he had little independence of action. In Mogadishu, Di Giorgio was given, as proof of the governor's displeasure, substandard lodgings. Neither of the men was conciliatory, and equivocation marked the issuing of each order of the day. The basic law only complicated the prob-

[5] *Responsa* of the Council of Discipline to the Foreign Minister, Rome, March 7, 1911, pp. 32–33, in ASMAI, pos. 86/5, f. 57.

[6] Foreign Minister, Rome, to Carletti, March 24, 1908, ASMAI, pos. 86/1, f. 4.

lem, for it failed to distinguish between the powers of the military and civil authorities in Somalia. Further confusion resulted from the fact that the personnel of the government office in Mogadishu, the civil authority, were for the most part military men on loan to the colonial government. The foreign ministry suggested that civilians be substituted, but this recommendation was never carried out.[7]

By June, Carletti and Di Giorgio were at loggerheads. The blurring of lines between civil and military jurisdiction affected a wide variety of topics: the nomination of vice-residents, who also served as commanders of the presidio in each vice-residency village, jurisdiction over lieutenants employed in both civil and military construction projects, questions of military discipline, and the meaning of a peaceful penetration that required, paradoxically, the use of military force. The strong-minded governor denied or delayed Di Giorgio's requests for funds to construct barracks and infirmaries. When the major complained, Carletti asked the foreign ministry to reaffirm the full powers granted to him by the basic law and suggested that the government recall Di Giorgio.[8] The foreign ministry replied that Carletti had every right to order military operations when he thought them opportune (hence placing Di Giorgio in the wrong for occupying Balad) but advised the governor to give "complete freedom of action to the commander of the troops in technical and military matters" (thereby recognizing Di Giorgio's right to occupy Balad).[9] Thus the dispute remained unresolved, and the two stubborn officials refused to abandon their respective positions.

The continuing personal dispute between the two men was obviously detrimental to the welfare of the colony. At one point the governor accepted as true a report by defeated

7 *Responsa* of Council of Discipline . . . , pp. 35–36, in ASMAI, pos. 86/5, f. 57.

8 Carletti report, No. 498, Mogadishu, June 14, 1908, ASMAI, pos. 86/1, f. 3.

9 Foreign Minister, Rome, to Carletti, July 11, 1908, ASMAI, pos. 86/1, f. 4.

Bimal chiefs rather than his military commander's account of the battle.[10] Morale suffered among the personnel, who did not know where their allegiance should lie. Carletti ultimately succeeded in obtaining Di Giorgio's recall and added a final blow by prohibiting him from reviewing his troops when he left Mogadishu on November 4, 1908.[11] There Carletti hoped the matter would end.

What neither Carletti nor Di Giorgio knew was that Giuseppe Piazza, a correspondent for the Rome *Tribuna,* had been an observant witness of their feud. Piazza had been sent by his newspaper to investigate the Bimal uprising, the dervish movement, and the Italian campaign to occupy the lands of the middle Webi Shebelle. On November 1, 1908, the *Tribuna* published an article by Piazza entitled "Internal Dissensions in our Colony," the first mention of the dispute in Italy. A month later another article appeared, "The Colonial Man," in which the journalist ironically recalled the feud as "something inevitable" in the affairs of the colony. On December 22 his third article appeared, "In the Benadir—under the Ashes." The next day Di Giorgio responded to Piazza's charges in letters to both the *Tribuna* and the *Giornale d'Italia.* He described the circumstances referred to by Piazza as invented or misconstrued by the journalist, declaring that he himself preferred to await the opinion of more competent judges.

The matter did not end there, for in reading that same article soon afterward, Foreign Minister Tittoni recognized excerpts from official documents; he immediately ordered an investigation of the leak. Five days later the rash Piazza published another article on the Benadir under the challenging headline of "Enough Experiments!" He attacked the investigating committee and lauded the work of Carletti in Somalia. Di Giorgio's reply was to sue Piazza and his newspaper for defamation of character. The trial, which ran from February

[10] *Responsa* of Council of Discipline . . . , p. 88, in ASMAI, pos. 86/5, f. 57.
[11] *Ibid.,* p. 93.

through May, 1910, ended in victory for Di Giorgio. Piazza was sentenced to a year in prison and a fine of 1,000 lire, reduced upon appeal to ten months and a fine of 833 lire; the manager of the newspaper received an identical sentence.[12]

Not only did Tittoni order an investigation, but on December 27, he recalled the vigorous Carletti to Italy for questioning. The investigating committee found that Piazza had obtained his material from Lieutenant Emilio Rovatti, a clerk in the government office at Mogadishu. But, even more important, the committee revealed all the facets of the Carletti-Di Giorgio dispute and felt compelled to investigate its background. Its conclusions in this matter were that Major Di Giorgio had acted properly in his dealings with the governor. As for Carletti, who had done so much for the administration and occupation of the colony,

the committee must conclude that in Governor Carletti's conduct it was not able to find that inspiration to high ideals of duty for the sake of which sentiments of a personal nature are placed behind the zealous defense of the general interest. . . . The committee must express with regret its opinion that under the circumstances the conduct of Governor Carletti was greatly at fault.[13]

During the period of the investigation, the government had already come to its own conclusions and on April 28, 1910, appointed a new governor, Senator Giacomo De Martino.

When the Di Giorgio–Carletti feud was settled, the metropolitan government, in consultation with Governor De Martino, issued a new administrative ordinance enabling De Martino to reconstitute the colonial government. The new government consisted of a civil governor and an executive

---

[12] Sentence of the Court of Appeal, Rome, November 26, 1910, ASMAI, pos. 86/5, f. 54. Despite eight months in prison, Piazza retained his enthusiasm for the Benadir, which he described as "Italy's Egypt," and for colonial ventures in general. His books include *La Nostra Terra Promessa: Tripolitania* (Rome, 1911), *Alla Corte di Menelik* (Rome, 1912), *Il Benadir* (Rome, 1913), and *Come conquistammo Tripoli* (Rome, 1914).

[13] *Responsa* of Council of Discipline . . . , pp. 99–100, in ASMAI, pos. 86/5, f. 57.

council composed of a director of civil and political affairs, a commander of the troops, directors of the various branches of government, special consultants for public works, agriculture, and legal affairs, and an accountant—an administrative system that continued until 1941. The territory of the colony was divided into administrative regions, which were divided in turn into residencies and vice-residencies. The governor was responsible to the Colonial Office of the Ministry of Foreign Affairs and, after 1912, to its successor, the Ministry of Colonies. The regional commissioners were directly responsible to the governor; the residents and vice-residents to the regional commissioners; and the commanders of stations and separate police posts, native chiefs, and Muslim cadis administering native law to the residents and vice-residents.[14] Both the basic law of 1908 and the ordinance of 1910 provided only for the administrative division of the colony into residencies, but effective occupation of the land beyond the Webi Shebelle called for an expanded administration, which De Martino was empowered to establish by gubernatorial decree. The governor felt the need for an administrative organ intermediate between the residency and the governor's office, which he filled by creating the administrative region.

During De Martino's rule, residencies were established at Afgoi, Audegle, Balad, Jelib, Margherita, Mahaddei Wen, Matagoi, and Wanle Wen, in addition to those already in existence at Bardera, Brava, Itala, Jumbo, Merca, Meregh, Mogadishu, and Warsheik.[15] Each residency was dependent on one or another of the four regions: Upper Juba, Middle Webi Shebelle, Upper Webi Shebelle, and Gosha–Lower Webi Shebelle.[16] The residents, almost all of them professional or retired soldiers, ruled Italian Somalia in a manner similar to that of the district officer of British Africa: indirect

[14] Mondaini, *La Legislazione coloniale italiana* . . . , I, 256–58.

[15] Gubernatorial Decree, No. 757, October 16, 1911, ASMAI, pos. 75/11, f. 122.

[16] Gubernatorial Decree, No. 488, May 5, 1910, ASMAI, pos. 75/11, f. 122.

rule was combined with paternalism to achieve the best results at the smallest cost.

Along with this paternalism, De Martino developed a native policy that served the Italians well throughout the colonial period. In 1914 the governor created a list of warrant chiefs and cadis. The warrant chiefs were the colonial government's main instrument for the administration of Somalia. They were the point of contact between the government and its colonial subjects. The chiefs were particularly important in the border regions, where they were held responsible for preventing raids upon tribes across the undefined Somali-Ethiopian frontier. On the local level, they were an invaluable source of information on tribal politics and customs for the Italian officials.

Each resident and regional commissioner nominated chiefs and cadis for a three-month experimental period, and the Italian authorities soon compiled lists of 577 chiefs, 72 cadis, and one dervish, all on the government payroll.[17] Depending on their good behavior, the chiefs and cadis received a monthly salary usually ranging from 6 to 50 rupees; the important sultan of Geledi received a monthly stipend of 150 rupees. Upon recommendation by the resident and seconding by the regional commissioner, the governor could decree stipend increases for particularly worthy chiefs or cadis. The resident was empowered to withhold up to 10 per cent of the monthly stipend for the punishment of unruly warrant chiefs; a higher percentage could be withheld by the regional commissioner. If a warrant chief continued to give the government trouble, his salary was suspended. As a check on each dependent chief and cadi, the residents submitted annual reports to the regional commissioners, who classified the chiefs and cadis in schoolmasterly fashion as "bad, mediocre, good, or excellent."[18] By 1917 the colonial minister could boast of the success of this variant of indirect rule: "With respect to the tribal

[17] *Bollettino Ufficiale della Somalia Italiana*, August 31, 1914, p. 6.

[18] Gubernatorial Decree, No. 1334, August 25, 1914, ASMAI, pos. 75/12, f. 142.

chiefs of our territory, we can now rely upon their loyalty to the government and upon their performance in the interest of the colony."[19]

To protect the traditional rights and powers of the chiefs, the Italian administration recognized as valid not only the Muslim Shari'a but also Somali customary law (*testur*), which occasionally differed from Muslim practices outside Somalia. The sole restriction on this general practice was a requirement that the native law administered by the cadis be compatible with the fundamental principles of Italian law.[20] Although the *testur* was consistently overruled in matters of slavery, the juridical system, which was unchanged from 1911 to 1941, guaranteed the preservation of much of native law. For the consideration of crimes not covered by native or Muslim law, a politico-military Tribunale dell'Indigenato was established in each of the four regions of the colony. The Indigenato, a new institution in Italian colonial law, was empowered to try natives on the following charges: smuggling of arms and ammunition; endangering the security of the colony through raids; commission of crimes against officials on duty; refusal to accept legal currency, to co-operate in supplying labor or requisitions for the public welfare, or to furnish correct information to the authorities; and failure to observe government decrees, laws, ordinances, and so on. The Tribunale dell'Indigenato, which in each region consisted of the regional commissioner, the local resident, and the commander of the local presidio, was given broad discretionary powers. Occasionally, a Somali notable would be called in for consultation. The Indigenato enforced its decisions through confiscation of goods or through collective punishment. Both methods were extremely effective because they were refinements of the Somali custom of tribal and clan responsibility for the behavior of the individual. In extreme cases offenders were deported

---

[19] Unsigned memorandum on chiefs and notables of Somalia (1916), ASMAI, pos. 89/18, f. 70.

[20] Royal Decree, No. 708, July 7, 1910, ASMAI, pos. 75/11, f. 122.

to Eritrea.[21] Appeal could be made to the governor and to the Supreme Court (Corte di Cassazione) in Rome. In cases of litigation between Italians and Somali, Italian law was applied, "in order to protect the prestige of the former, [which is] the basis of their rule . . . and a practical necessity of colonialism in Africa."[22] In its broad outlines and summary powers, the Indigenato closely resembled the French Indigénat, which flourished from 1887 to 1912 and may have served as a model for the Italians.

To enforce the peace and provide for the defense and security of the colony, the basic law of 1908 and the administrative ordinance of 1910 created a military force, the Colonial Troops Corps, of Somali, Eritrean, and Arab askaris under the command of Italian army officers. During the second campaign for peaceful penetration of the interior, De Martino created the Corpo di Polizia della Somalia ("Somali Police Force"), composed of *carabinieri* officers and Somali recruits.[23] On the eve of World War I the Colonial Troops numbered approximately four thousand Africans and Arabs under the command of a dozen Italian officers. For the most part the troops were recruited from Hadramaut, Aden, and Yemen; a smaller number came from Eritrea; and only 10 per cent of the troops were Somali. In September, 1912, a mobile militia was formed to aid the presidios of the interior; its members were recruited for three-year terms from the locale of each military outpost.[24]

After ten years of direct government administration in southern Somalia, the Italians had created an effective system of indirect rule and had formulated a conservative and prac-

21 Royal Decree, No. 937, June 9, 1911, ASMAI, pos. 75/11, f. 122; Governor's circular letter, "Instructions on the Indigenato," March 31, 1912, ASMAI, pos. 75/11, f. 127.

22 Mondaini, *La Legislazione coloniale italiana* . . . , I, 293.

23 Gubernatorial Decree, No. 913, January 13, 1912, ASMAI, pos. 75/12, f. 142.

24 Gubernatorial Decree, No. 972, September 17, 1912, ASMAI, pos. 75/12, f. 142.

tical native policy. They had mitigated the evils of slavery, safeguarded the interior, organized an administrative system, and provided for defense and security. In the realm of economic development, however, De Martino's otherwise forceful government failed to achieve notable successes.

When the government assumed direct administration of Somalia in 1905, total trade amounted to slightly more than 5,000,000 lire, an increase of 40 per cent over the period 1896–1900 and 180 per cent over that of the last year of the Filonardi Company, 1895–96 (see Appendix IV). After the government took over, imports rose sharply and total trade amounted to 6,300,000 lire, even with a slight decline in exports. From 1907 to 1909 imports and exports dropped severely, dipping down to pre-Benadir Company levels; during that period, the interior of the country was in turmoil, and the Bimal uprising affected the trade of both Mogadishu and Merca. (Not only until 1911 did exports return to the level of 1905.) Imports rose sharply in 1906–7 as the government ordered war matériel (not included in the statistics, however) and taxable non-military accessories for the several thousand askaris and the enlarged Italian administrative staff. But after that year imports, too, declined and did not rise again for a few years. By 1912 trade had become brisk; in that year total trade passed the 7,580,000 lire mark. Nevertheless, the colony still had an unfavorable balance of trade, the value of exports ordinarily amounting to approximately one-half the value of imports.

Attempts to interest investors in agricultural concessions met with scant success. From 1907 to 1909 the governor authorized the concession of 46,800 hectares (approximately 115,000 acres) along the Webi Shebelle and Juba rivers to fifteen different concessionaires. Eight grants were of 5,000 hectares each, one of 3,000, one of 1,000, one of 800, and four of 500 each. The conditions of the grants were for the most part quite favorable: a sixty-year contract, a schedule of development calling for cultivation of only 20 per cent of the land by the end of the fifth year, and a five-year tax exemption followed by a tax rate for twenty years of only 2 lire per hectare (doubled if the land was serviced by a railway). Sub-concessions were forbidden.[25] Despite the generous conditions, however, the governor reported in October, 1910, that of the eleven concessions put into operation seven had been abandoned; such was "the constant and painful history of first attempts in all colonies," a thought that did little to ease the disappointment of the concessionaires.[26]

The following year De Martino decreed that all uncultivated lands not used in a permanent fashion by natives or groups of natives or rightfully belonging to any European were to be at the disposition of the state. In essence, most of Somalia became the property of the state. The nomadic populations, except for small scattered groups along the two rivers, could lay no claim to permanent cultivation of any lands.[27] Despite its broad applicability, the decree was never invoked to infringe upon the lands of the nomadic tribes; domanial rights were exercised only in a small area along the Juba and Webi Shebelle. The same decree also changed the terms of concession. Within three years, 20 per cent of the concession had to be under cultivation; within five years, 50 per cent; and at the end of ten years, 100 per cent. To stimulate interest in concessions, the government granted a ten-year tax exemption and increased the maximum period of concession to ninety-nine years.[28] The governor himself proposed the establishment of a large plantation in the vicinity of Golwin and an association of small farmers along the rivers. In addition, he suggested that the government establish an experimental farm and provide loans to new concessionaires. Greater interest in Libya and the threat of war, however, distracted atten-

25 Royal Decree, No. 572, August 18, 1908, ASMAI, pos. 75/11, f. 122.

26 De Martino, "The Present and Future of the Colony," Mogadishu, October 10, 1910, ASMAI, pos. 75/12, f. 131.

27 Royal Decree, No. 695, June 8, 1911, ASMAI, pos. 75/11, f. 122.

28 Royal Decree, No. 120, June 8, 1911, ASMAI, pos. 75/11, f. 122.

tion from Somalia, and only a small part of the governor's program was realized.

To decide what might be profitably grown in the still untested Somali environment, De Martino brought a young agronomist, Romolo Onor, to the colony with him in April, 1910. A generation earlier Cecchi had suggested the cultivation of cotton in Somalia, and occasionally writers like Piazza referred to the Webi Shebelle as Italy's Nile; but thus far the Italians knew nothing about their colony's agricultural potential. De Martino was eager to produce results in agriculture as he had done in administration, and he attached Onor's study of agricultural conditions in Southern Italian Somalia to his annual report for 1911. As consultant for agrarian works, Onor traveled extensively and studied tropical agriculture in the British and German colonies of East Africa. In 1911 he established an experimental farm at Genale, where he tested different types of cotton, tobacco, grains, bananas, oil and coconut palms, and other possible export crops. But Onor's research did not produce results fast enough for the impatient governor, and although he gave Onor material support, he limited his range of action and even went so far as to suppress unfavorable conclusions about the agricultural future of Somalia.[29]

Onor was pessimistic about the future of the concessions; a location near Margherita that he had opposed because of irrigation limitations was being considered for a plantation by a company under the direction of Count Enrico di Frankenstein. Onor also criticized the governor's scheme calling for

[29] In the preface to her brother's posthumously published book, Irene Onor claimed that the government compelled him to remove the word *not* from his statement "the Benadir is not a rich region" in a speech to the second Congress of Italians Abroad. Signorina Onor also alleges that De Martino deleted from his own book, *La Somalia italiana nei tre anni del mio governo,* any mention of failure in the experiments with cotton "under the pretext that that would harm the colony's good name." See R. Onor, *La Somalia italiana: Esame critico dei problemi di economia rurale e di politica economica della colonia* (Turin: Bocca, 1925), pp. xiii, xvii.

Italian immigrants to operate the smaller concessions as not sound and advocated "native colonization" of the concessions. In May, 1913, two families arrived from Italy to settle on concessionary land along the Webi Shebelle, and Onor watched the pathetic experiment at white colonization fail. Throughout 1913, tension with the governor increased. De Martino insisted that the government farm established at Genale not only experiment but also produce a profit. For almost five more years Romolo Onor worked in loneliness, in bitterness and frustration. He gradually began to disintegrate under the pressure of isolation and unrewarding work, and on the night of July 25, 1918, gravely depressed and melancholic, he shot himself.

The work of Onor indicated to the metropolitan government the possibilities and limitations of agricultural development in Somalia. A government investigator, Francesco Fazi, supported the unfortunate agronomist's contention that "the natural resources of the colony do not respond to the hopes which superficial affirmations have created and which official reports and parliamentary documents have accepted as truth." According to Fazi, the agricultural possibilities of Somalia were limited by special conditions of soil and climate to some 150,000 hectares (about 371,000 acres) of irrigable land, discounting dry farming, which was not then considered feasible. As Fazi pointed out, this "not negligible quantity" of land was equal in potential to one of Italy's small Po Valley provinces. Another factor limiting the agricultural development of Somalia was the labor supply, a real problem in a sparsely populated country where the majority of the population held agriculture in contempt; it was estimated that two or three concessions of 5,000 hectares each would absorb the entire available labor supply of the Juba valley. Moreover, the importation of European labor was not practical. Fazi pointed out another difficulty: it was doubtful whether Bantu farmers would grow cash crops. "If you try to make a native understand that by cultivating cotton with the aid of irrigation he could have a product worth more than corn, he answers you *'You can't eat cotton!'* "[30]

World War I brought to an abrupt halt Italian concern with the economic development of Somalia. European events preoccupied the metropolitan government. The colonial government's political and administrative accomplishments assured the Italians that they had little to fear for their Indian Ocean colony. The system of administration, composed of elements of direct and indirect rule, functioned comparatively smoothly. Italian district officers kept intertribal difficulties at a minimum, and the warrant system secured the loyalty of Somali chiefs and religious figures. After the conversion of slavery into domestic servitude, the social question had faded into the background. Only in the field of economics was the colonial government unable to succeed. The full value of the colony was far from realized. Concession after concession either failed to materialize or succumbed to the rigors of the Somali environment. Trade statistics indicate no significant rise in exports that might reflect an improvement or expansion of the colonial economy. Somalia was far from self-sufficient. Had it not been for the intrusion of the war, the economic conditions of the colony might well have attracted greater attention in the halls of Parliament. For the time being, the economic development of Somalia was suspended, as Italy and the world focused on hostilities in Europe.

Throughout the war, Somalia remained quietly in a backwater of world history. The war rendered communications between motherland and colony even more infrequent. Before Italian involvement in the war in May, 1915, the home government had taken no measures to inform the colonial government of the progress of hostilities. In mid-August, 1914, Governor De Martino had cabled, "I would be grateful if [the colonial ministry] would see to it that the most important war news is communicated to me. We are in complete

[30] Fazi, Foligno, to Colonial Minister, August 18, 1915, ASMAI, pos. 171/4, f. 27.

isolation here."[31] By September, 1914, De Martino had made arrangements for the shipment of large quantities of provisions for stockpiling; every staple commodity was on the list, for the colony could furnish the Italians with little.[32] After Italy entered the war, the colonial ministry took steps to keep adverse war news out of Somalia. The primary concern of the Italians was that their declaration of war on Muslim Turkey not have political repercussions in Muslim Somalia. Governor De Martino assured the colonial ministry that "there is no trace of Turkish instigations in the colony. . . . The situation is completely tranquil."[33] In fact, the Italian declaration of war on Turkey in September, 1915, passed unnoticed in Somalia. When the activities at the battlefront went against the Allied cause, the government suppressed the news in the colony. The colonial minister urgently recommended that "the publication of war bulletins be made with maximum prudence and even avoided if judged necessary by the governor."[34] No news was published in the colony other than that officially distributed by the government.

In June, 1918, the colonial government first expressed its own ideas on the postwar development of Somalia. Acting Governor Iacopo Gasparini proposed, as part of a general scheme for Italian action in East Africa, the economic penetration of southern Ethiopia within the limits of existing treaties; a study of possible commercial relationships between the colonies and Italy and among the colonies themselves; creation of an economic agency to assure markets and raw mate-

---

31 De Martino, Afgoi, to Colonial Minister, August 17, 1914, ASMAI, pos. 153/1, f. 1.

32 De Martino, Mogadishu, to Colonial Minister, August 9, 1914, ASMAI, pos. 153/1, f. 1. Included on De Martino's list, in a mixture of English and Italian, were "flower [sic] best quality . . . pastes," butter, cheese, "vegetables preserve," olive oil, sesame oil, table salt, rice, wine, refined and raw sugar, washing soap, mineral water, coal, candles, matches, and "cotton tissues."

33 De Martino, Mogadishu, to Agnesa, August 21, 1915, ASMAI, pos. 153/3, f. 1.

34 Colonial Minister, Rome, to Cerrina Feroni, October 28, 1917, ASMAI, pos. 153/2, f. 9.

rials for the Italian economy; institution of a shipping line connecting Italy, the ports of Eritrea, Somalia, southern Arabia, Bombay, and Mombasa; and construction of railroads and port works in Somalia "in proportion to the extent of the above program of economic expansion." His program also called for the methodical organization of the fishing industry, the exportation of cattle and sheep, an increase in cotton production (which then amounted to only 110 tons), the utilization of northern Somali products like gums and incense, and the investigation of salt and other mineral deposits in northern Somalia. He suggested that Somalia export its skins and hides exclusively to Italy. In this complex program for the economic development of Somalia, Gasparini exhibited a vision and practicality that was to be put to use in the following decades as the *mise en valeur* of Somalia was begun.[35]

The Convegno Nazionale Coloniale per il Dopoguerra delle Colonie ("National Colonial Conference for the Post-War Future of the Colonies"), held in Rome from January 15 to 18, 1919, exerted additional pressure on the government to recognize the value of each colony. Speaking on the future of Somalia, Professor Giuseppe Stefanini, who had conducted a study of the colony's natural resources on the eve of the war, lamented the government's failure to expend enough effort to develop the colony's economy. Stefanini envisioned a prosperous Somalia with an economy based on commerce, agriculture, and pastoralism. He advocated the construction of a railroad from Mogadishu to Lugh and the allegedly rich provinces of southern Ethiopia, by which skins, hides, and coffee could more easily find their way to the new Italian port of Trieste. Referring to the edited Onor report appended to De Martino's *La Somalia nei tre anni del mio governo,* Stefanini evoked a picture of fertile plantations of rubber, cotton and other fibers, tobacco, and sugar cane along the Juba and the Webi Shebelle. He suggested that the non-irrigable

[35] Gasparini, Mogadishu, to Cerrina Feroni, June 16, 1918, ASMAI, pos. 171/2, f. 9.

lands of the dry plateau region should "generously" be reserved for the natives for traditional subsistence agriculture
(millet, corn, sesame, and a little tobacco). All this, however,
would take time. Stefanini foresaw more practical and immediate results from pastoralism, or more particularly, stock-
raising. With the great postwar rise in meat and leather prices,
this industry, together with agriculture, might well become
the basis of a prosperous colonial economy. To bring its point
home, the Convegno passed a three-part resolution urging
that the government develop animal husbandry in Somalia,
either by encouraging the native industry or by assisting the
work of private companies; that a thorough study be made of
the hydrology of the Juba and the Webi Shebelle; and that
work begin on a port and a railroad "that must push from
Somalia into the Kaffa region of southern Ethiopia."[36]

While Stefanini was expressing such resplendent hopes for
the economic future of the colony, the economic situation was
far from bright. Somalia was still the *Cenerentola delle Colonie* ("Cinderella of the colonies"). Governor De Martino's
long, glowing reports of 1910 to 1913 had been followed by
briefer annual reports concerned with the prosaic business of
making ends meet within the restricted colonial budget. In
1917, Colonial Minister Gaspare Colosimo's annual report
to Parliament on the conditions of the colonies devoted only
thirty of its more than five hundred pages to Somalia. In these
pages it was revealed that 75 per cent of Somalia's income was
derived from government sources. Now, additional funds
were necessary to promote economic progress "in order not to
let [the colony] perish." The shortage of capital and of labor
prohibited the large-scale development of agriculture, and
the colonial government turned to the idea of native cultivation of land with government assistance in mechanization and

[36] G. Stefanini, *Le Risorse idriche della Somalia italiana e l'avvenire della
colonia* (Rome: Convegno Nazionale Coloniale per il Dopoguerra delle
Colonie, 1919), p. 16.

marketing. For the first time the colonial government talked of taxing the tribes in at least part of the colony.[37]

A few years later, in the immediate postwar period, Governor Carlo Riveri expressed a general note of dissatisfaction in reporting on the condition of the colony: "There is still very much to be done." Riveri had been optimistic when he assumed office in June, 1920, but he was soon cured of that attitude. The war had had few repercussions on native life, but its effects on the homeland and on Europeans in the colony had created a general economic crisis. Native policy had progressed to the satisfaction of the governor, who found that "native policy to date . . . has drawn them increasingly into our orbit and has made them appreciate the paternalism of an impartial government that is always ready to aid them and to humor them." To continue these encouraging political developments, the governor looked forward to increasing the influence of local Italian authorities over the tribes and intensifying the work of the residents and regional commissioners. What was lacking was economic progress to act as a catalyst in "the natural improvement in the standard of living of the native populations, [and in] their political and social evolution."[38]

One factor limiting economic expansion was the colony's unhealthy monetary system. Before 1904 the Benadir did not have its own currency but used the Maria Theresa thaler, which was based on a free silver value, and the besa of Mombasa and Zanzibar as fractions of the thaler; also in circulation were the English and German besas from nearby colonies. But the thaler was exceedingly unstable. Although it was usually worth 150 besas, Arab and Indian merchants could buy their besas in Oman at the rate of about 500 to the thaler and

[37] G. Colosimo, *Relazione al Parlamento sulla situazione politica, economica ed amministrativa delle colonie italiane* (Rome: Tipografia del Senato, 1918), pp. 131–55.

[38] C. Riveri, *Relazione annuale sulla situazione generale della colonia, 1920–21* (Mogadishu: Ufficio del Governo, 1921), p. 8.

then speculate in the unstable thaler in Somalia. In 1905 Governor Mercatelli proposed the introduction of special silver and bronze coins minted in Italy. As a temporary measure, Mercatelli circulated 50,000 lire in nickel coins of 25 centesimi and 8,500 lire in bronze coins of 1 and 2 centesimi, and put the Italian centesimo on a par with the official Zanzibari besa. The Arab and Indian traders refused to co-operate, however, and the Italian besa fell in value to 300 to the thaler. Consequently, the government was forced to restore the old besa and keep the unstable thaler.[39]

In 1910 the colonial government again attempted currency reform by introducing the Italian rupee.[40] Between the years 1910 and 1920 almost three million silver rupees were put into circulation. To ease the way for the new monetary unit, which at 1.68 lire was on a par with the rupee of India and East Africa, the governor permitted circulation of the British East African and Indian rupees in the colony.[41]

During the war the colony experienced a grave coin shortage. Paper money was not acceptable to the Somali; and as the metropolitan lira depreciated and the price of silver rose, the rupee's intrinsic value doubled and even tripled. The rapid depreciation of the lira, moreover, posed difficult budgetary problems for the colony, which kept its books in lire. In September, 1919, the Italian rupee was revaluated at the rate of 15 to the English pound sterling.[42] The colonial rupee was thus finally stabilized, although its relation to the lira still remained in question. The rupee was withdrawn from circulation in British and ex-German East Africa, and the currency of most of East Africa was tied to the pound sterling. In an era of rising economic nationalism and neoprotectionism, the Italians were in the uncomfortable position of having the currency of one of their colonies dependent not upon the lira but

39 "Monetary circulation in Somalia, 1912," ASMAI, pos. 75/12, f. 139.

40 Royal Decree, No. 847, December 8, 1910, ASMAI, pos. 75/11, f. 122.

41 Gubernatorial Decree, No. 724, August 31, 1911, ASMAI, pos. 75/11, f. 122.

42 Royal Decree, No. 2339, September 19, 1919, ASMAI, pos. 75/12, f. 142.

upon the English pound. Financial reform came to Somalia in 1925 when the Fascist government, in imitation of British and French currency policy in their colonies after World War I, introduced the metropolitan currency into Somalia.[43] As late as 1931, however, Italian currency was still relatively unknown in northern Somalia and in the bush, where the Maria Theresa thaler still circulated.[44]

Riveri's faith in attracting private capital to Somalia was the one ray of hope in an otherwise grim economic picture. In 1914, Professor Giuseppe Scassellati-Sforzolini of the Istituto Agricolo Coloniale of Florence had investigated the economy and agriculture of Somalia and had seconded the findings of Romolo Onor that small concessions in Somalia failed because of lack of adequate capital. By 1919, only four concessions survived. Scassellati remained convinced, however, that an agricultural endeavor in Somalia could succeed—if it had ample financial backing. Recalling the earlier period of concessions, he wrote in 1926, "They dreamed of amazing earnings from the cultivation of 4 or 5 thousand hectares of cotton with the investment of a few tens of thousands of lire; there were also those who had never been to the colony but still thought of speculating . . . on the price of concession lands."[45]

Just when the agricultural future of colonial Somalia looked darkest, the situation changed. Prince Luigi Amedeo of Savoy, Duke of the Abruzzi, who had long been interested in Africa and had led an expedition to explore Mount Ruwenzori in the lake region of East Africa in 1906, became interested in the development of commercial agriculture in the Webi Shebelle valley. In 1919, he invited Scassellati to study the agricultural potential of Somalia. The following year the Società Agricola Italo-Somala (SAIS) was founded, with the Duke as president and Scassellati as manager. Banking, cotton

[43] Royal Decree, No. 1143, June 18, 1925; Gubernatorial Decree, No. 4444, July 1, 1925; Mondaini, *La Legislazione coloniale italiana* . . . , I, 327.

[44] *Atti del Primo Congresso di Studi Coloniali* (Florence: Centro di Studi Coloniali, 1931), VI, 358–59.

[45] Quoted in G. Corni, *Somalia italiana* (Milan: Arte e Storia, 1937), II, 383–84.

textile, sugar refining, and other industrial and private interests underwrote its initial capital of 24,000,000 lire, which was increased to 35,000,000 in 1923. The company was guaranteed financial resources many times the amount available to the Benadir Company for the administration of the whole colony before 1905. A site was selected on the middle Webi Shebelle between Balad and Mahaddei Wen, and in 1923 work began for the creation of a highly mechanized commercial plantation.[46] Naturally, SAIS could not produce immediate results, and Governor Riveri, who was eager for the economic development of the colony to begin, stressed the need for government action to supplement private initiative. "The absolute unpreparedness of Somalia to receive this sudden influx . . . has made even more evident the deficiency of government action."[47]

Indeed, government inaction marked the period from 1920 to 1923 in both the colony and the homeland. At the time of Mussolini's assumption of power as prime minister on October 31, 1922, it was difficult to predict what direction the new government would take. His public statements indicated that the world could expect at least a series of melodramatic gestures; yet because the Fascists were not in complete control of the government, hope remained that in foreign policy the new prime minister might be guided by more moderate voices. In colonial matters, an indication of future policy was given by the appointment of aggressively imperialistic Luigi Federzoni as minister of colonies; Carlo Riveri, however, remained governor until October, 1923. Mussolini and the Fascists first had to concern themselves with metropolitan politics before ranging farther afield. With the appointment of Quadrumvir C. M. De Vecchi as governor of the colony in October, 1923, it became apparent that Fascism and vigorous action would come to the sleepy colony on the Indian Ocean.

[46] A. Piccioli, *La Nuova Italia d'Oltremare* (Verona: Mondadori, 1934), I, 824–28.

[47] Riveri, *Relazione annuale . . . 1920–1921*, p. 7.

CHAPTER SIX

The Northern Protectorates, 1889–1923

When Sultan Yusuf Ali of Obbia requested Italian protection in December, 1888, Vincenzo Filonardi saw an opportunity to extend his commercial interest into northern Somalia, a region known for its ostrich feathers and incense. Filonardi was aware that Yusuf Ali wanted Italian support in his long dispute with the sultan of Zanzibar over the border region north of Warsheik.[1] Yusuf Ali was also interested in influencing the balance of power in northern Somalia against his traditional enemy, Sultan Osman Mahmud of the Mijjertein, with whom he contended for control of the interior and of the Nogal region; and Europeans could be useful as suppliers of firearms and ammunition. In brief, the sultan had much to gain and little to lose from making an agreement with the Italians, who gained the prestige of nominal control over an area of approximately 50,000 square miles.

During the negotiations, Filonardi discovered that Yusuf Ali's daughter was the favorite wife of Sultan Osman Mahmud and proposed that Yusuf Ali act as intermediary between the Italians and the Mijjertein sultan, over whose territory they also wanted to establish a protectorate. Although the British authorities at Aden were skeptical that the Mijjertein Somali would ever accept a protectorate, Osman Mahmud

---

[1] Filonardi, Zanzibar, to Foreign Minister, December 17, 1888, *Documenti diplomatici italiani presentati al Parlamento italiano dal Ministro degli Affari Esteri (Blanc): Somalia Italiana (1885–1895)* (Rome, 1895), doc. 2, p. 27 (hereinafter cited as *Libro Verde*).

agreed to negotiate with the Italians. The situation had changed, and Osman Mahmud saw the advantages inherent in "submitting" to the Italians—guns, a sure source of income, and a countermove against Yusuf Ali. On April 7, 1889, he formally accepted an Italian protectorate. The treaty was identical with that signed by Yusuf Ali, with the exception of the subsidy. Osman Mahmud drove a harder bargain than his father-in-law, who immediately demanded an equal sum— 1,800 thalers annually.[2]

The Italians did not visit their new protectorates again until the following year, when Filonardi made his first annual tour of inspection and presented the subsidies. Yusuf Ali also received twenty-five new rifles and five thousand cartridges, as well as cotton goods and other small gifts. The Obbians, who had great respect for Filonardi, took this to mean Italian approval of their seizure of El Hur, a trading center claimed by the Arab merchants of Mogadishu, then under the Zanzibari flag.[3] Filonardi close to ignore the incident, which indirectly worked in his company's favor.

In keeping with the policy of government by chartered company, the Filonardi Company in the Benadir was also responsible for the administration of the protectorates, as we have seen in chapter i (p. 36). In 1893, the government reminded Filonardi of the need to obtain the adherence of the northern sultans to the general acts of Brussels and Berlin, by which trade in slaves, arms, and liquor was limited in Africa.[4] Filonardi, beset with difficulties in the Benadir, could do nothing at the time, and in the following year Cecchi, then consul at Aden, visited the protectorates to carry out the government's instructions. Osman Mahmud complained to him

---

2 Treaty for Protectorate over the Mijjertein, *Libro Verde*, doc. 11, annex I, p. 39.

3 Filonardi, Rome, to Foreign Minister, March 2, 1890, *Libro Verde*, doc. 27, pp. 61–62.

4 Foreign Minister, Rome, to Filonardi, November 20, 1893, *Libro Verde*, doc. 103, p. 254.

THE NORTHERN PROTECTORATES

```
0      50    100         200         300
├───┼───┼───┴───────────┼───────────┤
              MILES
```

that no Italian ship had visited Alula since 1890; but after Cecchi had contented him with the usual gifts of arms, the sultan eagerly adhered to the general act of Brussels limiting traffic in arms and ammunition.[5] Cecchi also obtained Yusuf Ali's adherence. Inasmuch as the Mijjertein and Obbian Somali were stout Muslims, they readily accepted the clauses limiting trade in hard liquor. As for slavery, Cecchi found that the institution was virtually non-existent in northern Somalia and thus posed no problem. In this mission, too, Cecchi played the role of ardent imperialist. Pressing for more dynamic government action, he criticized the existing protectorates as having compromised Italian prestige and dignity. "Symbols of possession are not enough. . . . We need a valid political organization instead."[6] Not until thirty years later was this demand to be realized.

In 1896, a year of crisis for Italian colonialism in Ethiopia and in southern Somalia, the northern sultanates remained loyal. Acting together, Yusuf Ali and Osman Mahmud even proposed sending an expedition against Harar. They claimed that the Ogaden Somali would rise against the Ethiopians and join forces with the invaders. They promised that Obbia and the Mijjertein would raise some fifty thousand warriors, if only the Italians would agree to furnish them with rifles and ammunition.[7] Before the Italians could pay more attention to this proposal, however, the defeat at Adowa caused all their plans for East Africa to go up in smoke, and the proposed Somali invasion of Ethiopia did not materialize.

After Adowa, the two sultans renewed their aggressiveness. Yusuf Ali, the more enterprising of the two, had ambitions to

[5] Commander Rebaudi, Zanzibar, to Naval Ministry, January 1, 1895, *Libro Verde*, doc. 85, pp. 201–2.

[6] Cecchi, Zanzibar, to Foreign Minister, December 24, 1894, *Libro Verde*, doc. 84, p. 201.

[7] Vice-Consul V. Bienenfeld, Aden, to Governor Baratieri of Eritrea, January 3, 1896, Archivio Storico dell'ex Ministero dell'Africa Italiana (hereinafter cited as ASMAI), pos. 59/1, f. 13.

expand southward. In October, 1897, during the period of temporary, direct governmental control, Royal Commissioner Extraordinary Giorgio Sorrentino discovered that Yusuf Ali intended to gain control of Harardera, sixty miles southwest of Obbia. The Waesle tribesmen of that district had already placed themselves under Italian protection, and Sorrentino was confronted with a choice between the Waesle and the Obbians. But in 1897 the Italians were weak, and Sorrentino came to the sad conclusion that "it would not be opportune to make an issue of it; it is better to pretend to ignore the question."[8] Clearly, the Italians could not effectively intervene in northern matters. They had to appease their protégé by sacrificing the Waesle. The Italians also avoided embroiling themselves in the increased rivalry between the two sultans. To counter his father-in-law's growing power, Osman Mahmud established a town at the mouth of the wadi Nogal and immediately offered to place the region under Italian protection. The treaties of 1889 had recognized an Italian protectorate over this disputed region between Obbia and the Mijjertein, but it was unclear to which sultanate the region belonged.[9]

Matters worsened in May, 1900, when Osman Mahmud tried to seize control of the water wells of Alula, traditionally in the possession of followers of Yusuf Ali, although Alula was the seat of the Mijjertein sultanate. Osman Mahmud, who had never truly understood the nature of the protectorate, actually appealed to Italy for assistance.[10] Then in rapid succession, the Italians learned of increased gunrunning from French Somaliland into Alula and of Mijjertein pirate

[8] Sorrentino, Zanzibar, to Foreign Minister, October 20, 1897, ASMAI, pos. 59/2, f. 15.

[9] Foreign Minister, Rome, to Sorrentino, December 29, 1897, ASMAI, pos. 59/2, ff. 17 and 18.

[10] Acting Vice-Consul Lang, Aden, to Foreign Minister, May 9, 1900, ASMAI, pos. 59/2, f. 25.

attacks on pearl fishers in the waters of British Socotra.[11] How long they could ignore northern affairs was debatable. Governor Dulio of the Benadir Company was particularly worried about Osman Mahmud, who, in a bid for influence southward, was attempting to stir up the peoples of the Mudugh region against Obbia. Dulio was of the opinion that northern turmoil would soon threaten the precarious peace of the Benadir.[12]

In March, 1901, Giulio Pestalozza, Italian consul at Aden, was ordered to Alula to induce the sultan to give full recognition to the protectorate. Pestalozza met with Osman Mahmud at Bargal on March 12 and again at Hafun later that month, but the sultan continued to refuse to yield. Although the Italians had at first ruled out the use of force because they did not want to upset the uneasy balance of power between Obbia and the Mijjertein, which had worked to their benefit, Pestalozza was now determined to teach the recalcitrant Mijjertein a lesson. Osman Mahmud's intransigence had played right into the hands of his traditional rival, Yusuf Ali. On April 1, Pestalozza sailed from Obbia with Yusuf Ali and 117 askaris. As Osman Mahmud fled into the interior, the *Volta* bombarded the coastal villages of Bereda and Bender Kassim. The Italians and their Obbian mercenaries confiscated more than five hundred rifles and thirty thousand cartridges at Alula, Bender Filuk, Bereda, Bender Kassim, and Bender Merhagno. Yusuf Ali occupied Alula.[13]

In a vain effort to avoid capitulating to the Italians, Osman Mahmud sent his cousin Muhammad Musa to Aden to ask for a British protectorate. In mid-May Muhammad Musa sailed

11 Acting Vice-Consul Lang, Aden, to Foreign Minister, June 6, 1900, ASMAI, pos. 59/2, f. 25; British Chargé d'Affaires, Rome, to Foreign Minister, September 14, 1900, and British Agent Hardinge, Zanzibar, to Dulio, September 8, 1900, ASMAI, pos. 59/2, f. 26.

12 Dulio, Mogadishu, to Foreign Minister, February 6, 1900, ASMAI, pos. 59/2, f. 27.

13 Commander of the *Governolo*, Aden, to Naval Ministry, March 14, 1901, ASMAI, pos. 59/2, ff. 28 and 29.

for Dar es Salaam, where he was equally unsuccessful in pressing his case with the German authorities. Meanwhile, the Italian minister in Cairo intercepted a letter ostensibly seeking a Turkish protectorate over "independent Mijjertein Somalia, whose confines extend to the region of Kismayu." All of these attempts came to naught, and with no alternative Osman Mahmud came to terms with the Italians.[14]

By the convention of Bender Ollok on August 18, 1901, the sultan of the Mijjertein again recognized his dependence on Italy. Osman Mahmud's subsidy was restored, and the Italians even promised to compensate him for the bombardment of the coastal villages.[15] All that Italy gained from the new convention was the right to build a lighthouse at Cape Guardafui. Pestalozza could have extracted much more from the sultan, but he chose not to press for the installation of an Italian agent at Bender Kassim or to demand the right to minerals in the Mijjertein or to the salt deposits at Hafun. Once more Yusuf Ali and Osman Mahmud were placed on a more or less equal footing. The Nogal remained a disputed area, and the protectorates continued to be loosely administered by Italy from the consulate at Aden. No Italian agent resided in either Obbia or the Mijjertein, and the Italians had few sources of information about developments in the mountainous north. Oddly enough, although Pestalozza felt that he had been pursuing the government's own policy, the foreign ministry strongly criticized him for humoring the sultan and following the path of least resistance in negotiating with the northern Somali.[16]

14 Lang, Aden, to Foreign Minister, May 18, 1901, and Italian Minister Tugini, Cairo, to Foreign Minister, April 14, 1901 (containing the Italian translation of a letter in Arabic from a certain Sheik Idris, supposedly on mission from the Mijjertein), ASMAI, pos. 59/2, ff. 28 and 29.

15 Bulletin of the Agenzia Stefani [news service], No. 101, Rome, August 26, 1901.

16 Foreign Minister, Rome, to Pestalozza, September 13, 1901, ASMAI, pos. 59/2, f. 33.

The restoration of the status quo in northern Somalia was not to be accomplished easily; inevitably, new elements entered the picture. The relations of the Italians with the sultans of northern Somalia were complicated considerably by the appearance of a religious leader who was to keep northern Somalia, British Somaliland, and the Ogaden province of Ethiopia in turmoil for two decades.

In 1899, Muhammad Abdullah Hassan, leader of the Salihiya religious brotherhood in British Somaliland, broke with the British authorities and declared a holy war against all infidels.[17] His dervish movement spread like wildfire and became very powerful in the north. In hopes of gaining an ally on the flank of his Obbian enemy, Osman Mahmud began to sell Muhammad Abdullah some of the rifles he had smuggled in from Djibouti in French Somaliland.[18] As the dervish movement spread, trade came to a standstill in the Ogaden and in the British protectorate. Then in March, 1900, the dervishes attacked the Ethiopian fort at Jijiga and caused great alarm at Harar. The Ethiopian government proposed a joint Anglo-Ethiopian expedition against the dervishes to the British authorities in Somaliland, who, although they numbered only ten, excluding a small force of one hundred thirty Indian askaris, anticipated a speedy end to the uprising.[19]

Faced with the advance of fifteen thousand Ethiopians, one thousand British Somali, and a few hundred Anglo-Indian troops, Muhammad Abdullah withdrew into the Mudugh oasis of northern Somalia. The dervishes were not safe there, however, for Yusuf Ali jealously guarded the important water holes. The dervishes then moved north to just within the Mijjertein sultanate. The British ignored orders from London and pursued the dervishes across the border into Italian

17 A. Baldini, "Somalia italiana," *Enciclopedia Italiana,* XXXII, 115.

18 J. J. Vianney, "Mohamed Abdulla Hasan: A Reassessment," *Somali Chronicle* (Mogadishu), November 13, 1957, p. 4.

19 D. Jardine, *The Mad Mullah of Somaliland* (London: Herbert Jenkins, 1923), p. 49.

Somalia, burned several villages, and then retired to the British protectorate. By the end of July, 1901, the British had withdrawn completely. They had failed to weaken the dervishes, let alone end the threat. The Ethiopians had succeeded only in preventing the dervishes from moving west.[20] From his base in the Mijjertein, Muhammad Abdullah Hassan regrouped his forces and raided the British protectorate again. A second British expedition in 1902 also ended in failure.

After the failure of the first two expeditions, the British decided to initiate a three-pronged Anglo-Italo-Ethiopian attack against the dervishes. The Italian government, however, refused to undertake expensive military operations; Italian public opinion was still influenced by the disaster at Adowa. All that the Italians would permit was a British landing at Obbia. The British plan of attack called for almost two thousand Central African, Sudanese, and Indian troops to land at Obbia in December, 1902, and proceed northwest. A second force of two thousand English, Indian, Somali, and Boer troops was to move southeast from Berbera. Fitawrari Gabre's five thousand Ethiopians would march down the Webi Shebelle valley. At the end of March, 1903, the two British forces met without having encountered the dervishes. After the onset of the rainy season in May, the dervishes attacked, and by the end of June the British were in retreat. The "Mad Mullah," as the British came to call Muhammad Abdullah Hassan, then swept down to the Indian Ocean and occupied the whole Nogal valley from the British border to Ilig on the sea.

From its very beginnings, Italian co-operation with the British disturbed the loose arrangement with the northern sultans. Commander Giovanni Lovatelli, who was the Italian liaison officer at Obbia, felt that it was his duty to co-operate fully with the British, with whom he had served at Kismayu

<hr/>

[20] A. Gaibi, *Manuale di storia politico-militare delle colonie italiane* (Rome: Ministero della Guerra, 1928), p. 170; Jardine, *The Mad Mullah of Somaliland,* pp. 85–86.

ten years earlier. When the British, through General W. H. Manning, wrongly accused Yusuf Ali of favoring the dervish cause, Lovatelli gave Manning a free hand to arrest the sultan and his son, Ali Yusuf, and transport them to Aden. Yusuf Ali, who had co-operated with the Italians in previous ventures, soon found himself exiled in Eritrea. The whole matter was handled clumsily, and Italian popularity and prestige at Obbia diminished to the vanishing point as a result of Lovatelli's strong Anglophilia. When the foreign ministry heard of Manning's high-handed action and Lovatelli's acquiescence, it immediately protested the deposition of Yusuf Ali and relieved Lovatelli of his mission.[21]

Lovatelli's successor, Captain Eugenio di Robbiate Airoldi, in contrast, did not trust General Manning and was suspicious of British motives in northern Somalia. He even suggested that the British had designs on the sultanate of Obbia.[22] In the face of a threatened rebellion by the Obbians, the foreign ministry ordered his superior, Admiral Carlo Mirabello, to bring Ali Yusuf back to Obbia to serve as regent in his father's absence. Mirabello shared Airoldi's opinion that in northern Somalia the Italians had as much to fear from the English and the Ethiopians as from the dervishes.

British intervention in northern Somalia was also manifested in the Mijjertein. During the fourth expedition against Muhammad Abdullah in 1903, a new crisis with Osman Mahmud was triggered near Alula. In retaliation for the death of an Italian naval officer, the Italian gunboat *Antilope* and the H.M.S. *Mohawk* bombarded the village of Durbo. When Osman Mahmud refused to yield, the Italians blockaded the Mijjertein coast and bombarded several other villages. The British, who did not want to alienate a possible ally against the "Mad Mullah," intervened on Osman Mahmud's

---

[21] Foreign Minister, Rome, to Consul Ferdinando Sola, February 20, 1903, ASMAI, pos. 59/3, f. 43.

[22] Captain Airoldi, Obbia, to Minister of War, September 7, 1903, ASMAI, pos. 59/3, f. 50.

behalf, and the Mijjertein sultan expressed his willingness to co-operate in their plans by occupying part of the Nogal.[23] Thus the British were backing the Mijjertein while the Italians favored Obbia. Neither course brought stability to the troubled north.

Meanwhile, the campaign against the dervishes got under way in January, 1904, as Ali Yusuf's Obbians occupied Galkayu and the dervishes suffered a major defeat at Jidbali in British Somaliland. By March the British had driven the dervishes into the Mijjertein, and an alarmed Osman Mahmud sent eight hundred men against them to cut the rebels off from contact with their forces at Ilig. On April 21, the British landed five hundred men at Ilig and, when it appeared that they would soon be victorious on the battlefield, magnanimously offered Muhammad Abdullah Hassan safe conduct into permanent exile at Mecca.[24]

Rather than surrender to the British, Muhammad Abdullah saw another way out. There was strong sentiment in some Italian quarters to negotiate a separate settlement with the dervish leader. From the beginning, it had been obvious that the Italians did not want to undertake an expensive campaign against him; and British experience since 1899 had indicated to them that the outcome of any military operation was highly uncertain. On October 16 and 17, 1904, Muhammad Abdullah met with Giulio Pestalozza at Ilig, and the Italian consul listened to what he had to say. Muhammad Abdullah was resentful of both the English and the Mijjertein Somali and was willing to negotiate for peace: "My people and I will be the Italian government's people, and we shall be dependent on it, if it will favor us . . . and permit us to build a town on the coast."[25]

23 Gaibi, *Manuale di storia politico-militare delle colonie italiane*, p. 172.

24 F. S. Caroselli, *Ferro e fuoco in Somalia* (Rome: Ministero delle Colonie, 1931), p. 57. Jardine makes no mention of this offer in his semi-official account, *The Mad Mullah of Somaliland*.

25 Muhammad Abdullah to Pestalozza, Ilig, October 17, 1904, in Caroselli, *Ferro e fuoco in Somalia*, pp. 78–79.

After obtaining the approval of Obbia, the Mijjertein, and Great Britain, Pestalozza returned to Ilig to conclude negotiations with the dervish leader. On March 5, 1905, Pestalozza and Muhammad Abdullah signed a peace treaty. The "Mad Mullah," regarded by the British as a brigand and fanatic, was given the Nogal territory between Obbia and the Mijjertein and was recognized as the lawful ruler of a third Italian protectorate in northern Somalia.[26]

Although the Nogal now served as a buffer state between Obbia and the Mijjertein and the threat of a dervish invasion of the Benadir was eliminated at a time when Italy was particularly concerned over the future of southern Somalia, it was uncertain whether Muhammad Abdullah would settle down or foment trouble between his new protector and the dissident elements of southern Somalia. Both the Italians and the dervishes had gained time, but the basic problem of defining Italy's role in northern Somalia was unresolved.

After the establishment of the Nogal protectorate and the Italians' recognition of Muhammad Abdullah Hassan as its ruler, his prestige rose high throughout Somalia. Although his religious message had not been well received outside the Darod tribal regions of northern Somalia, he now became a symbol of political rebellion against foreign domination. Dervishism had come to mean revolt, and the Bimal and Wadan tribes of the Benadir were among the first to understand the nature of Muhammad Abdullah's victory. They welcomed dervish emissaries, who supplied them with arms and preached their message of revolt throughout the Benadir.[27]

To contain the Bimal revolt and to prevent a Bimal-dervish alliance, the Italians called upon the forces of Obbia and the Mijjertein. Although the foreign ministry had approved the use of force in penetrating the Webi Shebelle valley, it still ruled out direct intervention in northern affairs. The weak-

[26] E. Hertslet, *The Map of Africa by Treaty* (3d ed.; London: His Majesty's Stationery Office, 1909), III, 1120–22.

[27] Caroselli, *Ferro e fuoco in Somalia,* p. 163.

ness of this policy became evident as the two sultans and the dervish pursued their own goals and upset the delicate balance in the north. It was rumored that the Machiavellian Osman Mahmud planned to attack Muhammad Abdullah, his erstwhile friend, in league with Yusuf Ali, his traditional enemy, who had been restored to power several years earlier.[28]

Obviously the Italians could only be alarmed about the situation in the north. In March, 1906, Eugenio Cappello, consul at Aden, frankly declared, "Politically our position could not be worse."[29] After a visit to Obbia and the Mijjertein later that year, Cappello, who had long experience in Somalia, wrote, "I have the impression that not only is our present position in Somalia false, but it is also beginning to be ridiculous."[30] To improve a situation in which Italy was sovereign over northern Somalia only on sufferance of the local rulers, Cappello urged that the foreign ministry give serious thought to the occupation of Bender Kassim, Ilig, and Obbia.[31]

Although Foreign Minister Tittoni had given his fullest support to the military operations in southern Somalia, he hesitated to commit himself to such action in the north. Giacomo Agnesa, the head of the Colonial Office, warned him of the complications that would come from intervention in northern Somalia: the need to suppress arms-smuggling, the delicate problem of dealing with rumored equivocal relations of Yusuf Ali and Osman Mahmud with the Ethiopians and the English, and the impossibility of acting without first establishing Italy's full authority over the three protectorates. The only effective remedy, commented Agnesa, was one that Parliament was unwilling to endorse—a military expedition of one thousand men at an estimated cost of 1,000,000 lire,

[28] Memorandum on northern Somalia, January, 1908, ASMAI, pos. 59/4, f. 59.

[29] Cappello, Aden, to Foreign Minister, March 20, 1906, ASMAI, pos. 59/4, f. 59.

[30] Cappello, Aden, to Foreign Minister, August 15, 1906, ASMAI, pos. 59/4, f. 59.

[31] Cappello, Aden, to Foreign Minister, August 22, 1906, ASMAI, pos. 59/4, f. 59.

which could disarm the northern Somali as a preliminary to further political action.[32]

At this time, many Italians still believed that a political solution could be found. Thus the basic law providing the outline for colonial rule in southern Somalia, which was passed in the next year—April 5, 1908—entrusted the governor at Mogadishu with the administration of the northern protectorates. The distance between Mogadishu and Obbia, however, was so great that Governor Carletti proposed to the foreign ministry the constitution of northern Somalia as a separate colony. The foreign ministry ignored Carletti's proposal and ordered the colonial government to prepare for the gradual installation of residencies along the coast of the protectorates, the first to be installed at Obbia.[33]

Because of Yusuf Ali's increasing difficulties with his belligerent neighbor to the north, the new Italian consul at Aden, Gino Macchioro, was able to obtain the sultan's reluctant agreement in principle to the installation of a resident at Obbia. By September, 1908, the dervishes were more daring in their attacks on Obbian territory. They invaded the Mudugh in an attempt to establish contact with the Bah Geri on the upper Shebelle. At the same time, in conjunction with the Warsangeli, they again invaded British territory. Dervish raids on the Ogaden and on Obbia increased in the months that followed, and northern Somalia's thirty months of relative peace came to an end.

Macchioro was less successful with the "Mad Mullah" at Ilig, where his only means of contact was by letter. Muhammad Abdullah doubted the good intentions of the Italians, who dared not put ashore for fear that the dervishes would capture them as hostages. They were more successful farther

[32] Memorandum from Central Directory of Colonial Affairs to Foreign Minister, Rome, July 15, 1907, ASMAI, pos. 59/4, f. 59.

[33] G. Mondaini, *La Legislazione coloniale italiana nel suo sviluppo storico e nel suo stato attuale (1881–1940)* (Milan: Istituto per gli Studi di Politica Internazionale, 1941), I, 246.

north, although it was clear that the Mijjertein Somali were hostile to the Italians. Osman Mahmud reluctantly agreed to accept a resident in Mijjertein territory.[34]

Meanwhile the British planned a new campaign against the dervishes. By mid-February, 1909, they had amassed a force of four thousand men in British Somaliland and had stationed three warships off the coast. On March 12, however, only five weeks after the military operations had been ordered, the secretary of state informed the British authorities in Somaliland that the cost of maintaining a large force in the interior was so great that the whole question of British policy in Somaliland was going to be reconsidered.[35]

At this time the British and the Italians were encouraged by the defection of Abdullah Shahari, Muhammad Abdullah's friend and adviser, who had concluded most of the arrangements for the Ilig agreement of 1905. The dervish leader had alienated Abdullah Shahari by denouncing his marriage to a Mijjertein woman, and Abdullah Shahari sought revenge. Armed with accusations against the conduct and religious orthodoxy of the "Mad Mullah," he went to Mecca, where he had an audience with Muhammad Salih, the founder of the Salihiya. Abdullah Shahari then appeared at Aden, bearing a letter to Muhammad Abdullah from Muhammad Salih, to confer with the Italian acting consul to determine how the strongly worded message could be put to political use against the dervish leader. Late in March, 1909, Abdullah Shahari and Acting Consul Renato Piacentini sailed from Aden to Ilig, where they sent a messenger to the dervish with Muhammad Salih's letter:

I have before my eyes the news that you and your people have got into bad ways and no longer respect the Shariʿa. Of this I have proof, for you and your people raid, and rob, and enjoy the women and wives of those men whom you kill and whose goods you take

[34] Macchioro report, 1908, ASMAI, pos. 59/5, f. 80.

[35] Jardine, *The Mad Mullah of Somaliland*, p. 183.

for your own. . . . I do not approve of this, for it is against the law and the word of our holy prophet Muhammad. . . .

From this moment on I wish to have nothing to do with you and your people; I will not write to you again, and I do not want you to write to me. Those who follow the path of God have his protection, but those who do evil shall surely be punished. . . .

What you have done is now enough; leave off your bad ways. For if you do not change I will not write you again, nor will I have anything to do with you, and I shall inform all the faithful brethren of your wicked actions, and you shall no longer belong to [the Salihiya].[36]

In effect, Muhammad Salih excommunicated Muhammad Abdullah. When the cadi of Ilig declared in his presence that he approved of Muhammad Salih's decision, the "Mad Mullah" ordered him and eight other men killed on the spot.[37] The news of the excommunication and of the cadi's death caused great consternation in the dervish camp, and many abandoned Muhammad Abdullah and returned to their tribes in the Ogaden and the Mijjertein and among the Dolbahanta.

Assuming that the dervish power was now broken, Piacentini continued on to Obbia, where he sought to instal a resident. Yusuf Ali, whose fear of the dervishes was lessened by news of the excommunication, yielded to the Italian demand for an agreement only after Piacentini threatened to bombard Obbia. It was agreed that the resident "would in no way be in charge of the administration of the sultanate, neither in matters of customs revenues or commerce, nor in matters of justice, unless there should arise questions between subjects of the Italian government and peoples subject to Yusuf Ali, in which case the resident would act as the natural

[36] An Italian translation of the Arabic letter appears in Caroselli, *Ferro e fuoco in Somalia*, pp. 129–31, and a not entirely accurate English translation in Jardine, *The Mad Mullah of Somaliland*, pp. 184–85.

[37] Jardine, *The Mad Mullah of Somaliland*, p. 186; Caroselli, *Ferro e fuoco in Somalia*, p. 131.

judge." It was explicitly stated that the resident was to have no direct authority over the affairs of the sultanate but would come "to Obbia as the sultan's friend and adviser." The sultan also agreed to provide the new resident, Lieutenant A. Ardinghi, with a house.[38]

News soon reached Obbia that the bulk of the dervishes had remained loyal to Muhammad Abdullah Hassan, and the new resident's immediate task was the organization of the forces of Obbia to withstand a dervish invasion. Yusuf Ali had in his possession not more than eight hundred rifles. If the Italians intended to use the Obbians as a shield to protect the Benadir against a dervish drive southward, the resident had his work cut out for him.[39] The practical effects of the excommunication were felt primarily, not in northern Somalia, but in the Benadir, where letters from Muhammad Salih to the principal religious leaders propagandized against Muhammad Abdullah and his alleged heresy. His prestige, though lessened, was still great enough in northern Somalia to create uneasiness among his immediate neighbors in the Mijjertein, Obbia, and British Somaliland.

The British, in particular, overestimated the importance of Muhammad Salih's letter to Muhammad Abdullah. In April, 1909, Sir Reginald Wingate and Rudolph Slatin Pasha were entrusted with a mission to persuade the supposedly weak dervish leader to come to terms with the British. For several months there were fruitless negotiations between the British and an emissary of Muhammad Abdullah, who apparently enjoyed playing a cat-and-mouse game with the British. The Wingate mission failed completely; the much-vaunted colonial experience of Wingate and Slatin in the Sudan amounted to little in dealing with the wily dervish. An organized campaign was out of the question because a costly military occupation of indefinite duration could not be justi-

---

38 Caroselli, *Ferro e fuoco in Somalia,* pp. 119–20.

39 *Ibid.,* p. 121.

fied to the House of Commons.[40] Accordingly, on November 12, 1909, the protectorate government was ordered to withdraw from the interior of British Somaliland and to concentrate its small forces at three towns on the coast. The Somali of the interior were armed for their own protection against the dervishes of the Nogal.

By the Wingate mission and the subsequent decision to withdraw to the coast, the British undid whatever good the letter of excommunication might have accomplished. Their abandonment of the interior left the door open for the dervishes to return to British Somaliland, and the prospects for expansion from the narrow confines of the Nogal valley allowed Muhammad Abdullah to rally his followers with the promise of earthly success.

The Italian Colonial Office evaluated the dervish threat in entirely different terms. The director, Agnesa, was of the opinion that the main threat from the dervishes was an invasion not of British Somaliland but of the Benadir. He was convinced that "of all the projects attributed to the Mullah, the oldest and the one dearest to him, the truest and most convenient, his endless dream, is to go to the Benadir . . . rich in water and in livestock."[41] If his analysis were true, and if Muhammad Abdullah and his estimated five thousand rifles and three thousand lances were to move south, the Italian position in southern Somalia was in grave danger.

The policy of isolating the dervishes in the Nogal protectorate had failed. Direct military action had long been ruled out as too costly and, in the light of British experience, as sheer folly. The foreign ministry continued to base its northern Somalia policy on the two sultans. Reliance upon Osman Mahmud, however, was an uncertain proposition; as in the past, the Mijjertein Somali preferred to act independently of the Italians. In 1909, the sultan was exceptionally in-

40 Jardine, *The Mad Mullah of Somaliland*, p. 189.

41 Agnesa, Rome, to Foreign Minister (confidential), July 27, 1909, ASMAI, pos. 171/2, f. 13.

transigent and refused to fly the Italian flag. The Italians suspended his subsidy and bombarded the coastal villages to assure the proper respect for their national flag. Yet naval bombardment was never really effective, for the villages were easily rebuilt at no great cost. The commanders of the Italian ships stationed in Mijjertein waters could only lament the ineffectiveness of existing policy.[42]

Disgusted with the disloyalty of the Mijjertein sultan, Piacentini attempted to establish direct contact with local chiefs and elders and bypass the sultan, whose control over his subjects had always been loose. This new policy was freely applied by Piacentini and the naval commanders, and near anarchy came to prevail among the Mijjertein Somali.[43] Those who dared to deal directly with the Italians were subjected to punitive attacks by the sultan, who controlled the interior. The inability of the Italians to protect those chiefs who defected from Osman Mahmud only lessened whatever authority and prestige Italy had in northernmost Somalia.

Within a matter of months, however, events in British Somaliland had influenced Osman Mahmud to come to terms with the Italians. As the British withdrew from the interior, Muhammad Abdullah stepped up his raids into the eastern part of the protectorate. Anarchy spread as old intertribal rivalries were renewed. First the Dolbahanta were raided, and eight hundred warriors fell before the dervish onslaught. Then the Isa Mahmud, an Italian-protected tribe, felt Muhammad Abdullah's wrath. And finally, he directed his forces against those of the sultan of the Mijjertein himself.[44] Osman Mahmud now had to face the dervishes, dissident chiefs, and the Italians. He had dallied with the dervishes in the past

---

[42] Naval Minister, Rome, to Foreign Minister, December 9, 1909, ASMAI, pos. 59/6, f. 88; Naval Minister, Rome, to Foreign Minister, December 12, 1909, ASMAI, pos. 59/6, f. 88.

[43] Admiral G. Bettolo, Rome, to Foreign Minister Francesco Guicciardini, March 2, 1910, ASMAI, pos. 59/6, f. 92.

[44] Caroselli, *Ferro e fuoco in Somalia,* pp. 138–40.

and had supplied arms and ammunition to them for use against Yusuf Ali. At one time he had even presented one of his daughters to Muhammad Abdullah as a bride. But with the onset of dervish raids into the Mijjertein, Osman Mahmud broke off all relations with them, and when Muhammad Abdullah cut the throat of his new bride in retaliation, Osman Mahmud turned to the Italians and demanded an honorable settlement with them.

The Italians had Osman Mahmud in an unenviable position. Rather than depose him and thus eliminate all resistance to the dervishes in the Mijjertein, the foreign ministry decided to negotiate for the renewal of an effective protectorate. Early in March, 1910, Piacentini sailed from Aden, took Osman Mahmud and several other Mijjertein leaders aboard at Bender Kassim, and headed for Hafun, where negotiations were concluded on March 6. By the Hafun agreement, the Mijjertein sultan promised to observe rigorously the stipulations of the Bender Ollok accord of 1901. For his past misdeeds, he agreed to a penalty of 1,800 thalers, that is, the amount of the subsidy for 1909. Local chiefs were given the right to deal directly with the Italian consul at Aden, who was to act as commissioner for the protectorate. The sultan gave the Italians full right to institute residencies "in all places that the government shall establish them." Lastly, Osman Mahmud again promised not to deal directly with foreign powers.[45]

In summarizing the Hafun negotiations, Piacentini underlined the need for Italy to maintain her promises or threats to the sultans in order not to compromise Italian prestige. In the past the Italians had backed down from threats of direct, though limited, government action in the north when a crisis arose, thereby giving the sultans the impression that the Italians were either weak or unwilling to expend the effort necessary to maintain the status quo. With the evacuation of British Somaliland and the increased activities of the der-

[45] *Ibid.*, p. 144.

vishes, Piacentini foresaw the need to organize the Mijjertein forces for the double purpose of resisting Muhammad Abdullah and of indirectly protecting the Benadir. To achieve these goals, he proposed, as a maximum program, the institution of residencies at Hafun, Alula, Bender Kassim, Bender Beila, and Bargal and, as a minimum program, residencies at Bender Kassim and Alula.[46]

After Yusuf Ali and Osman Mahmud submitted to the surveillance of Italian agents, the dervishes had to be faced. The British, having abandoned the interior of their protectorate, indicated a willingness to co-operate with the Italians wherever possible in blockading the coast and the trade of hostile tribes and in promoting collaboration among those tribes still under British influence and those in the Italian protectorates. In December, 1910, the British Warsangeli and the Italian Mijjertein Somali agreed to act together in fighting the dervishes. This accord marked the first success for the Italians and the British in their policy of containing Muhammad Abdullah.[47]

In the first half of 1911, the dervishes maintained a steady series of raids against the Mijjertein Somali, who were able to launch a counterattack with the aid of their Warsangeli allies in June. By the end of the year Muhammad Abdullah and his followers were cut off from arms and ammunition ordinarily smuggled in from the coast and were driven out of Italian Somalia into British Somaliland; with great cruelty, they occupied Bohotleh and oppressed the Dolbahanta, who had shifted their allegiance back to the British. Thus the dervishes completely abandoned the Nogal valley, and the last vestige of the Ilig accord of 1905 was erased. As the Italians slowly gained some control of the political situation in northern Somalia, the Somali tribes showed greater respect for their protector power.

[46] Piacentini, Aden, to Foreign Minister, March 16, 1910, ASMAI, pos. 59/6, f. 92.

[47] Caroselli, *Ferro e fuoco in Somalia*, p. 148.

Meanwhile, the illness of the aged Sultan Yusuf Ali enabled the Italians to strengthen their hold on Obbia. When the sultan finally died on September 28, 1911, Governor De Martino's special assistant, Iacopo Gasparini, was on hand to regulate the succession.[48] Yusuf Ali's five sons could not agree on the division of their father's estate. The younger sons preferred a five-way division of the sultanate, but this would have greatly complicated the politics of northern Somalia. Thanks to the work of the resident at Obbia—and the increased prestige of the Italians—Gasparini was invited to settle the dispute.

Gasparini declared Ali Yusuf, eldest son of the late sultan, to be his successor. Gasparini's role in regulating the succession, so similar to that of the British agent in Zanzibar twenty years earlier, placed Ali Yusuf under heavy obligation to the Italians, who did not hesitate to press their advantage. To win complete Italian support against his brothers, the new sultan reaffirmed his acceptance of the protectorate and of expanded Italian control over the sultanate: he recognized the resident as the representative of the Italian government in all matters; he agreed to halt Obbian expansion southward in the direction of Meregh; and he accepted the resident's authority to approve all military movements by Obbian askaris.[49]

In 1912, Governor De Martino brought both Obbia and the Mijjertein into closer contact with the colonial government by the appointment of a commissioner for northern Somalia with regional headquarters at Alula. As provided by the basic law of 1908, the northern protectorates were finally removed from the jurisdiction of the consulate at Aden, which for several months of the year was not in com-

[48] Gasparini, Obbia, to Foreign Minister, October 1, 1911, ASMAI, pos. 59/7, f. 104.

[49] De Martino, Mogadishu, to Foreign Minister, October 8, 1911, and Gasparini report annexed to De Martino report of October 8, 1911, ASMAI, pos. 59/7, f. 105.

munication with them. De Martino, under whose administration the vast trans-Webi hinterland of the Benadir was
occupied, decided that the time was not right to press for
further controls on the northern sultans: Osman Mahmud
had received the governor at Bargal with every indication
of loyalty to the Italian government, despite his very check-
ered past; the new sultan of Obbia, who was weak and uncertain of his control over Obbian tribesmen, had willingly
turned to the Italians and permitted the resident a great deal
of interference in Obbian matters; and the dervishes had withdrawn from Ilig to Bohotleh. (In January, 1913, Muhammad
Abdullah moved his headquarters to Taleh, where he remained for the next seven years.) On the whole, the colonial
government regarded the situation in northern Somalia as
satisfactory.[50]

In February, 1914, a residency was established at Alula
that soon acquired an influence over Osman Mahmud's followers similar to that of the residency created in Obbia five
years earlier.[51] Osman Mahmud, however, continued to re-
side at Bereda or Bargal, and thus the usefulness of the resident at Alula was lessened. Ali Yusuf of Obbia remained a
friend of the Italians. After the dervishes' evacuation of the
Nogal, Obbian forces turned again toward the Mudugh and
the Ogaden. From the Benadir the Italians continued their
penetration of the interior, occupying Bulo Burti in May,
1914. Bulo Burti soon became the advance post against the
Bah Geri allies of the dervishes. From the region of Belet Wen,
the Bah Geri harassed the Shebelle and Makanne tribes along
the Webi Shebelle and occasionally penetrated farther down-
river. The Bah Geri also attempted in vain to spread their
message of religious and political revolt among the Hawiya
tribes that had submitted to Italian rule. By 1915, however,

[50] De Martino, *La Somalia italiana nei tre anni del mio governo* (Rome:
Tipografia della Camera dei Deputati, 1912), p. 44.

[51] Unsigned and undated memorandum on *Atti di Governo* (Mogadishu, 1913),
ASMAI, pos. 151/1, f. 3.

the Bah Geri found themselves facing the Obbian forces in the Mudugh and at El Bur and the Italian-led forces at Bulo Burti.[52] In this way the Italians and their Somali subjects contained the dervish movement.

The outbreak of World War I thus found the Italians in a relatively secure position in both southern and northern Somalia. The war itself had little influence upon the protectorates, despite the fears of the foreign ministry of a general Muslim uprising. A graver preoccupation was occasioned by events in Ethiopia. Rumors reached Mogadishu of Muslim Ethiopian leaders in the camp of Muhammad Abdullah and of the expected conversion of Emperor Iyasu to Islam. The appalling prospect was raised of an alliance of the Muslims of Ethiopia and northern Somalia to drive out the Christian invaders. In April, 1916, Italian fears appeared to have been realized with the announcement of Iyasu's conversion to Islam. The announcement, however, unleashed a storm of opposition in Ethiopia, and Iyasu was deposed on September 27. Before his deposition, the young Iyasu had contracted a marriage alliance with Muhammad Abdullah Hassan. In August, 1916, he sent a mission to Taleh to fetch the bride, but his fall in September prevented the celebration of the marriage.[53]

Although captured documents indicate that Muhammad Abdullah was negotiating with Iyasu, the dervish leader haughtily denied it.[54] Nevertheless, he began to look farther afield for Muslim allies to help him in his seventeen-year-old revolt. In the summer of 1917, Osman Mahmud informed the Italian authorities at Alula that Muhammad Abdullah had sent an agent to enlist the aid of Ottoman troops in southern Arabia. The Italians apprehended Sheik Ahmad Shirwa bin Muhammad and found in his possession corre-

52 Caroselli, *Ferro e fuoco in Somalia*, pp. 210–14.

53 Jardine, *The Mad Mullah of Somaliland*, p. 246.

54 The Italian consul in Harar informed the governor of Eritrea of Iyasu's relationship with Muhammad Abdullah on August 14, 1916 (see Caroselli, *Ferro e fuoco in Somalia*, p. 219).

spondence from the dervish leader offering to place himself and his followers under Turkish protection.[55]

Immediately after the war, the dervishes diminished in number. Four years of limited action by the Italians and their protected sultanates, by the Ethiopians, and by the British had confined their activities to southeastern British Somaliland, where chances of gaining new recruits became increasingly meager. The anarchy in the interior had resulted in the death of one-third of the population of British Somaliland, according to British estimates.[56] Stagnating at Taleh, the dervishes passed their peak of power. In October, 1919, the British government decided to undertake a final military campaign against the rebels. For the first time the British used air power, and by February 1, 1920, British land and air forces were at the gates of Taleh. On February 12, the British took Taleh, only to find that Muhammad Abdullah and a small band of followers had slipped out of the fortress a few nights earlier.[57] When British land forces blocked his path into the Italian protectorates, Muhammad Abdullah Hassan fled into the Ogaden in Ethiopia. Pursuit was useless, as the remaining dervishes moved ever to the south. At the headwaters of the Webi Shebelle, disease and famine struck the camp of Muhammad Abdullah and the faithful remnant of his once mighty dervish movement. On February 10, 1921, news reached Mogadishu that the "Mad Mullah" had died more than a month earlier. Later reports indicated that the proud religious leader had died of pneumonia, probably following an attack of influenza.[58]

[55] The Arabic original and Italian translation of the treaty of protection and related correspondence appear in Caroselli, *Ferro e fuoco in Somalia*, pp. 222–25.

[56] Jardine, *The Mad Mullah of Somaliland*, p. 315.

[57] Foreign Minister, Rome, to Italian Embassy in London, March 19, 1920, ASMAI, pos. 161/2, f. 12.

[58] British sources contend that his death occurred November 23, 1920. Italian sources consistently claim that the date was the first week of January, 1921. Muhammad Abdullah's son Abdurrahman Muhammad asserts that his father

With the death of Muhammad Abdullah Hassan, the dervish movement came to an end, but the problem of the disposition of the Nogal arose again. As in the past, the sultans of Obbia and the Mijjertein presented their conflicting claims for possession of the disputed territory. During the course of the long struggle with the dervishes, both the Obbians and the Mijjertein Somali had come into possession of a large number of modern rifles. The peace of northern Somalia was again jeopardized. The Italians had put off settling the Nogal dispute since 1889. Their inability to face and settle the issue was a reflection of their policy as a whole in the northern protectorates. In the summer of 1923, Governor Carlo Riveri proposed the institution of a commissariat in the Nogal territory with headquarters at Ilig.[59] His proposal, which was accepted by the colonial ministry, called for presidios along the frontier with British Somaliland and the Italian occupation of the disputed area between Obbia and the Mijjertein. A temporary halt was made in the realization of this plan with the recall of Riveri in October, 1923; but an observer of events in Italy could safely have predicted that his plan would be revived and that Riveri's successor would attempt to instil the new Fascist militaristic spirit in the Indian Ocean colony and protectorates.

---

died on December 21, 1920. Cf. Jardine, *The Mad Mullah of Somaliland,* p. 307; Caroselli, *Ferro e fuoco in Somalia,* p. 299; B. W. Andrzejewski and I. M. Lewis, *Somali Poetry* (Oxford: Clarendon, 1964), p. 55.

59 Renato Lefèvre, *Politica somala* (Bologna: Cappelli, 1933), p. 43.

CHAPTER SEVEN

La Grande Somalia:
The Fascist Era, 1923–41

Fascism came to Somalia with the arrival of Governor Cesare Maria De Vecchi di Val Cismon on December 5, 1923. Governor De Vecchi brought with him new ideas of forceful colonial rule, and the Fascists anticipated a new order in their Indian Ocean possessions. Hitherto, only one-third of the area of the colony had been subject to the direct rule of the colonial government. This was an intolerable situation for a party that believed in rule by force and not by indirection. De Vecchi, a military man, looked forward to the occupation of the northern sultanates, which had been a source of so much trouble for Italy in the past. After the occupation of Obbia, the Nogal, and the Mijjertein and the completion of negotiations for the annexation of Kismayu and the Jubaland, the colonial government could devote itself to the intensified economic development of the new Somalia, called by Fascist publicists *La Grande Somalia*.

After the collapse of Muhammad Abdullah Hassan's dervish movement, tribal relationships in northern Somalia reverted to the traditional pattern of disputes over grazing and water rights and intertribal raids. Old rivalries were renewed between the tribes of the two northern sultanates and the Warsangeli, Dolbahanta, and Ogaden tribes across the border in British Somaliland and Ethiopia. Border disputes flared, and De Vecchi found the British to be increasingly unco-operative. The northern tribes, like those under direct administration in the south, were armed, but the two sultanates were still in great measure free of Italian control. De Vecchi estimated that Somali tribesmen had in their possession more than sixteen thousand rifles, or six times as many as those assigned to the local defense forces.[1] His first task, therefore, was to disarm the populations of the Benadir hinterland and of the sultanates of Obbia and the Mijjertein.

The governor's first move was to reconstitute the old Somali Police Corps into a more efficient colonial force, the Corpo Zaptié.[2] Feverishly, the colonial government worked to prepare the new colonial force. The ranks of the older and less effective police corps were purged; new Somali, Arab, and Eritrean recruits were enlisted to bring the total strength of the Zaptié to eight hundred men. Barracks were built; language and tactical schools were organized. In March, 1924, *carabinieri* officers were assigned to train and supervise the new corps. Within a short time, De Vecchi was ready to use force against the Somali.

In January, 1924, the regional commissioner at Mahaddei Wen had presented the governor with a résumé of the "old-style" pre-Fascist policy of arming the tribes of the upper Webi Shebelle against the incursions of Ogaden Somali. With characteristic vigor, De Vecchi had denounced this "policy of weakness," which he found to be not only not Fascist but "pacifist and Masonic liberalism."[3] On February 2, he gave the order to disarm the Somali of the upper Webi Shebelle region, where most of the arms of the southern Somali were concentrated. Early in March the regional commissioner informed the chiefs and elders of the Somali tribes of the gov-

---

1 C. M. De Vecchi di Val Cismon, *Orizzonti d'impero: Cinque anni in Somalia* (Milan: Mondadori, 1935), p. 10.

2 M. A. Vitale, *L'Opera dell'Esercito (1885–1943)* (Vol. I of *L'Italia in Africa, serie storico-militare;* Rome: Istituto Poligrafico dello Stato, 1960), p. 150.

3 De Vecchi, *Orizzonti d'impero . . .* , p. 25.

ernor's order to surrender all firearms and ammunition within forty days. Most chiefs complied with the order, but Sheik Haji Hassan of the Galjal Hawiya arrogantly replied:

I do not accept your order. We will not come to you at any cost because you have broken our pact. All our slaves escaped and went to you and you set them free. We are not happy with the [antislavery] order. We abandoned our law, for according to our law we can put slaves in prison or force them to work. . . .

The government has its law and we have ours. We accept no law other than our own. Our law is that of God and of the Prophet.

We are not like other people; you have not seen any of our people enrol in the Zaptié. Not one. . . .

If you come into our land to make war we will fight you in every way, just as we fought the dervishes. God has said: The few can defeat the many. The world is near its end; only 58 years remain. . . . We do not want to stay in this world; it is better to die following Muslim law. All Muslims are one.[4]

Old grudges did not die easily, and the sheik was seeking revenge for the Italian antislavery policy of ten years earlier. Now he rallied his tribesmen to oppose the Italian order to surrender their only means of resistance against an unpopular regime.

Impatiently, De Vecchi ordered out the colonial forces on March 27. If the policy of disarmament were to succeed in the south, Somali resistance had to be broken at its first appearance. Upon the sheik and his Galjal tribesmen fell the honor of becoming for all Somalia the example of Italy's new Fascist decisiveness. Seven hundred Italian rifles, two machine-gun units, and two pieces of artillery soon convinced the Somali rebels that the few can indeed defeat the many. After several encounters betwen the Galjal and the colonial forces, the Italians captured Haji Hassan on April 4. The Galjal surrendered their arms; and in the next ten months, with the exception of a brief uprising among the Bantu Eile tribesmen

4 *Ibid.*, p. 27.

near Bur Acaba, the disarmament of southern Somalia proceeded comparatively smoothly. De Vecchi felt that he had "removed the wrecks of the past from the path and cleared the way to the future."[5]

While the collection of arms was under way in southern Somalia, the governor turned to the northern protectorates. In May, 1924, De Vecchi visited Obbia and compelled Ali Yusuf to take an oath of subjection and complete obedience. To the proud northern Somali, the oath must have been humiliating: "Command me and I shall obey any order the government may give; once I was ignorant, but now I know the truth and I am in your power." In July De Vecchi installed new Italian commissioners at Obbia and Alula. The commissioner at Obbia was a Fascist colonel who would brook no insubordination on the part of the Somali sultan. Ali Yusuf soon found his position intolerable. He was recognized as sultan, but the Italians refused to show him any deference. To his complaints, the governor responded: "The commissioner is just and tolerant; it is your duty to treat him with respect and deference and obedience in the name of the government which protects you."[6]

For more than a year, Ali Yusuf obeyed the new regime. Then, in the spring of 1925, he attempted to contact Osman Mahmud to end their bickering over the status of the Nogal and present a united front to their new common enemy, the colonial government. The Italians intercepted the letter, however, and nothing came of Ali Yusuf's plans. On July 10, 1925, Mussolini, having consolidated his position as prime minister, authorized the political and military occupation of northern Somalia and allotted some 12,000,000 lire for the purpose.[7] By October 1, De Vecchi's plans were put into ac-

[5] De Vecchi, *Relazione sul progetto di bilancio della Somalia italiana* . . . *1925/26* (Mogadishu: Bettini, 1924), pp. 4–5.

[6] De Vecchi, *Orizzonti d'impero* . . . , pp. 68–69.

[7] De Vecchi, *Relazione sul progetto di bilancio della Somalia italiana* . . . *1926/27* (Mogadishu: Bettini, 1925), p. 10.

tion. Three columns of the newly trained Zaptié occupied the sultanate. One column advanced along the coast from Meregh to Obbia; a second column, from Bulo Burti, occupied El Bur; and the third column, composed of the reorganized frontier police, marched from Belet Wen to Galadi and Galkayu. By the end of the month the occupation of the sultanate was complete, and Ali Yusuf had no choice but to yield to the Italians. Obbia was transformed from a sultanate into an administrative region, with residencies at Obbia, Galkayu, El Bur, and Ilig.

Meanwhile, the government also prepared to occupy the Mijjertein. The new commissioner at Alula, E. Coronaro, enjoyed a position similar to that of the commissioner at Obbia. In 1924, Coronaro had aided the Stefanini-Puccioni expedition for the exploration of the Mijjertein. The work of this expedition, outwardly purely scientific, proved invaluable, for no European had ever before traveled so extensively in the interior of the Mijjertein and the Italians had gained useful knowledge of that *terra incognita*. After the successful operations in Obbia, De Vecchi planned to occupy the Nogal and then the Mijjertein. In anticipation, one hundred troops were landed at Hafun and Alula.[8]

On October 21, Commissioner Coronaro presented Sultan Osman Mahmud with an ultimatum to disarm. Two days later, open rebellion broke out, and the first blood was shed at Bargal. On October 29, the sultan indicated he was willing to negotiate, but his forces shot at the Italian negotiations party as it disembarked. In retaliation, the Italians bombarded Bargal and razed it. Osman Mahmud was not alone in his resistance to the Italians, however, and the traditional chiefs urged outright war. They found a leader in Herzi Bogor, Osman's son and heir apparent.[9]

Before the Italians could concentrate operations in the Mijjertein, they were distracted by events at El Bur. After the

8 De Vecchi, *Orizzonti d'impero* . . . , pp. 68–69.

9 Renato Lefèvre, *Politica somala* (Bologna: Cappelli, 1933), p. 92.

occupation of El Bur, the Italians had appointed Omar Samantar as chief of the local population. Although he at first collaborated with the Italians, Omar had ambitions of his own. On November 9, he led a revolt at the El Bur fort, seized its store of arms, and entrenched himself and his followers in the fort's central building. The Italian forces that besieged him were in turn besieged by the surrounding population led by Sultan Ali Yusuf's district military commander, Herzi Gushan. On November 15, the Zaptié retreated to Bud Bud, leaving behind thirty-eight dead.

The uprising at El Bur was exactly what the Italians had hoped to avoid; it now seemed that the revolt might spread and that the whole sultanate of Obbia would have to be reconquered.[10] Undaunted by this prospect, De Vecchi called for two battalions of Eritrean reinforcements. As a precautionary measure, he removed Ali Yusuf and his family to Mogadishu. On November 30, the Italian forces suffered another defeat in an ambush at Bot. Impatiently awaiting the arrival of the Eritrean forces and dissatisfied by the performance of his Zaptié, De Vecchi abruptly reversed his tactics. Rather than rely on his much-vaunted Corpo Zaptié, he fell back on the pre-Fascist policy of using armed bands of askaris recruited from the local tribes. The colonial troops were given the task of defending the presidios. The Italians then won the support of the anti-Obbian Hawiya tribesmen of the southern part of the sultanate and, in January, 1926, rearmed the Habr Gedir. The new policy met with success, and on January 14, the Somali irregulars defeated the rebels at Shillave in the Ogaden and forced Omar Samantar and the remnant of his men to flee deeper into Ethiopia.[11]

Concurrently, the Italian forces in the Mijjertein were advancing up the Darror valley into the interior. The main Italian bases at Ras Hafun were the target of the rebels led by Herzi Bogor, who, early in December, 1925, drove the

10 De Vecchi, *Orizzonti d'impero* . . . , p. 143.

11 *Ibid.*, pp. 160–61.

Italian forces out of Hordio. A second large rebel attack six weeks later threatened Italian installations at Cape Guardafui. With the support of a warship, however, the Italians forced the rebels to withdraw seven to nine miles inland, just outside the range of the *Berenice*'s guns. Rather than press his advantage in the Mijjertein, De Vecchi decided that it was more important strategically to advance north from Obbia, occupy the Nogal, and thus hem the rebels in. For this task the Somali irregulars were employed once more, at a great savings of money and men. Confronted by the Italian advance, the Omar Mahmud and the Isa Mahmud, traditionally bitter enemies, united under Herzi Bogor, who fortified Eil at the mouth of the Nogal. On February 17, the Italians advanced on Eil from Ilig and dispersed the rebels. The Omar Mahmud reluctantly agreed to disarm. When Herzi Bogor announced that he would recapture Eil at any cost, however, they again rallied to his side. On May 15, 1926, the rebels assaulted Eil but met with complete defeat. Many of the Omar Mahmud returned to the Italian side; "yesterday's enemies thus became a precious instrument for Italian action."[12] By late June the complete disarmament of the Omar Mahmud had been achieved. A month later, the Eritrean forces occupied the Nogal.

In the summer and autumn of 1926, the Italians tried to tighten their circle about Herzi Bogor and his rebels. Mijjertein opposition and a high mortality rate among transport camels slowed down the campaign considerably. The first attempt to occupy the Darror Valley ended in failure. Late in October, after Eritrean forces occupied the northern coast of the Mijjertein and sealed off the interior from contraband in arms, the operations began to move favorably again. The Italians concentrated large irregular forces of Habr Gedir and Omar Mahmud and repeated the march on the Darror. They took Skushuban, and in January, 1927, the Somali irregulars

12 Lefèvre, *Politica somala,* pp. 102–7.

and regular troops from Hafun closed in on the upper Darror.

Faced with the prospect of desertion by his forces unless he won a major victory, Herzi Bogor unsuccessfully challenged the Italians at Skushuban. The rebels were forced to flee into British Somaliland, and the Italians completed the occupation of the Mijjertein. The three-month second Darror campaign had cost the Mijjertein Somali dearly. On March 3, Yusuf Mahmud, brother of the sultan, surrendered to the Italians. Shortly afterward, Osman Mahmud surrendered to the British at Berbera and was sent to Mogadishu, where he joined his brother, other members of his family, and the exiled sultan of Obbia. On November 6, 1927, the formal act of submission took place. Osman Mahmud dramatically consigned his sword to Governor De Vecchi and renounced his rights as sultan.[13] An era had come to an end in northern Somalia.

From 1925 to 1927, while northern Somalia was the scene of military operations, Italy peacefully incorporated the Juba-land into the colony of Italian Somalia. The negotiations with Great Britain for the transfer of the Jubaland to Italy took place intermittently from 1919 to 1924. The first phase of negotiations was concluded on September 13, 1919, when Lord Milner agreed to transfer a tract of the Jubaland, in-cluding the port of Kismayu, to Italy. This was the one posi-tive result of Article XIII of the secret wartime Treaty of London, by which the British promised to compensate Italy if Britain enlarged its African holdings at the expense of Ger-many. Inasmuch as the British offer was considerably less than Italy had demanded, the Italians broke off negotia-tions.[14] The following year Lord Milner and Foreign Min-ister Vittorio Scialoja exchanged a series of letters in which

---

13 De Vecchi, *Orizzonti d'impero* . . . , p. 224.

14 Colosimo, Rome, to Sonnino, May 25, 1919, and undated memorandum on Jubaland discussions (1924), Archivio Storico dell'ex Ministero dell'Africa Italiana (hereinafter cited as ASMAI), pos. 158/2, f. 14.

an enlarged region was offered to the Italians, but the foreign ministry was unwilling to accede to a British condition that Italy first recognize the British protectorate over Egypt.[15] In 1922, after Egypt was proclaimed independent, the British again bargained with the Italians for the Jubaland, but this time they demanded that Italy renounce its claim to the Dodecanese Islands.

Four months after his appointment as prime minister, Mussolini announced his intention of coming to a Jubaland settlement with Great Britain as soon as possible.[16] The Jubaland question was reopened, but the Italian ambassador in London had strict orders to keep the Jubaland discussions independent of the Dodecanese issue.[17] After the Treaty of Lausanne (July 24, 1923) confirmed Italy's possession of the Dodecanese, Italian demands for the inclusion of additional territory in the Jubaland delayed agreement with Great Britain. The Italian ambassador in London also suggested to the British that their recent stand on the Corfu incident had offended the Italian public and press and that only British cooperation would bring Italian support on the questions of the Ruhr and reparations.[18]

Early in 1924 Great Britain and Italy resumed negotiations. The Jubaland coast, it must be remembered, still belonged in name to the emasculated sultanate of Zanzibar, but this was a technicality that mattered little to the protector power. The sultan, like so many of his predecessors, was "irritated and dissatisfied about the cession of Kismayu, about which it [was]

[15] Minutes of colloquia between Italian and British colonial officers, March 8, 1920, ASMAI, pos. 161/2, f. 12.

[16] Mussolini, Rome, to Ambassador Pietro Tomasi della Torretta, February 12, 1923, *Documenti diplomatici italiani, settima serie, 1922–1935* (Rome: Libreria dello Stato, 1953), I, 350.

[17] Mussolini, Rome, to Tomasi della Torretta, March 9, 1923, *Documenti diplomatici italiani, settima serie, 1922–1935,* I, 420.

[18] Tomasi della Torretta, London, to Mussolini, October 11, 1923, *Documenti diplomatici italiani, settima serie, 1922–1935* (Rome: Libreria dello Stato, 1955), II, 284.

rumored he was not even consulted."[19] When the Italians withdrew their claims for more land, the last obstacle was removed. On July 15, 1924, the British ceded the Jubaland to Italy on the basis of the boundaries agreed upon by Milner and Scialoja five years earlier.

On June 29, 1925, at a solemn ceremony at Kismayu, the English colonial authorities transferred the territory to Corrado Zoli, high commissioner for the new territory of Oltre Giuba ("Trans-Juba"). The transfer went smoothly, to the delight of the Italian government, which had been concerned about the condition in which the British would leave the Jubaland. Governor De Vecchi was convinced that British officials in the Jubaland had opposed the cession of their colony to Italy and that they had spread anti-Italian propaganda among the Somali.[20] Commissioner Zoli reported to the colonial ministry that the British commissioner "did not stop spreading sharp anti-Italian propaganda until the last day of his stay at Kismayu."[21]

The Jubaland presented some unknown factors. In the southern part of the new territory, intertribal warfare between the Harti and the Muhammad Zubeir had until recently disturbed the peace. The Harti were apprehensive of the Italian occupation, partly because of the anti-Italian feeling stimulated by the British commissioner, and partly because of their fear that any colonial administrator would favor the cause of the Muhammad Zubeir. Along the coast, the Abdullah Talamoje exhibited a good deal of animosity toward the Harti. In the northern zone, where the Marehan and the Aulihan lived, there had never been political or administrative organization of any sort. The tribes there were as free as all Somali had been before the arrival of the British and the Italians thirty-five years earlier. The only

19 Foreign Minister, Rome, to Tomasi della Torretta, June 18, 1924, ASMAI, pos. 89/6, f. 18.

20 De Vecchi to Colonial Minister, August 8, 1924, ASMAI, pos. 89/6, f. 18.

21 Corrado Zoli, *Relazione generale dell'Alto Commissario per l'Oltre Giuba* (Rome: Arti grafiche, 1926), p. 99.

symbol of British authority had been the military post at Serenli, across the Juba from Bardera. The effective rule of the British had been limited to the European and commercial quarters of the towns and larger villages. "British police patrols could not enter the native quarter of Kismayu, not even to intervene in case of murder."[22]

High Commissioner Zoli assumed control over the new territory by the simultaneous entry of Italian colonial troops from Lugh, Bardera, Jelib, and Jumbo. Unsure of what was in store for the Italians, he immediately constituted military presidios and reinforced all defensive positions. In a show of strength, a mobile column consisting of a machine-gun unit and a section of camel artillery spent six weeks marching across the territory from Lugh to Kismayu. Police stations were organized in all large villages and towns. To prevent disorder, British laws and regulations remained in force until further notice. Zoli made every effort to convince the Somali of Italian impartiality and justice. His first success was a peace settlement concluded between the Harti and the Muhammad Zubeir on October 24, 1925.[23] At the end of the first year of Italian occupation, on July 1, 1926, the territory of Oltre Giuba was formally annexed to the colony of Italian Somalia as the Juba region.

With the annexation of the Jubaland and of the northern sultanates, all of Somalia came under the direct administration of the colonial government. By mid-1928, the period of Fascist heroics had come to an end. The colony settled down to a new regime, and De Vecchi returned to Italy. Significantly, his successors, Guido Corni (1928–31) and Maurizio Rava (1931–35) were members of the colonial service. This was indicative of the more peaceful development that followed De Vecchi's "act of faith," as he liked to call his militaristic administration.[24]

[22] *Ibid.*, p. 100.   [23] *Ibid.*, pp. 106–7.

[24] De Vecchi, *Relazione sul progetto di bilancio . . . 1926/27*, p. 3; *Orizzonti d'impero . . .*, pp. 1–2.

In line with the new "tough" policy, the colonial government applied economic pressure on recalcitrant chiefs and cadis to co-operate with the regime. The most effective method of dealing with a dissident chief, other than military force, was the suspension of his stipend. New colonial officials, in fact, were reminded of the scale of punishments they were entitled to use to coerce the chiefs: verbal reproof in public, suspension of the stipend, suspension of the chief's authority, and ultimately, removal of the unco-operative chief.[25] In this respect, Fascist policy was but a continuation of the policies established by Governor Carletti in 1908 and by Governor De Martino in 1910 and 1912. Colonial officials were also explicitly instructed to "safeguard the natives' religious liberty in the fullest sense of that term."[26] Here, too, the Fascist government followed the precedent set by earlier policy.

The one new direction in native policy was the field of taxation. Before the Fascist era, the Somali were not subject to government imposts other than cadi fees and import and export taxes. To place the colony's expanding budget on sounder financial ground, Governor De Vecchi instituted the first direct tax imposed on the Somali. The tax, in the form of an annual hut tax varying from 8 to 24 lire, produced good results. In the residency of Bur Acaba alone, the Somali contributed to the local treasury 159,920 lire on a total of 19,141 huts, or an average hut tax of 8.35 lire. The new tax expanded the resident's revenue from 147,444 lire in 1925–26 to 326,181 lire in 1928–29. In effect, the hut tax more than doubled the residency's revenue of the pre-1926 period.[27]

In addition to the hut tax, other new taxes were imposed.

25 E. Bono, *Vade Mecum del R. Residente in Somalia* (Mogadishu: R. Stamperia della Colonia, 1930), pp. 17–18.

26 A. Bertola, *Il Regime dei culti nell'Africa italiana* (Bologna: Cappelli, 1939), pp. 20–21.

27 E. Bono, *La Residenza di Bur Hacaba* (Mogadishu: R. Stamperia della Colonia, 1930), p. 13.

Most of them did not affect the Somali population of the interior. A graduated tax ranging from 1 to 5 per cent on net business incomes and on rents above 1,500 lire was applied unevenly in the residencies. Personal income was taxed on a graduated scale from 2 to 8 per cent; this measure fell mostly on Italians, the coastal Arabs, and town Somali. In general, taxes were somewhat higher in the older administrative regions. In 1930, all unmarried male Italians between the ages of twenty-five and sixty-five years were required to

TABLE 1

COLONIAL REVENUES

(In Lire)

Year	Business, Income, Hut, and Other Taxes	Customs Receipts	Total
1926–27..........	3,157,000	11,071,000	14,228,000
1927–28..........	3,449,000	15,118,000	18,567,000
1928–29..........	4,241,000	14,437,000	18,678,000
1929–30..........	3,627,000	15,560,000	19,187,000
1930–31..........	3,909,000	14,003,000	17,912,000
1931–32..........	3,239,000	12,799,000	16,038,000
1932–33..........	3,455,000	10,836,000	14,291,000
1933–34..........	3,409,000	10,171,000	13,580,000
1934–35..........	3,799,000	31,808,000	35,607,000
1935–36..........	11,996,000	69,264,000	81,260,000

Source: Guido Corni, *Somalia italiana* (Milan: Arte e Storia, 1937), II, 74, 93.

pay the same bachelor tax previously imposed in metropolitan Italy.[28]

The total revenue derived from the colony from 1926 to 1936, however, continued to be based largely on customs receipts (see Table 1). The drop in total income from 1930 to 1934 reflects the impact of the growing world depression, which strongly affected Somalia's export trade (see Appendixes III and IV). The figures for 1934–36 reflect the onset of the second Ethiopian war; income tax rates in Somalia were increased to help meet the cost of the campaign. The rise in customs receipts is an indication of the increased

[28] G. Corni, *Somalia italiana* (Milan: Arte e Storia, 1937), II, 63–71.

importation of taxable goods for the large influx of civil and
military personnel brought into the colony to build up the
southern front against Ethiopia. The rise did not, however,
take place until after the Walwal incident (December 5–6,
1934), which precipitated a crisis between Italy and Ethiopia
and served as a pretext for the Italian invasion of Ethiopia
in 1935. The first shipment of mobilization materials left
Naples on December 23, 1934, eighteen days after Walwal.[29]

Although the colony's income had increased over that of
the pre-Fascist period, the colony was far from self-supporting.
The military campaign for 1926–27 alone cost more than
23,000,000 lire, excluding the reorganization of the Corpo
Zaptié. In fact, budgetary expenditures for that year totaled
just under 70,000,000 lire, in strong contrast with the colonial
revenues of slightly more than 14,000,000 lire. The state,
which had set aside an ordinary contribution of 44,000,000
lire for Somalia, contributed an additional sum of nearly
23,000,000 lire for extraordinary expenses. The following
fiscal year, 1927–28, De Vecchi requested a contribution of
35,000,000 lire for military expenses in northern Somalia, as
well as an extraordinary contribution of 14,000,000 lire for
civil and other military expenses. Compared with these sums,
the colonial revenues of 18,567,000 lire were a paltry contribution indeed. In the following two years, the metropolitan
government gave the colony a total of 112,000,000 lire in
grants-in-aid.[30]

Italy's great hope for Somalia lay in a new emphasis on the
colony's agricultural potential. Until the outbreak of the
war with Ethiopia in 1935, the energies of the colonial gov-

29 "Military Preparation in Eritrea and Somalia," January 5, 1935, ASMAI,
pos. 181/3, f. 18.

30 De Vecchi, Relazione sul progetto di bilancio . . . 1926/27, p. 11; De Vecchi,
Relazione sul progetto di bilancio . . . 1927/28 (Mogadishu: Stamperia della
Colonia, 1926), p. 10; Corni, Relazione sulla Somalia italiana . . . 1928/29
(Mogadishu: Stamperia della Colonia, 1929), p. 146; Corni, Relazione sulla
Somalia italiana . . . 1929/30 (Mogadishu: Stamperia della Colonia, 1931),
pp. 202–3.

ernment were devoted largely to agriculture and to public works connected with agriculture. The export of skins and the production of salt and incense in the north were of only secondary importance. Indicative of the new interest in agriculture in Somalia was the growth in the number of concessions and in the amount of land under cultivation. When the Società Agricola Italo-Somala (SAIS) was founded in 1920, only four active concessions survived in the colony. As of June 30, 1933, the colonial government had granted one hundred fifteen new concessions for a total of 60,995 hectares, of which almost 30,000 were under cultivation.[31]

By far the largest single concession was that of SAIS at Villaggio Duca degli Abruzzi (Villabruzzi). Of its 25,000 hectares, SAIS had placed 10,000 under cultivation and reserved the balance for pasture land. From 1921 to 1926 the company spent great sums of money to prepare the way for mechanized agriculture. More than thirty thousand tons of equipment were brought in by camel, truck, and boat; huge earth-moving machines then cleared and leveled the land at an expense of 3,400,000 lire. Nineteen miles of primary and secondary irrigation canals were excavated, and a complex irrigation system of more than 420 miles of channels brought water from the Webi Shebelle to SAIS's fields of cotton, bananas, sugar cane, castor beans, sesame, durra, maize, kapok, and coconut palms. Experiments to grow peanuts, tobacco, ramie, barley, oats, Brazil rubber, pineapples, sugar beets, potatoes, and forage crops all failed or were only partially successful. But SAIS successfully introduced the sunflower, hemp, legumes, lemon grass, and eucalyptus. At the end of the first phase of development, the director of SAIS, Giuseppe Scassellati-Sforzolini, wrote, "We can look with satisfaction upon the completion of this first stage . . . and serenely anticipate a pleasant future. . . . SAIS is assured of prosperity and of ultimate success."[32] Scassellati could indeed be satis-

[31] M. Rava, *Parole ai Coloniali* (Milan: Mondadori, 1935), p. 245.

[32] G. Scassellati-Sforzolini, *La Società Agricola Italo-Somala in Somalia* (Florence: Istituto Agricolo Coloniale Italiano, 1926), pp. 73–74.

fied; at the end of its fourth year (June 30, 1925), SAIS showed a profit of 2,267,909.66 lire.[33]

Much of SAIS's profit was the indirect result of government aid. The company bought war surplus materials at cheap prices; it secured its loans at low interest rates; and the government purchased its hydraulic and other public works and financed the construction of the sixty-eight-mile railroad that ran from Mogadishu to Villabruzzi. The railroad alone cost the government more than 7,500,000 lire. After successful experiments with sugar cane, the company formed a subsidiary, the Società Saccarifera Somala (SSS). Its sugar refinery had a capacity of 250 to 300 tons daily. In 1935 the SSS refinery produced 4,400 tons of sugar. The refinery operated far below capacity, and transportation costs from Villabruzzi to Mogadishu and abroad made the industry uneconomical.[34] SSS also operated an alcohol distillery and the railroad system, which consisted of one steam and four diesel engines and ninety railroad cars. In 1929–30 SSS carried 51,000 tons of cargo and 15,000 passengers on its railroad. In July, 1928, SSS began operation of an oil press and refinery and undertook the electrification of the SAIS establishments.[35]

SAIS developed its own means of attracting native labor to its concession. The neighboring Shidle tribesmen, a Bantu group despised by the nomadic Somali, willingly worked on SAIS's plantation. Each native family that settled on the plantation was given about one hectare of irrigated land. The company insisted that the Shidle worker raise food crops on half his land and a cash crop of cotton on the other half; the food crop went to the Shidle family, and the cotton became SAIS property as a rental payment for the improved land that had been given the worker. The company also supplied the laborers with huts, tools, livestock, wells, medical assistance,

[33] *Ibid.*, p. 75.

[34] In 1959, SSS produced 8,800 tons of sugar. Today the refinery still operates much below capacity.

[35] Corni, *Relazione sulla Somalia italiana . . . 1928/29*, p. 21.

and money loans. SAIS employed some twenty-four hundred Shidle families, or about six thousand individuals, who signed a contract with the company that was notarized by the local resident. On the plantation, the Shidle were grouped into sixteen villages, each with its own tribal chief, mosque, and well.[36] All in all, it was an effective paternalism.

Second in importance to SAIS for the development of commercial agriculture in Somalia was the Azienda Agraria Governativa at Genale, begun in 1912 during the De Martino administration and directed by Romolo Onor until 1918. After the death of Onor, the agricultural station at Genale rapidly declined, although the government spent large sums on it. In 1924, inspired by the example of SAIS, Governor De Vecchi proposed a new program for the development of Genale and the hinterland of Merca. De Vecchi's plan called for the concession of small tracts of land to private settlers, who could benefit from the government's investments in irrigation works, roads, buildings, cotton gins and presses, and warehouses. By 1926 the government had constructed dikes and nine canals for the irrigation of up to 24,000 hectares.[37] By 1933 it had granted one hundred concessions at Genale for a total of 20,142 hectares, of which almost 18,000 were under cultivation in cotton, bananas, oilseeds, and grains for local consumption.[38] Most of the cotton exported by the colony continued to come from the SAIS plantation, but Genale provided the larger part of the equally important banana export crop. (Few small concessionaires could afford to grow cotton after the world drop in prices in the early 1930's.) The State Banana Monopoly in Italy ensured the profitability of the Genale plantations by licensing only Somali bananas for importation into Italy. The Italian consumer, who ultimately subsidized the Somali banana industry, had to pay almost

[36] A. Piccioli, *La Nuova Italia d'Oltremare* (Verona: Mondadori, 1934), I, 838.

[37] Rava, *Parole ai Coloniali*, p. 241.

[38] L. Federzoni, *L'Africa Orientale* (Bologna: Zanichelli, 1936), p. 104.

twice as much for the short red Merca banana as other Europeans paid for Central American bananas.

The Corni administration, which succeeded De Vecchi's, took two steps to improve the position of the concessionaires. In January, 1929, the colonial government modified the 1911 decree regulating the concessions. To encourage new concessionaires, Governor Corni decreed that concessions would no longer be limited to ninety-nine-year leaseholds; the government would grant outright ownership of concessions as private property or in perpetuity with option to purchase.[39] The second step was the establishment of a standard form of contract for hiring native labor at Genale. There, as at Villabruzzi, a Bantu people accustomed to agriculture (in this case, the Tuni Torre) afforded a labor supply. Each native who agreed to work for a concessionaire of the Azienda Agraria Governativa was provided with a hut or a substitute annual payment of 25 lire. He was given half a hectare of irrigated land or credited at a rate of 100 lire per hectare of unimproved land he received. Each worker, male and female, was provided with four hens and a cow. The work week consisted of five days, at the end of which the men received a daily pay of 2.50 lire and the women 2 lire.[40]

A third important group of concessions, fourteen individual enterprises totaling 15,483 hectares, was located at Afgoi, at Avai on the lower Shebelle, and in the region between Margherita and Jelib on the lower Juba. These concessions were less successful than SAIS and the Azienda Agraria Governativa; as they were supported for the most part by small private capital, they could cultivate only a limited portion of the land that had been allotted—in actual practice, about 10 per cent. Here, indeed, were failures in abundance. The Juba Company of Italy, a successor to one of the earliest concessionaires (Carpetti), grew cotton, coconut palms, and agave on several hundred hectares near the mouth of the Juba; but, as

---

[39] Corni, *Somalia italiana*, II, 404.

[40] Corni, *Relazione sulla Somalia italiana . . . 1928/29*, pp. 138–39.

an example of its difficulties, its irrigation pumps sometimes pumped salt water from the Juba. The Società Romana di Colonizzazione, founded in 1910 and still under the direction of its founder, Count Enrico di Frankenstein, was the most important enterprise in the Juba region. Its mechanized plantation at Cansuma produced cotton, which alternated between profitable and very poor yields. The Gallinara concession, on the Webi Shebelle near Caitoi since 1912, produced kapok and fruit, which it transported to Merca and Mogadishu with the greatest difficulty. The original proprietor had lost the concession in 1924 for failure to meet the government's terms. Still another concession, that of a Signor Natale southwest of Caitoi, had raised cotton, sesame, and castor beans, beginning in 1921. The concessionaire, however, did not have a good year until 1923; he rented his concession out in 1924 and ceded it to another in 1925.[41]

Although Governor Corni came to the conclusion that the small enterprises would fail miserably unless they had government support, as was the case with both SAIS and Genale, official government publications of the Fascist era spoke glowingly of the future of Somalia.[42] By 1935, however, the results obtained by large government and private investments were less than spectacular (see Appendix V). The export crops of concessionaires amounted in value to one-third of the colony's exports, and in that sense, they were important. (In 1930, they amounted to approximately 13,000,000 lire, or triple their value in 1927.) But those who benefited from this trade were few in number. After 1930 and the onset of the great depression, investments did not increase. Moreover, it should not be forgotten that whatever success the concessions had, rested on a 96,500,000 lire investment, 70 per cent of which had come from SAIS.[43]

[41] Scassellati-Sforzolini, *La Società Agricola Italo-Somala* . . . , pp. 20–22.

[42] Corni, *Relazione sulla Somalia italiana . . . 1928/29*, p. 46.

[43] *Ibid.*, p. 143.

Ranking in value with the agricultural exports were animals and animal products. In 1930 exports in this category amounted to more than one-third of all exports; their value of more than 16,000,000 lire was slightly more than that of agricultural exports for the same year. In value, cattle hides accounted for 50 per cent of these exports. Trade in hides did not, however, enrich the colony. The regional commissioner of the Mijjertein, which accounted for 45 per cent of the exports of sheep- and goat-skins, reported that all exported skins went to Aden, in return for which the Mijjertein Somali received durra, wheat, rice, and cloth—necessities of life in the bleak mountains of the north.[44]

Of strictly tertiary importance among exports from the colony were limited quantities of luxury commodities like incense, myrrh, and gums. Somalia may have exported 90 per cent of the world's incense and myrrh, but in 1930 this amounted to little more than 3,000,000 lire, or under 7 per cent of the colony's exports.[45] The salt deposits at Ras Hafun, where a Lombard firm had invested 43,000,000 lire, were of greater promise. By 1933–34, the Hafun salt works were producing more than 200,000 tons annually, most of which was exported to the Far East. Salt exports were valued at more than 5,000,000 lire in that year.[46]

If Italy's great hopes for the future of agriculture in Somalia were misplaced, there was even less room for optimism in other fields of economic development. Rapid geological surveys of Somalia revealed that the colony offered little other than Hafun salt for commercial development; and in vain, Italian geologists sought oil and iron ore to buttress Italy's sorely deficient industrial base.

Except in the zone of agricultural plantations along the

44 Corni, *Somalia italiana*, II, 614.

45 A. Ferrara, "Le Industrie rurali indigene della Somalia italiana," *Atti del Primo Congresso di Studi Coloniali* (Florence: Centro di Studi Coloniali, 1931), VI, 381.

46 Corni, *Somalia italiana*, II, 556–61.

Webi Shebelle and the Juba, life for the Somali was un-changed by Italian colonialism. Although the colonial econ-omy was meant to be an overseas extension of the metropoli-tan economy, no attempt was made to Italianize the Somali. Throughout most of the colonial period, there was practically no educational system in the colony other than the traditional koranic schools. The history of European education in Italian Somalia could, in fact, be characterized as virtually complete neglect. In 1907 the Dante Alighieri Society established a school at Mogadishu to teach Italian to the Somali. Its one teacher received a salary of 60 lire monthly, and the school did not last long.

Until 1922, the government ignored public education. A small school at Mogadishu was run by the Trinitarian Order; it had one priest and few students. Two years later the gov-ernment agreed to subsidize the Mission of the Consolata, which undertook to organize elementary schools for the sev-eral dozen Italian children in the colony. The mission school educated Italian children side by side with mulatto "orphans" and a few Somali and Arab children who had been placed in the care of the mission. The government assumed responsibil-ity for the educational system in 1929, but it continued to work through the mission. Previously, the government had given the mission an annual subsidy of 300,000 lire. In 1929, the colony budgeted 3,000,000 lire for educational purposes. By 1935 a superintendent of schools directed ten government schools and five orphanage schools. Yet the statistics reveal how inadequate the system of public education was to sup-port any Italian claim to a civilizing mission in Somalia (see Table 2).

Christian proselytism among the Muslim Somali was not permitted at first or encouraged later. The estrangement of church and state in Italy accounts for the absence of Roman Catholic activity in Somalia before the Fascists came to terms with the Church. There were but few priests in Somalia, and they were to be found mostly in the schools, the orphanages, and the leprosarium at Alessandra on the Juba. The only active missionary work permitted by the government took place among the pagan Bantu populations of the Juba valley. Significantly, that work was carried on by Swedish Protestant missionaries who had been carefully scrutinized by the colonial government.

TABLE 2

EDUCATION IN SOMALIA
(1934)

Type of School	Italians	Somali	Mulattoes	Arabs	Total
Elementary Schools					
Mogadishu (Europeans)....	71	....	....	......	71
Mogadishu (natives).......	....	28	29	6	63
Merca....................	8	301	....	....	309
Afgoi....................	4	72	....	....	76
Villabruzzi..............	6	66	....	....	72
Brava....................	6	100	....	....	106
Baidoa...................	....	274	....	....	274
Jelib....................	....	81	....	....	81
Kismayu.................	3	197	....	....	200
Middle Form					
Mogadishu..............	46	....	....	....	46
Orphanage Schools.........					
Mogadishu (boys).........	4	43	12	....	59
Mogadishu (girls)........	....	20	22	....	42
Mogadishu (infant asylum).	....	26	6	....	32
Baidoa...................	....	25	....	....	25
Brava....................	....	32	....	....	32
Totals					
Males..............					1,378
Females............					110
Both..............	148	1,265	69	6	1,488

Statistics derived from ASMAI, pos. 89/15, ff. 57 and 58 *passim*.

By 1935, Somalia had made little progress, even though for the first time the metropolitan government had accorded sustained interest to its economic development. Previously, the government had regarded the colony only as a means to maintain imperial prestige or to penetrate Ethiopia; such were the goals of Mancini and Cecchi and Crispi. With the rise of Fascism, the government began to stress the intrinsic value of Somalia to the homeland. And indeed, in the first decade of

Fascism the Italians secured direct dominion over the whole country, added the Jubaland in vain hopes of increasing the wealth of the colony, and poured time and money into the agricultural development of several small but important areas.

It is difficult to determine the main purpose of the Fascists in Somalia. Renato Lefèvre, who reflected official opinion in his *Politica somala*, published in 1933 under the auspices of the Istituto Coloniale Fascista, claimed that Somalia had been renewed by Fascism and that its young economy was assured of unlimited growth when international economic conditions returned to normal after the depression.[47] This was the Fascist dream of what Lefèvre and others called "Greater Somalia." Yet elsewhere, there were indications of concern with goals beyond Somalia. In 1924, before the campaign for the pacification of northern Somalia, Governor De Vecchi had described Somalia as "the sure and infallible way of access for the inevitable penetration of the great Ethiopian plateau."[48] Exactly when Fascist thought turned to Ethiopia is difficult to say. Certainly, Italy's failure to expand its African empire during World War I was a contributing factor to the rise of Fascism. The public had generally been aware during the war of Colonial Minister Colosimo's strong advocacy of the renewal of Italian activity in the horn of Africa at the expense of Ethiopia, British Somaliland, French Somaliland, and the Jubaland.[49] Governor De Vecchi, one of Mussolini's closest comrades in the Fascist march on Rome, had also enthusiastically voiced this expansionist sentiment. In 1925, the British and Italian governments exchanged notes on Ethiopia. The British promised to aid Italy in the development of its sphere

[47] Lefèvre, *Politica somala*, p. 9.

[48] De Vecchi, *Relazione sul progetto di bilancio della Somalia italiana . . . 1925/26*, p. 13.

[49] R. L. Hess, "Italy and Africa: Colonial Ambitions in the First World War," *Journal of African History*, IV (1963), 105–26.

of influence in Ethiopia in return for Italian support of British efforts to secure a dam at Lake Tana. After the Ethiopian government protested against the Anglo-Italian notes and what appeared to be the preparations for a new partition of the horn, both sides gave assurances to Ethiopia that they had no designs on the independence of that country. In 1928, in fact, the Italians concluded a treaty of Italo-Ethiopian friendship that was supposed to endure for twenty years.

Speaking before the Chamber of Deputies in March, 1927, Colonial Minister Luigi Federzoni envisioned a Somalia whose economic problems would be solved in the long run. At the same time, however, he graphically pictured the continuation of the railroad, then approaching Villabruzzi, beyond the Benadir and into the Ethiopian highlands.[50] For the Italians, Ethiopia was a Lorelei, luring them on to disaster; and like the Lorelei, the riches of Ethiopia were to remain elusive. Federzoni was only dreaming the same dreams as Mancini, Cecchi, Crispi, and a hundred others. The flaw in Italian plans for colonizing the horn of Africa was the temptation to succumb to the attractions of Ethiopia and ignore Somalia.

In 1932, the colonial government in Somalia assumed a policy of "inflexible reciprocity" in its dealings with Ethiopia and began to talk of the solution of the "Italian colonial question" in terms of expansion into the southern and western territories of Ethiopia, regions which it described as Ethiopia's colonies. Residents and regional commissioners were instructed to reorganize the frontier police and to prepare the Somali for auxiliary military service.[51] On May 31, 1934, seven months before the Walwal incident, Mussolini met with his chief of staff, Marshal Pietro Badoglio, the colonial minister, General Emilio De Bono, and Undersecretary of State F. Suvich to discuss "defensive arrangements" for Eritrea's

---

50 Federzoni, *L'Africa Orientale*, p. 105.

51 Governor's circular letter, No. 400, "Direttive per l'Oltre Confine: Segreta," Mogadishu, August 1, 1932.

border with Ethiopia. Mussolini summarized his program as follows:

1. Completion of defensive arrangements in the shortest possible time.

2. Upon completion of defensive arrangements, study of the problem of indirectly provoking an action on the part of Ethiopia.

3. Regarding our general policy toward Ethiopia, pursuit of a policy that tends to avoid anything that could upset our military preparations and therefore a policy that applies the Treaty of Friendship in the greatest measure possible. . . .

4. Absolute silence about the policy of military preparation with the governments of France and Great Britain.[52]

At this early stage of preparation, the Italians anticipated an Ethiopian attack on Assab. No mention was made of Somalia.

Early in December, 1934, Italian and Ethiopian forces clashed at Walwal, sixty miles west of the provisional frontier between Somalia and Ethiopia. The Italians, who claimed that Walwal was in Italian territory, demanded an apology and the payment of reparations; the Ethiopian government, which considered Walwal to be Ethiopian, insisted on an investigation to fix the responsibility for the incident. In the ensuing months Mussolini deliberately refused to come to terms with Ethiopia and continued his preparations for invasion. On January 7, 1935, Mussolini came to an understanding with France. The Franco-Italian agreement called for a cession of part of French Somaliland to Italy and the sale of shares in the Djibouti–Addis Ababa railroad. But more important, France renounced her political interests in Ethiopia and limited her economic interest to the zone of the railroad. France's Laval also gave Italy verbal assurances of a free hand to expand in East Africa and to settle once and for all every question with the government of Ethiopia.[53]

[52] Minutes of meeting with Mussolini, Rome, May 31, 1934, ASMAI, pos. 181/2, f. 5. Cf. P. Badoglio, *La Guerra d'Etiopia* (Milan: Mondadori, 1936), p. 6.

[53] W. C. Askew, "The Secret Agreement between France and Italy on Ethiopia, January, 1935," *Journal of Modern History*, XXV (1953), 47–48.

At the end of January, the Italians began in earnest to prepare Somalia for war with Ethiopia. Colonial Minister De Bono sent instructions to General Luigi Frusci, commander of the troops in Somalia:

Assure for Somalia . . . enough forces to guarantee the territory's integrity in concurrence with the operations on the northern front, where we will have taken the initiative; assure 100 per cent probability of initial success. . . . Be ready by October.[54]

Somalia's role was to be defensive. But when Governor Rodolfo Graziani arrived in Somalia in March, 1935, he found that the colony's preparations for war existed only on paper. Roads had to be built, transportation had to be organized, bases had to be constructed, and inadequate port works had to be improved. Not until August were the troops in a state of readiness. By October 1, Graziani had prepared his war machine of 51,000 rifles, 112 pieces of artillery, 1,585 machine-guns, 1,800 trucks, 70 tanks and armored cars, and 38 airplanes.[55] Two days later, the Italian invasion of Ethiopia began. In the campaign against Ethiopia, the Somali colonial troops eagerly fought against the Ethiopians, their traditional enemy. Six thousand Somali Zaptié served loyally under Graziani and their Italian commanders.

Shortly after the Walwal incident, the government had instituted the office of high commissioner for the East African colonies and had placed Marshal Emilio De Bono, and later Marshal Pietro Badoglio, in charge of political and military matters. On June 1, 1936, after the fall of Addis Ababa and the proclamation of the new Italian Empire, the Italians reconstituted their colonial possessions in the horn of Africa. Eritrea, Ethiopia, and Somalia were united as one colony, Africa Orientale Italiana ("Italian East Africa"). The huge new colony was administratively subdivided into six *governi:* Amhara, Galla-Sidama, Harar, Shoa, Eritrea, and Somalia.

54 R. Graziani, *Il Fronte Sud* (Milan: Mondadori, 1938), p. 35.

55 *Ibid.*, p. 144.

The *governo* of Somalia was not identical, however, with the former colony of Somalia. For ethnic and administrative purposes, the Italians attached to the old Somalia the Ogaden, a province inhabited largely by Somali tribes. In this way the Fascists created *La Grande Somalia,* increased in area if not in wealth.

The enlarged African empire of which Somalia had become just one province barely had time for administrative reorganization and a return to peacetime economic development before Italy became involved in World War II. In 1940 the empire briefly expanded again as the troops of Africa Orientale Italiana overran British Somaliland, but by 1941 Italy's fortunes had reversed. From Kenya and from the Sudan, the forces of the British Empire and Commonwealth moved in on the vulnerable Italian empire. The Italian military machine, so overwhelmingly victorious five years earlier, literally crumbled, and Italy precipitously withdrew from Somalia. On February 25, 1941, only weeks after the British crossed the Jubaland border, Mogadishu was occupied and the colonial government ceased to function. With the fall of Somalia, the way was open to Harar, and the victorious British troops swept inexorably onward. Addis Ababa—and Italy's dream of empire—fell on April 5. The last Italian flag in the horn of Africa was lowered at Gondar in northwestern Ethiopia on November 27, 1941.

CHAPTER EIGHT

Perspective on Italian Colonialism

From Mancini to Mussolini, Italian colonialism in East Africa was characterized by its lack of full commitment to the responsibilities of being a colonial power. That Italy operated in East Africa in the late nineteenth century first under the aegis of Great Britain and then through Filonardi's chartered company reflects this basic weakness. Italian political leaders like Mancini and Crispi—and later, Mussolini—were not incapable of devising grand strategies and impressive colonial programs for the extension of Italian influence over the horn of Africa; but there was a great contrast between such comprehensive formulations and the actual achievements of Italy overseas.

A partial explanation for this state of affairs may be found in Italy. Before 1884 the new kingdom of Italy was little interested in events in Africa, except for Tunisia. Only when the industrial north became seriously interested in overseas markets and resources in the mid-1880's were the prospects for colonialism improved. Mancini felt that the time was ripe for his African proposals in the Chamber of Deputies only when the obvious pressures of emigration had received public airing. But this was not enough to carry through his plans or even part of them. Italian colonialism had no ideological basis. The only principle followed was to seek "colonies of settlement," and this had no relevance in the arid steppes of Somalia.

The lack of a consistent colonial ideology was also evident after Italy entered the East African scene, when the narrow economic motives of Filonardi contrasted with the sweeping imperial ambitions of Cecchi. Yet neither man could gain any real encouragement from a government unable to mobilize public opinion in favor of colonial adventures.

The result of this situation was a certain amount of self-delusion, as well as a deliberate ignorance of internal African affairs in Zanzibar, in Somalia, and especially in Ethiopia. Hence, Italian activity was characterized by confusion, uncertainty, hesitancy, and inner contradictions. As for the motive of prestige, which loomed large in the minds of men like Cecchi and Crispi, the necessity to act under the aegis of Great Britain and the Imperial British East Africa Company led only to a co-operative imperialism in which Italy was the junior partner. The retention of Kismayu by the British attested to the uneven arrangement. Although Italy wished to increase its economic and political influence in East Africa, Italian actions in Zanzibar amounted to little more than hollow threats and feeble accomplishments. To vacillation and wish fulfilment was added reliance on minimal means. The agents of Italian expansionism—propagandists, traders, missionaries, explorers, diplomats, administrators, and the employees of the chartered company—were always too few in number; they made little impact in Italy or in East Africa, an area several times the size of Italy. Nevertheless, Italy strove to act as a third force in East Africa, as an equal of Germany and Great Britain, who, although they too worked with minimal means, were capable of a greater effort than a country which had yet to consolidate its national unity.

Italy was a relative latecomer in the race for colonies. The partition of Africa was almost completed in 1889. It was then that Italy extended a protectorate over northern Somalia in hopes of raising Italian prestige, but the results were meager. After a series of costly military operations in Eritrea, the government was unwilling to commit itself to a policy of open

expansionism in Somalia. After all, Ethiopia was more promising. From the beginning of the period of government by
chartered company, it was abundantly clear that the metropolitan government did not wish to spend money on the colony or to assume any responsibility for its defense. Filonardi's
company suffered from years of painfully slow negotiations to
lease, not purchase, the Benadir from the declining sultanate
of Zanzibar. Despite itself, however, the government was compelled to subsidize the chartered company, which had become
the agent for its venture in shoestring colonialism. It should
have come as no surprise that the first experiment in government by chartered company was a failure.

Ethiopia's decisive defeat of Italy in 1896 turned Italian
ambitions away from the highlands of Ethiopia for more than
a third of a century. After Adowa and the death of Cecchi at
Lafolè, a large number of influential Italians hoped that their
colonial holdings would be completely liquidated. Yet, if this
had been done, Italy would have suffered an even greater loss
of prestige. Rather than abandon Somalia, Italy chose to make
another attempt at government by chartered company.

The second period of government by chartered company,
from 1900 to 1905, in some ways repeated the experiences of
the Filonardi Company. The basic problems of exploiting the
Benadir profitably remained to be solved, as did the definition
of the company's relation to the government. An effective
administrative system had to be devised, and the precarious
security of Italy's holdings in southern Somalia had to be
maintained. Somalia was an isolated colonial outpost, and demoralization of the administrative personnel was not uncom-
mon. The company, whose capital was not large enough to
permit the occupation of the interior, was confined to limited
operations on the coast. The government did as little as possible. Only a full-blown slavery scandal brought the colony to
national attention. Then and only then did the government
take steps to purchase the Benadir from Zanzibar.

The period of government by chartered company is especially significant for an understanding of the operation of colonialism in Africa. The Filonardi Company and the Benadir Company were not merely private trading companies that had been given a concession to administer southern Somalia. The companies were a curious mixture of public and private elements. As private companies, both attempted to create a trading empire in Somalia. This would have been a difficult enough task in itself, but the companies' charters also stipulated their responsibility for a whole set of functions not generally within the range of private business enterprise. Thus the companies formulated native and land policies and were required to attempt the effective occupation of southern Somalia with their own armies and police forces. The companies levied taxes, made laws, and were the government in their own right. The Italian chartered companies, like those elsewhere in Africa, were agencies with paragovernmental functions; they were semiofficial overseas extensions of the metropolitan government. This arrangement permitted the home government to shift all responsibility for the colony onto the company. It gives the lie to any suggestion that an aggressive imperialism was at work in Somalia. Yet the arrangement also burdened the companies with responsibilities that they could not handle and financial burdens that nearly drove both companies to bankruptcy. Aside from complete withdrawal, there was only the alternative of a still lesser degree of involvement, as in the so-called protectorates of northern Somalia, where the name of Italy was not respected. The northern protectorates enhanced the name of Italy in Europe, but not in Somalia.

Although the companies failed to achieve the government's purpose, they did perform a very necessary function in the colonial history of Somalia. In undertaking paragovernmental operations, the Filonardi Company laid the basis for indirect rule in Somalia. Filonardi's judicial system was based on the traditional role of the cadis and on the Shari'a. The Benadir Company continued this practice; the government

ıter extended it to the warrant chiefs. Filonardi's expropria-
ιion of all uncultivated lands set the stage for De Martino's
agricultural concessions and for the Società Agricola Italo-
Somala. Company agents in Somalia performed the same
function as the residents and regional commissioners after
1905. Moreover, many of the employees of the chartered
company, on loan from the navy, stayed on in the service of
the government. The early colonial government was but a
continuation of the chartered company's government. The
chartered companies thus established the main lines of Italian
colonial policy in Somalia. The Tittoni government, the first
to provide for direct administration of the colony, merely followed existing directions; and the colonial policy of the Fascist
government for *La Grande Somalia* differed little from that
of pre-Fascist days.

Even when forced to administer the Benadir directly, the
government attempted to avoid responsibility and to keep
its commitments to a minimum. Italian behavior in Somalia
at this time was in sharp contrast to the usual stereotypes of
imperial and colonial activity. The eighteen years of Italian
colonialism before the advent of Fascism were characterized
by beneficent paternalism. More than one Italian colonial
officer described the Somali as children under the guidance
of their Italian "father." In that period the government continued the chartered companies' policy of not disturbing the
political and social order of the Somali tribes or of Islam; the
Shari'a and the *testur* tribal law were enforced almost *in
toto*. The relatively few Italians in Somalia—fewer than one
thousand in 1923—were subject to Italian law. Occasionally,
the Italians deposed a chief, but in general, they used them
in the governmental administration. The warrant chiefs, for
example, were drawn from the ranks of traditional society.
Italian indirect rule in Somalia evolved not through convic-
tion of the intrinsic worth of such a system but through
necessity. The number of personnel stationed in the colony
was limited. Moreover, before the Fascist era, vast areas of

the country were—in practice, if not in theory—under the rule of traditional chiefs. For their own purposes, the Italians preserved the chieftainship system, but they never completely understood or studied it. In general, they were unaware that northern chiefs had less power than the southern Rahanwein and Digil chiefs, although the Italian experience had been that indirect rule worked in southern Somalia but failed in Obbia and the Mijjertein.

The eighteen years of Fascist rule were little different from the earlier period in that the Fascists did nothing to destroy traditional tribal institutions or to encourage political awareness. The very nature of indirect rule, in fact, inevitably produced a system of weak authority; and in Somalia indirect rule was further limited by the highly segmented nature of Somali society. All the Italians could do was to put a stop to interclan and intertribal warfare. Occasionally, this was done with a brutality sanctioned by Fascism. They were unable, however, to create a sense of national solidarity among their Somali subjects. In the Ethiopian war, they sponsored a Somali identity in order to stimulate anti-Ethiopian feeling. Yet they soon discovered that the Ogaden Somali were hostile to other Darod and to the Hawiya Somali; in fact, some Ogaden chiefs fought on the Ethiopian side to preserve tribal interests. The creation of an administrative greater Somalia with the annexation of the Ogaden region did little to promote protonationalist feelings.

By and large Somali opposition to the Italians was local in nature and at no time involved all Somali tribes. The Bimal revolt, for example, was easily put down with the aid of Somali allies among the Geledi. The single important large-scale movement, the dervishes under the leadership of Muhammad Abdullah Hassan, was not directed primarily against the Italians. The Bah Geri terrorized the Bantu tribes of the Webi Shebelle valley and indirectly threatened the Italians in the Benadir but had no reason to be sworn enemies of the colonial regime. Only when the Fascists occupied the northern sultanates was there an attempt at rebellion, but Obbia and the Mijjertein were torn by tribalism and factionalism and could not present a united front. Similarly, the Galjal of the south, like the Bimal before them, were overwhelmed by Somali irregulars. Although there was a cultural and ethnic Somali nation, it had no political manifestation in resistance to Europeans.

From the point of view of Italian colonialism, the venture in Somalia met with only limited success beyond the establishment of an Italian presence in East Africa. The colony was always a great economic burden for a nation that advocated economic self-sufficiency. Yet the Ethiopian crisis in 1934 clearly demonstrated Somalia's strategic worth. From the perspective of an independent Somali Republic today, some of the Italian policies can be seen to have hindered the development of those skills and institutions essential to the operation of an independent state. At no time, however, did the Italians contemplate the eventual independence of their Indian Ocean holding. Nevertheless, significant changes took place in the political and economic life of the territory. Although fewer changes were apparent in the educational system and in social organization, it is obvious that, all in all, Somalia at the end of the Italian colonial period had undergone a variety of experiences markedly different from the traditional life of its tribes.

The politics of neither precolonial nor colonial Somalia were conducive to the establishment on a national scale of the preconditions for political independence. No political parties existed in the Italian colony, other than those Fascist groups to which only Italians belonged. Nor is there any evidence of the emergence of protopolitical groupings comparable to those found in British or French Africa. Political life, such as it was, existed on two separate levels—the Somali tribal and the Italian administrative. At the beginning of Italian activity in the region, tribalism was a disruptive force, a constant threat to the maintenance of public order. The Italians were aware that one of the prime requisites for the development of a productive colony would be the suppression of intertribal warfare and the establishment of peace and order. Indeed, the failure of the experiments in government by chartered company may be attributed in large part to the disturbed condition of the interior. A half-century of Italian influence did not eliminate all conflict, but in the last fifteen years of Italian rule intertribal hostility diminished to nearly negligible proportions.

To do away with one cause of intertribal disputes, Italian administrators formally established the borders of the areas occupied by each tribe. Limitations were placed on the movements of each tribe in a first step toward what the Italians hoped would be the civilizing of a nomadic people and their eventual settlement in agricultural communities. In the interior, however, life on the arid steppes demanded seasonal migrations in search of water and pasture. For this reason, the Italians made treaty arrangements with Great Britain to permit the free movement of the northern tribes between Somaliland and Somalia. Before 1935 the long border with Ethiopia was ignored by the nomadic tribes; and after 1935 there was no border separating the Ogaden Somali from the original colony of Italian Somalia.

Although the freedom of movement of nomadic tribes was limited to a certain extent, the general effect of the Italian system of indirect rule was to confirm existing tribal institutions and practices. The great tribal assemblies (*shir*) were used by Governor De Martino and his successors to organize a tribal consensus in favor of government policy, which left the clan system virtually untouched. The creation of warrant chiefs, and their assimilation into the colonial administration, strengthened rather than weakened tribal solidarity. It is worth noting also that the Italians fought against or contained the greatest challenges to tribalism—the religious order of Muhammad Abdullah Hassan and the opportunism of sultans like Yusuf Ali. The Italian administrative system was, in fact, superimposed on the tribal political structure.

Some elements of the Italian colonial administrative structure in Somalia have endured to the present. The system of regional commissioners and residents, paralleling the district officers of British Africa, has been modified only slightly by Italy's heirs in Somalia—the British military administration, the United Nations trusteeship administration, and the Somali Republic. Titles have changed, but the system remains basically the same. The residents' practice of consulting with local leaders has evolved into formalized residency councils, which have the earmarks of thriving democracies on the local level. Thus, although the quality of Italian administration always depended largely on the caliber of individual officials, many of whom were isolated from contact with Mogadishu even during the period of comparatively vigorous Fascist administration, these same officials appear to have imposed an over-all administrative unity on Somalia which has survived to the present and has provided a strong foundation for the independent Somali Republic.

It was also Italian policy not to tamper with the indigenous judicial institutions. Elements of the Italian judicial system were grafted onto the traditional Islamic and Somali systems. The result of this policy was that much of the Somali *testur* and the Muslim Shari‘a survived the colonial period in pure form.

Just as the political development of colonial Somalia was marked by the continuance of precolonial indigenous patterns of political life, although with an overlay of Italian innovations, so the economic life of colonial Somalia was characterized by the persistence of nomadic stock raising in the north and mixed farming in the less arid regions of the south. Few Somali were drawn out of the traditional pattern into the new forms exemplified by plantation agriculture along the Juba and the Webi Shebelle rivers. The concessionaires did not affect the economic pattern within the colony, although it was they who were responsible for Somalia's cash economy. Indeed, Somalia had two coexistent economies, the indigenous and the Italian-introduced plantation.

It has already been demonstrated how significant the Società Agricola Italo-Somala (SAIS) was for the emergence of a non-traditional sector in the economy. Although the achievements of SAIS were encouraging, Somalia did not prove to be the El Dorado of the colonial dreamers. Government and private investment in the colony's economy greatly outweighed the material benefits that it reluctantly yielded. The balance of trade was inevitably adverse. The usual ratio of imports to exports was two to one. Compared with the other Italian colonies, Somalia offered little. Tripolitania and Cyrenaica, with 70 per cent of Somalia's population of approximately 1,400,000, had exports valued at nearly 40,-000,000 lire in 1928/29, whereas Somalia's exports amounted to little more than 25,000,000 lire. And Eritrea, with 40 per cent of Somalia's population, exported twice as much as the two Libyan colonies. Somalia's customs and internal revenues amounted to 22,000,000 lire, or slightly more than those of Eritrea, but the Italians collected six times that amount from their North African holdings.[1] The relative positions of Somalia and the other colonies remained the same until the end of Italian colonialism in Africa. Moreover, the cold hard facts of economics in Somalia have continued into the present.

In all fairness to Somalia, however, it should be noted that the other colonies were also far from being self-sufficient. Libya's internal revenues of approximately 138,000,000 lire did not cover its expenses of 536,000,000 lire. Similarly, Eritrea's internal revenues covered less than half the colony's budget. As a result, the metropolitan government had to subsidize Libya, where it could sponsor Italian settlers, to the amount of more than 400,000,000 lire annually and Eritrea,

[1] Angelo Piccioli, *La Nuova Italia d'Oltremare* (Milan: Mondadori, 1933), II, 1379–86.

with its much smaller budget, to the amount of at least 56,000,000 lire. Thus, although Somalia was relatively poor, its budgetary problems were neither unique nor less severe than those of the other Italian colonies. If autarchy was Mussolini's economic goal, he stood no chance of achieving it in Africa. Colonialism was no solution to Italy's economic problems. Like the other colonial powers, Italy discovered that colonies were literally not a paying proposition.

Perhaps because the Webi Shebelle did not become Italy's Nile in Somalia, the Somali were spared the hardship of being deprived of large areas of their land. Although the Filonardi ordinances set a precedent for state seizure of all unoccupied lands, there was no reason for the Italians to confiscate land. Only one-tenth of the land area of Somalia was suitable for agriculture of any kind. A Somali had more to fear from other tribesmen who coveted his clan's grazing area and water holes than he did from the Italians. Consequently, through-out the colonial period the Somali did not suffer alienation of their lands, and the traditional way of life was little af-fected by the activities of the Italian concessions along the rivers.

As in the political and the economic areas of life, in which new ways were to some extent successfully introduced—al-though old ways continued to predominate—Italian influence on the socially conservative Somali in the social and educa-tional fields was superficial. Although new products came into the country and a plantation agriculture was developed in the area of the sedentary Bantu, Rahanwein, and Digil tribes, the nomad's way of life remained essentially un-changed. The Somali of the interior continued to live as their ancestors had lived centuries earlier. They despised agriculture and the sedentary life and avoided the Italian tax collector. The nature of Italian colonialism prior to World War II did not call for greater changes on the part of the native.

All the Italians asked was obedience (to force or to the

threat of force), reduced tribal warfare, and a restricted area for nomadism. Other than this and the lure of Ethiopia, the Italians were more concerned with their frankly exploitative but unsuccessful program for the economic development of the colony. The positive values embodied in the United Nations Charter find no counterpart in the Italian colonial program for Somalia. It is not possible, therefore, to talk of Somalia's political advancement along the lines followed by other African colonies that were prepared for independence through changes in the imperial policies of the European powers that claimed their territory.

Although Governor De Martino claimed in his annual report of 1911–12 that it was Italy's duty to bring about the moral, intellectual, and social regeneration of the Somali— Italy's civilizing mission in Africa—no attempt was made to Italianize the Somali through education.[2] Of all the Italian colonies, Somalia received the least aid for schools. Because of the neglect of education in the period under study, it is impossible to speak of the formation of an educated native elite comparable to that, for example, of West Africa. To obtain an education, the Somali had the choice of attending either the traditional koranic schools or the highly suspect mission-run government schools. The former, preservers of traditional Muslim learning, were neither helped nor hindered by the government. Their language of instruction, however, was Arabic, not Somali. The mission schools trained the Somali only for subservience to his Italian masters. The fifteen schools of the country had a Somali enrolment of less than one-tenth of 1 per cent of the population. A large number of Somali served in the military force and as irregulars, but few of them were trained as clerks; most of them worked in a capacity that was not very different from that of the traditional askari. No Somali was given a position of

2 R. R. De Marco, *The Italianization of African Natives: Government Native Education in the Italian Colonies, 1890–1937* (New York: Teachers College, Columbia University, 1943), pp. 8, 19.

command, except at the lowest echelons, either in the army or on the plantations. Those few Somali who had been influenced by Italian culture had no political outlet for their energies and no educational opportunities beyond the elementary curriculum. Moreover, the Somali language, unlike tens of other African languages, had no written form. There was a formidable communications barrier between Italian and Somali, perhaps greater than in most other African territories.

With the exception of a handful of orphans, all Italian children who went to school in Mogadishu attended the two European schools. The slightly smaller number of Somali and mulatto children who attended school in Mogadishu never sat in the same classroom with European students. Outside Mogadishu, those Italian children who were not sent home to Italy for their education went to the same elementary schools as the Somali, but for the Somali education ended with the elementary school. The middle form was exclusively for Italians, and there was no higher education in the colony.

Despite this implicit separation of the races, outside the school system there was little indication of strong racial feelings among the Italians. The Somali retained their traditional disdain for all foreign elements, especially white Christian Europeans. The Italians, on the other hand, were for the most part unconcerned about race. In Mogadishu there were a number of marriages as well as informal liaisons between Italian men and Somali women. In general, a laissez faire attitude prevailed, although the Italians did tend to be condescending and paternalistic toward the Somali. Nineteenth-century European attitudes toward Africans were thus preserved throughout the history of the colony. Symptomatic of this was the Italian adoption of British colonial terms for servants: *il boy* and *la boyessa.*

Not until late in the Fascist period was there racist talk in Italian colonial circles. When Angelo Piccioli, a high official of the Ministry of Italian Africa (successor to the Ministry of Colonies), lectured on race and empire in 1938, his talk contained none of the racist elements found in the ideology of Italy's ally north of the Alps. He paid little attention to allegedly scientific investigations into racial intermixture. Rather, he pointed to the practical disadvantage of intermarriage: the creation of a social class of mixed-bloods accepted by neither ruler nor subject race. Piccioli, whose lecture was sponsored by the Fascist government, had little patience with arguments about physical differences. Appealing to the rich historical past, he argued that the "basis of Italian racism is . . . the justifiable pride in all that Italians have done for world civilization in the centuries of their history."[3] In other words, Piccioli returned to a Mazzinian concept of nationalism, to which he added an imperialist corollary. Although this type of nationalism contributed historically to the development of European racism, it is not racism per se. The Fascists spoke of race only in Italy and used the vocabulary current at the time. In Somalia there were too few Italians to spread an official racist doctrine, especially one that did not interest the money-oriented concessionaires. Perhaps for this reason individual Italians are liked and respected in independent Somalia, as in Ethiopia, although colonialism as a whole is condemned by both countries.

3 *Annali dell'Africa Italiana,* II (1938), 417–22.

Epilogue

With the conquest of Ethiopia and the formation of the Italian empire in 1936, Somalia was combined with the former Ethiopian province of Ogaden to form a united province within Africa Orientale Italiana. Ethnically and religiously, the union was justifiable in that both areas were Somali and Muslim. Five years later, the Somali, who had fought against the Ethiopians with the victorious Italians, were surprised at the ease with which the Italians were defeated by the British in a lightning campaign. After the British had occupied Italian East Africa in 1941–42, they set up a military administration which governed the former Italian colony of Somalia until 1950. Until 1948, the Ogaden remained united with Somalia, despite the protests of Ethiopia.

At the end of the war, the disposition of the Italian colonies posed a problem for the Allied victors. At Yalta, at San Francisco, and at Potsdam, they discussed the Italian colonies, but they could reach no agreement about their future status. In September, 1945, at the first session of the Council of Foreign Ministers in London, the United States proposed a collective trusteeship for the former colonies under Article 81 of the United Nations Charter. France, Great Britain, and the Soviet Union opposed the plan for varying reasons. The following April in Paris, the British foreign minister proposed the union of the Ogaden, British Somaliland, and Italian Somalia to form a "Greater Somalia" under the trusteeship or protection of Great Britain. This plan was overshadowed,

190

however, by a French proposal that Italy be considered as the trusteeship administrator.

Italy renounced all right and title to her former colonial possessions in the peace treaty signed in Paris in 1947. It was agreed that within one year the United States, Great Britain, France, and the Soviet Union would decide the future of the colonies. When the Big Four failed to reach an agreement, the matter was referred to the General Assembly of the United Nations. In 1948 the four powers sent a commission of investigation to Somalia. The question of Italy's future in Europe influenced both the Western bloc and the Soviets. The Italians, who had joined the Allied cause after overthrowing Mussolini in 1943, did not consider themselves to be a defeated enemy and sought the return of their colonies. In a compromise measure, Libya was given its independence, Eritrea was federated with Ethiopia, and the new democratic Italian republic received a limited trusteeship over Somalia. On December 2, 1950, the General Assembly ratified the trusteeship agreement, and Italy commenced a ten-year term of administration, at the end of which Somalia was to receive her independence.

In Somalia the possible return of Italy to her former colony had been met with mixed feelings. The Somali Youth League, the territory's first political party, declared its opposition to the Italian Trusteeship Administration. In January, 1948, the party was involved in riots with Italian and pro-Italian groups in Mogadishu, Kismayu, Merca, and Brava. Forty-two Italians and eleven Somali lost their lives in the disturbances. In April, 1949, a party leader, Abdullahi Issa, appeared before the United Nations Trusteeship Council and condemned the return of an Italian administration in any guise. Not all Somali opposed an Italian trusteeship, however. A group of pro-Italian parties, the Conferenza della Somalia, sent its representative to the United Nations to express satisfaction with the trusteeship arrangements. Both the Somali Youth League, which was heavily influenced by northern

Darod, and the Conferenza della Somalia, which represented southern tribes, claimed the support of an overwhelming majority of Somali.

Another side of the question was expressed by the Ethiopian government. Immediately after the war, Emperor Haile Selassie had stressed Ethiopia's claims to Eritrea and Somalia "as territories incontestably belonging to the Ethiopian Empire since before the Christian era and stolen through Italian aggression." The claim was hotly disputed by Somali leaders. What Addis Ababa seemed to fear most was a renewed threat of Italian aggression.

After the assumption of the trusteeship administration, Italy turned to the development of the territory along lines drastically different from those of the prewar period. Italy chose to demonstrate through its administration its good faith in training an ex-colony for independence. The political situation was fluid; yet, the Italian Trusteeship Administration had only ten years in which to prepare Somalia to stand alone. The problem was immense, for 70 per cent of the population was nomadic. The political parties, which had not appeared until after 1945, were in sore need of guidance.[1] Other organs of self-government than a vigorous party system had to be developed. The Somali had to be educated to take over the ranks of the civil service. As if this were not enough, the trusteeship administration also faced the continuing task of making the economy viable, a task which fifty years of colonialism had failed to perform.

For the purpose of giving advice to the Italian administration and of allaying the fears of those who were suspicious of Italy's motives in returning to one of her former colonies, the United Nations appointed an advisory council to act as

[1] The Somali Youth Club, founded in 1943, became a full-fledged political party, the Somali Youth League, in 1945. In 1947, the Hisbia Digil and Mirifle was formed to protect the interests of the Digil and Mirifle tribes. Within short order, more than a half-dozen other parties, mostly based on tribes, sprang up.

a watchdog over its operations. The advisory council gave useful advice to the Italians on the establishment of a municipal council in Mogadishu and on various modifications of Italian policy. It also served as a convenient agency for receiving Somali petitions to the United Nations and to the Italian Trusteeship Administration.

Italy's immediate political problem was to win the confidence of its former colonial subjects. This the Italians attempted to do by granting amnesty to the Somali who had been imprisoned following the disturbances in 1948, by training Somali administrative personnel, and by encouraging the development of democratic institutions on all levels. It was a slow and difficult process, but by 1955, the Italian administration had apparently succeeded in convincing the Somali that it was only a temporary agency. In that year the Somali Youth League executed a *volte-face* and announced a policy of collaboration with the Italian Trusteeship Administration.

Within a remarkably short time, the Italian administration helped the Somali political parties to develop the institutions of self-government. In its first year, it authorized the creation of thirty-three municipal councils in an effort to introduce the concept of self-government on the local level. During the colonial regime, only eleven municipalities had self-sufficient budgets, that is, were financed by local taxes. For political reasons, the administration broadened the definition of municipality to cover most of the territory's largest villages. As in the colonial period, the local resident or commissioner consulted with local interests. Now, however, those consulted were at first appointed and later elected to regularly constituted municipal councils. Elections were held in the municipalities for the first time in March, 1954. An attempt to modernize the *shir*, or traditional tribal councils, and convert them into district (provincial) councils failed.

At the end of the Italians' first year back in Somalia, a territorial council, the precursor of a Somali national assembly,

came into being. Its members were at first appointed and
then, in gradually increasing numbers, elected. The advisory
council recommended that no more than 75 per cent of Somali representatives be nominated through tribal gatherings.
In this way it was hoped that the influence of tribalism could
be lessened. Elections were held again in 1955. In 1958, a
constitutional assembly was elected, for a term of two years,
as the last step in the progress toward self-government.

By 1958, the Italians had helped to create the institutions
necessary for a peaceful transfer of power to the elected representatives of the Somali people. In the civil service, a pro-
gressive Africanization of personnel had taken place, and 85
per cent of the civil offices were held by Somali. In two areas,
however, the Italians did not solve important problems of the
nascent Somali Republic: the question of the border with
Ethiopia and the creation of a viable economy. During the
colonial period, the delimitation of the Somali-Ethiopian
border had not been a problem because both Italy and Ethiopia preferred to leave the question open. Each hoped that
the frontier would eventually be settled to its advantage. Both
the Treaty of Addis Ababa (1896) and subsequent negotiations in 1908 failed to arrive at a mutually satisfactory settlement. The Ethiopians claimed a good deal of Somalia—in
fact, to within less than one hundred miles of Mogadishu.
The Italians, on the other hand, continued to feel that by
leaving the border question unsettled, the way would be
open to them for encroachment upon Ethiopian borderlands.
The Somali tribes took no stand; the only borders that interested them were those between tribal grazing lands. The
nature of the nomadic life made conflict over grazing lands
almost inevitable between the Somali of the Ethiopian
Ogaden and the Somali of Italian Somalia. The issue had
been temporarily settled after the Italian invasion of Ethiopia
and the amalgamation of the Ogaden and Somalia. After the
war, the British military administration refused to change
existing borders. Thus when Italy returned to Somalia in

1950, the trusteeship administration had to govern a territory with a boundary problem. The policy of the Italians was to postpone negotiations until such a time as the Somali themselves could handle the question. The Ethiopians, wary of the creation of an independent Somali Republic and its implications for Somali irredentism in the Ogaden, continued to claim large areas of Somalia. When the Somali Republic became independent on July 1, 1960, Somali irredentist nationalism was immediately given impetus by the unification of British Somaliland with ex-Italian Somalia. The enlarged Somali Republic proceeded to claim large areas of eastern Ethiopia, the North Eastern Region of Kenya, and French Somaliland; and to the present, it has refused to surrender its concept of a greater Somalia based on the concept of national self-determination.

The problem of creating a viable economy has continued to plague the Somali Republic. In ten short years, the Italian Trusteeship Administration could not do what Fascist Italy had tried and failed to do over an eighteen-year period. In an attempt to create a new image for itself in Africa, Italy poured a large annual subsidy into Somalia. But in 1954, a United Nations mission predicted that, despite attempts to change the economic pattern of Somalia, the country would not be self-supporting at the time of independence. The herculean task of modernizing the Somali economy continues to challenge the country today and to influence its political direction. Colonial Somalia was dependent on large subsidies from Italy in order to maintain its governmental services and to provide a minimal stimulus for the economy. The independent Somali Republic is also dependent on foreign aid for the same purposes, and Italian support has been supplemented by aid from the Soviet Union, China, the United States, and the United Arab Republic.

When Somalia became independent on July 1, 1960, the day after the Belgians freed their one African colony, the developing Congo crisis overshadowed the passing of an era in the horn of Africa. Although the Italian colonial administration had officially bowed out twenty years earlier, Italy had returned for an encore in which it was successfully cast in an entirely new role, a role analogous to that of other European powers compelled by a changing world to revise their colonial policies and prepare their one-time colonial subjects for independence.

Ultimately, the Italian colonial experience in Somalia was far from unique. Like Great Britain, France, Belgium, and Portugal, Italy was confronted with the common problems of the colonial powers in Africa: resistance from supposedly docile subject peoples, the necessity to embark—often unwillingly—upon a program of conquest, insufficient support from the metropolitan government, general public apathy at home occasionally interrupted by violent outbreaks of anticolonial sentiment (as after Adowa), inadequate funds to effect rapid development, and, by a strange turn of history, the obligation to train Africans for independence and nationhood. The uniqueness of Italian colonialism in Somalia lies not in the trusteeship period or in the Fascist period when Italian colonialists consciously emulated the more vigorous colonialism of other European powers but in its unusual dependence in its early stages on the good offices of another European power, its unhappy experiments in minimal colonial involvement and continuing aversion in the pre-Fascist period to large-scale colonial activity, and its sorry history of failures.

Agreement between the Imperial British East Africa Company and the Italian Government

Agreement entered into this 3rd day of August, 1889, between the Imperial British East Africa Company, hereinafter called "The British Company," of the one part, and M. Catalani, Chargé d'Affaires for His Majesty the King of Italy in London, for and on behalf of the Royal Italian Government, of the other part, whereby it is agreed as follows:

Whereas, negotiations have been carried on for some time past, and are still pending, between the British Company and His Highness Seyyid Khalifa, Sultan of Zanzibar, for the cession by the said Sultan to the British Company of certain lands, territories, and countries which lie on the coast from and including Kismayu and north of the mouth of the River Juba, including the ports of Brava, Meurka, and Magadisho, with radii landwards of 10 sea miles, and of Warsheikh, with a radius of 5 sea miles:

And whereas, His Highness the said Seyyid Khalifa, Sultan of Zanzibar, by a letter dated the 15th January, 1889, to His Majesty the King of Italy, through Her Britannic Majesty's Agent and Consul-General at Zanzibar, authorized His Maj-

Source: E. Hertslet, *The Map of Africa by Treaty* (3d ed.; London: His Majesty's Stationery Office, 1909), III, 1088–91.

esty the King of Italy's Government to arrange with the British Company for the joint occupation of Kismayu:

And whereas, the Royal Italian Government are desirous of acquiring territories and ports in the East Coast of Africa, and the British Company are anxious to assist the Royal Italian Government in attaining such object:

1. Now, it is hereby mutually agreed between the parties hereto, that when His Highness Seyyid Khalifa, Sultan of Zanzibar, concedes to and hands over according to his promises and declarations to the British Company the said lands, territories, and countries lying on such coast from and including Kismayu and north of the mouth of the River Juba, including the ports of Brava, Meurka, and Magadisho, with radii landwards of 10 sea miles, and of Warsheikh, with a radius of 5 sea miles, the British Company shall, with the consent and approval of the Sultan, but at the expense of the Italian Government, transfer, or cause to be transferred, to the duly authorized Agents of the Italian Government, the aforesaid lands, territories, and countries, and the above ports of Brava, Meurka, Magadisho, and Warsheikh, to be held by the Italian Government on the same terms and conditions as those which may be contained in the Concession to be granted for the aforesaid ports and territories to the British Company, or on the best terms obtainable from the Sultan.

Except as to Kismayu and its adjoining territory, which is to be jointly occupied by the parties hereto, as hereinafter provided.

2. The Italian Government hereby agrees to indemnify the British Company from all expenses, reasonable demands, and claims, if any, that may arise by reason of the provisions of the Agreement, or in the carrying out of the same.

3. The British Company agree with the Italian Government upon an equal joint occupation of Kismayu and its adjoining territory as conceded by the Sultan, which will be jointly and equally held and administered by the two Contracting Parties. Both the British Company and the

Italian Government shall possess at Kismayu and its adjoining territory perfect equality of rights and privileges, but subject always to terms, if any, of the Concession to be granted as aforesaid. The Italian Government and the British Company shall bear and pay an equal share of the cost of administration, and shall divide equally the net returns from Kismayu and its adjoining territory. The detailed provisions for arriving at a *modus vivendi,* and carrying out in the most friendly way the provisions of this clause, are to be agreed upon and settled at Kismayu by the Agents of the Italian Government and the Agents of the British Company duly authorized as soon as possible after Kismayu has been handed over by the Sultan of Zanzibar to the British Company, and by the British Company to the Italian Government.

4. The Italian Government bind themselves to limit the Italian sphere of influence and operations on the East African continent by refraining from exercising any political or other influences, accepting Protectorates, making acquisitions of lands, or interfering with the extension of British influence on the territories or over the tribes lying to the west or south of a line drawn from the north bank of the mouth of the Juba River, and intended to keep always on the north and east sides of the River Juba to the point where the 8th degree of north latitude intersects the 40th degree of east longitude, and a line drawn direct from the above-named point and running over the parallel intersecting the 35th degree of east longitude of the meridian of Greenwich.

On their part the British Company agree and bind themselves to limit the said British Company's sphere of influence and operations on the East African continent by refraining from exercising any political or other influence, accepting Protectorates, making acquisitions of lands, interfering with the extension of Italian influence on the territories or over the tribes lying to the east and north-east of the lines above specified, provided, nevertheless, that if the course of the Juba River should, on survey, be ascertained to flow at any points to the north or east of the above-mentioned lines, then the northern or eastern bank of the said river, as the case may be, shall at such points be accepted as the line of demarcation between the said parties. This proviso, however, shall only extend to deviations of the said river up to the point where the 8th degree of north latitude intersects the 40th degree of east longitude. The above-mentioned lines are distinctly marked in red on the Map annexed hereto, and which Map, for the purposes of identification, has been signed by the parties hereto.

5. It is hereby further agreed that the Italian Government shall have joint and equal rights with the British Company of navigation on the River Juba and its tributaries so far as it may be requisite to give the Italian Government free access to the territories reserved to its sphere of influence as above mentioned.

6. The two contracting parties agree that any controversies which may arise respecting the interpretation or the execution of the present Agreement, or the consequences of any violation thereof, shall be submitted, when the means of settling them by means of an amicable arrangement are exhausted, to the decision of the Commissions of Arbitration, and that the result of such arbitration shall be binding upon both Contracting Parties. The members of such Commissions shall be elected by the two Contracting Parties by common consent, failing which, each of the parties shall nominate an Arbitrator, or an equal number of Arbitrators, and the Arbitrators thus appointed shall select an Umpire.

7. The Royal Italian Government reserve to themselves full power to delegate all their rights, powers, and privileges belonging to them, or acquired through the present Agreement, to an Italian Company, in course of formation, to be called "The Royal Italian East Africa Company," or some such similar name, binding themselves, however, that the said Italian Company shall comply with all obligations undertaken herein by the Italian Government, who will themselves

remain responsible for the strict compliance with the obligations herein contained. This Agreement to be construed according to English law.

Done and signed at London, in duplicate, in the English and Italian languages, with the understanding that the English text shall be binding, this 3rd day of August, in the year 1889.

W. Mackinnon.

T. Catalani.

Signed by the said Sir W. Mackinnon and Signor Catalani in the presence of

George S. Mackenzie.

3rd August, 1889

Administration of the Benadir, 1893–98

1893–1896
V. Filonardi e Compagnia

Income (Lire)		Expenditures (Lire)		Net Profit or Deficit (Lire)
1893–94				
Government subsidies	350,000	Rental to Zanzibar	256,000	
Customs revenues	104,657	Ordinary expenses	237,934	
Other taxes	8,418*			
Total	463,076	Total	493,934	− 30,858
1894–95				
Government subsidies	350,000	Rental	256,000	
Customs revenues	115,879	Ordinary expenses	87,631	
Other taxes	8,418			
Total	474,297	Total	343,631	130,666
1895–96				
Government subsidies	350,000	Rental	256,000	
Customs revenues	115,879*	Ordinary expenses	103,296	
Other taxes	8,418*			
Total	474,297*	Total	359,296	115,001
Three-year total	1,411,670	Three-year total	1,196,861	214,809

July 15, 1896—April 30, 1898
Provisional Government Administration

Income (Lire)		Expenditures (Lire)		Net Profit or Deficit (Lire)
1896–97				
Customs revenues	179,115	Rental	222,000	
		Ordinary expenses	220,280	
Total	179,115	Total	442,280	−263,165
1897–98				
Customs revenues	223,293	Rental	222,000	
		Ordinary expenses	220,280*	
Total	223,293	Total	442,280	−218,987

* Estimated.

Source: Two memorandums on the administration of the Benadir, undated, ASMAI, pos. 75/4, f. 34. The first was compiled largely from figures derived from the reports of F. Quirighetti, the second on estimates by E. Dulio.

202

Convention between the Italian Government and the Benadir Company, May 25, 1898

ARTICLE I. The government agrees to hand over to the "Società Anonima Commerciale Italiana del Benadir (Somalia Italiana)," having its head office at Milan, the administration of the towns and territories of the Benadir, with their respective hinterland, as at present exercised by the government, and that at the risk of the company and without guarantee.

The convention will be in effect from May 1, 1898.

On its part, the company agrees to further the civil and commercial development of the colony and to furnish a detailed account of its administration to the Italian government, which will have the right to supervise the company's operations. The company will also develop in the most suitable manner the economic condition of the towns conceded to it and for that purpose will undertake all works which may be thought necessary.

There not being fixed beforehand a detailed program of such works to be undertaken by the company in order to obtain the above-mentioned ends does not lessen its legal obligation to do whatever may be recognized as its duty, given the circumstances and under the sanction of law.

Source: ASMAI, pos. 75/4, f. 30. Author's translation.

In case of disagreement, disputes will be handled in the manner laid down by Article XVII.

Art. II. The government agrees to pay to the company from May 1, 1898, to April 30, 1910, the annual sum of 400,000 gold francs and from May 1, 1910, to July 16, 1946, 350,000 gold francs, for the maintenance of existing stations, as well as of those which the company may hereafter found.

Art. III. Should the territory of Lugh remain in the Italian zone of influence, or should it in accordance with future treaties pass to another state with Italy retaining the right to maintain a trading station there, the administration of Lugh in the first case, or of the Italian trading station at Lugh in the second case, will, with all its rights and responsibilities, fall upon the company, as in the case of the other stations.

Art. IV. The government will make use of the company and will hand over to it regularly the sum necessary for the payment of the annual subsidies to the sultans of Obbia and of Alula, that is to say, in all 3,600 Maria Theresa thalers, so long as the government is under obligation to the said sultans.

Art. V. The government will apply, as regards the company, Article III of the Anglo-Italian protocol of March 24, 1891 [Equality of treatment between British and Italian subjects and protected persons at Kismayu].

Art. VI. The government agrees to grant to the company free and gratuitous enjoyment of mines with the power of transferring concessions of the same to third persons, although only with the consent of the government if third persons are foreigners.

The enjoyment of mines and the concessions to third persons must not be of longer duration than that of the administration of the company.

The government also agrees to give to the company without payment the power to occupy all lands which at the time the company takes possession are recognized as state domains and all real property of which it may have obtained the use and enjoyment from the sultan of Zanzibar. The company will have the power to give concessions for the use of these lands, for a term not longer than that of its administration, to Italians or to dependent natives resident in the colony. It will have the power, moreover, to give concessions to foreigners so long as the term does not exceed that of its administration and so long as the concession has the previous consent of the government.

The government, with the consent of the company, will have the right to make concessions both to foreigners and to Italians for terms exceeding that of the company's administration.

ART. VII. The company will collect the customs duties for its own account on the basis of existing treaties and existing taxes; it can also levy new taxes or repeal existing ones and reduce customs duties, subject to the approval of the government.

ART. VIII. The products of the territories to which the present convention refers will receive the same customs treatment as those of the Eritrean colony on their importation into the kingdom.

ART IX. The company agrees—a) to fly the national flag; b) to pay to the sultan of Zanzibar the annual rent of 120,000 rupees or whatever lesser sum may be agreed on hereafter; c) to pay the annual subsidies due the sultans of Obbia and of Alula as mentioned in Article IV; d) to maintain in good condition all the buildings received from the government; e) to maintain at least six hundred askaris for the internal security of the colony; f) to administer justice according to the rules in force in the towns and territories conceded to it; g) to apply the general acts of Berlin (February 26, 1885) and of Brussels (July 2, 1890) in regard to [suppression of] the slave trade and trade in arms and spirituous liquors; and h) to operate the postal service in accordance with the conditions laid down by the Postal Union.

ART. X. The government does not contract any obligation to defend the colony from external attacks but reserves to itself full liberty of action to take such steps as it may consider necessary in the public interest.

ART. XI. On request by the government, the company will be obliged either to expel from the colony any Italian or foreigner or to hand over to the government any offender taking refuge there.

ART. XII. The statutes of the company are annexed herewith as an integral part of the present convention.

No changes can be introduced in the said statutes under pain of forfeiture without the prior assent of the foreign minister.

ART. XIII. The government does not assume responsibility of any sort for credit operations made by the company, even in the interest of the colony, and the company in such operations can offer as guarantees only its own private property and its private credit.

ART. XIV. The present convention, which will come into effect on May 1, 1898, will remain in force until July 16, 1946, at which time it will *ipso facto* expire without any need of mutual notification.

The government, moreover, reserves the right to cancel the convention on July 16, 1921, with two years' previous notice, should it wish to exercise its own powers and administer directly the towns and territories subject to the present convention, or should it not feel disposed to continue to exercise its right of option toward the sultan of Zanzibar according to the convention of August 12, 1892.

The power of cancelling the present convention is also given to the company after twelve years from May 1, 1898, with a year's previous notice.

ART. XV. Permanent works constructed at the initiative and expense of the company, of such a nature as to ameliorate the financial condition of the colony, will at the expiration of the contract be accepted by the government and paid for at a set valuation, provided the execution of such works and the plans relating to them had received the previous consent of the government and reserving always to the company its right to cede to third parties those works not accepted by the government.

ART. XVI. Should the government cancel the convention at the end of twenty-three years, as provided for in Article XIV, the company will have a right to compensation, even for works undertaken without the authorization of the government at a valuation calculated at a sum between the expenses of the works in question and the greatest profit shown.

No indemnity will be due from the government if the cancellation of the convention results from an act or fault of the company.

ART. XVII. The value of the works for which compensation may be due will be determined by three arbitrators. Each party will name an arbitrator; these two arbitrators will choose a third; and in the case of disagreement over the choice of the third, the matter will be referred to the president of the Court of Cassation at Rome, where the seat of arbitration will be.

Any question of civil law arising between the government and the company in the execution or interpretation of this convention will also be decided by arbitration.

The judgments of the arbitrators will be arrived at without formality or procedure, and there will be no appeal against them.

ART. XVIII. The company must respect the laws of the state and the treaties in force and other treaties which the government may think fit to conclude or publish.

In the case of disputes, or other difficulties, between the company and the sultan of Zanzibar, or the chiefs of the various tribes, or the English authorities of the neighboring territory, the company must submit to the decision of the foreign minister.

In the case of disagreement between the parties, the arbitrators will determine whether the convention has suffered material alterations by reason of new treaties or by the measures taken as a result of conflicts.

In the case of an affirmative decision, the company will have the right to demand the cancellation of the convention with compensation for the value of the works executed.

Art. XIX. The company's charter will be registered with a tax of 1 lira.

The salaries of the employees of the company resident in the colony will be exempt from income tax.

Art. XX. The company will have the right to withdraw from the government depots, and possibly from those at Massawa, arms and ammunition at cost price which the government may consider strictly necessary for the security of the stations. Beyond this, all trade in arms is forbidden to the company.

Art. XXI. The government will make arrangements to keep a warship on the coast or in the waters of Zanzibar.

Art. XXII. The present convention and the privileges derived from it cannot be transferred by the company to third parties.

Art. XXIII. The present convention will be registered with a tax of 1 lira and will not be valid until approved by law.

G. Mylius	Rudinì
Dr. S. B. Crespi	Visconti Venosta
A. Carminati	Branca
	Luzzatti
	A. Di San Marzano
	A. S. Vimercati

Rome, May 25, 1898

Imports and Exports

(In Millions of Lire)

Year	Imports	Exports	Total	Per Cent of Total Trade with Italy	Customs Revenues
1890–91.....	2.10	4.50 est.	....	....	0.27
1891–92.....	....	....	....	....	0.33
1892–93.....	....	....	....	....	....
1893–94.....	....	....	....	....	0.10
1894–95.....	....	....	....	....	0.11
1895–96.....	....	....	1.83	....	0.12
1896–97.....	1.10	1.15	2.25	....	0.19
1897–98.....	1.54	1.19	2.73	....	0.23
1898–99.....	2.18	1.33	3.51	....	....
1899–1900...	2.35	1.51	3.86	....	....
1900–1901...	1.56	1.82	3.38	....	....
1901–2......	1.94	1.98	3.92	....	....
1902–3......	2.84	2.09	4.93	....	....
1903–4......	2.26	1.90	4.16	....	....
1904–5......	2.32	1.90	4.22	....	....
1905–6......	2.94	2.23	5.17	....	....
1906–7......	4.26	2.08	6.34	....	0.55
1907–8......	2.26	1.29	3.55	....	0.35
1908–9......	2.80	1.56	4.36	....	....
1909–10.....	4.52	1.80	6.32	....	....
1910–11.....	4.29	2.03	6.32	....	....
1911–12.....	....	....	7.58	....	....
1917–18.....	....	....	14.52	....	....
1918–19.....	13.87	6.24	20.12	....	....
1919–20.....	13.76	7.55	21.31	9.3	1.96
1920–21.....	39.41	17.62	57.03	13.2	4.23
1921–22.....	71.11	12.12	83.24	11.6	5.51
1922–23.....	50.96	10.98	61.94	18.7	4.71
1923–24.....	52.95	12.23	65.18	25.3	5.25
1924–25.....	59.40	16.78	76.18	25.5	5.36
1925–26.....	75.71	28.51	104.22	31.7	7.42
1926–27.....	129.44	29.03	158.47	33.3	11.07
1927–28.....	156.24	25.30	181.54	30.5	15.11
1928–29.....	134.15	42.33	176.48	32.3	14.43
1929–30.....	143.90	49.98	193.88	34.3	15.56
1930–31.....	136.12	47.95	184.07	30.1	14.00
1931–32.....	128.78	78.82	207.60	31.3	12.79
1932–33.....	55.54	24.05	79.59	52.4	10.83
1933–34.....	58.66	30.25	88.91	52.6	10.17
1934–35.....	59.19	30.39	89.58	60.4	31.80
1935–36.....	....	....	....	....	69.26
1936–41.....	Not available	....	....	....	....

These figures were gleaned from various official documents in the ASMAI. Unfortunately, the records are far from complete, but the above table will serve the purpose of this study.

APPENDIX FIVE

Agricultural Production

Year	Hectares	Tons	Value in Lire
	A. Production of Sugar		
1921–22......	3	....	....
1922–23......	6	....	....
1923–24......	22	....	....
1924–25......	17	....	....
1925–26......	30	....	....
1926–27......	200	....	....
1927–28......	600	1,161	1,922,988
1928–29......	502	2,226	3,339,300
1929–30......	645	2,398	3,611,700
1930–31......	630	2,298	3,694,764
1931–32......	584	2,035	1,017,600
1932–33......	600	1,991	992,170
1933–34......	660	2,224	1,556,400
	B. Production of Bananas		
1925–26......	45	....	....
1926–27......	53	....	....
1927–28......	253	51	51,200
1928–29......	377	186	186,186
1929–30......	584	725	725,105
1930–31......	1,235	1,781	1,781,486
1931–32......	2,031	5,836	4,494,000
1932–33......	2,644	11,255	10,105,000
1933–34......	3,808	14,421	11,713,840
	C. Production of Cotton		
1921–22......	100	20	49,046
1922–23......	600	230	735,628
1923–24......	1,000	277	1,020,726
1924–25......	1,500	417	6,916,278
1925–26......	2,500	459	9,167,343
1926–27......	3,000	476	4,745,098
1927–28......	5,500	938	9,380,040
1928–29......	7,250	1,259	12,590,520
1929–30......	9,850	850	7,495,915
1930–31......	5,892	901	7,773,614
1931–32......	6,141	1,210	4,250,400
1932–33......	5,222	727	2,522,060
1933–34......	4,859	739	2,264,970

Source: Guido Corni, *Somalia italiana* (Milan: Arte e Storia, 1937), II, 583, 605, 608, 615, 620, 625, 628; figures not available for later years.

Year	Hectares	Tons	Value in Lire
		D. Production of Castor Beans	
1925–26......	73	....	....
1926–27......	193	....	....
1927–28......	18	....	....
1928–29......	37	....	....
1929–30......	715	....	....
1930–31......	3,391	....	....
1931–32......	3,263	....	....
1932–33......	2,467	556	353,470
1933–34......	950	283	245,690
		E. Production of Incense	
1926–27......		229	945,662
1927–28......		664	2,511,070
1928–29......		998	4,538,064
1929–30......		611	2,625,564
1930–31......		889	3,898,875
1931–32......		699	909,740
1932–33......		752	630,270
1933–34......		328	546,430
		F. Exportation of Cowhides	
1921–22......		1,153	6,892,141
1922–23......		725	5,719,020
1923–24......		671	6,171,905
1924–25......		1,118	15,234,531
1925–26......		1,113	12,509,516
1926–27......		1,007	13,879,144
1927–28......		1,549	20,104,922
1928–29......		1,623	18,492,733
1929–30......		1,110	13,730,417
1930–31......		1,015	12,951,815
1931–32......		1,597	....
1932–33......		2,129	6,007,560
1933–34......		1,706	5,525,830

Year		Number	Value in Lire
		G. Exportation of Cattle	
1921–22......		9,582	874,597
1922–23......		4,504	452,624
1923–24......		2,155	261,312
1924–25......		4,631	521,378
1925–26......		10,539	1,332,137
1926–27......		11,958	1,126,434
1927–28......		7,583	858,055
1928–29......		17,922	1,245,680
1929–30......		18,390	2,073,376
1930–31......		18,896	2,217,395
1931–32......		21,329	....
1932–33......		13,993	509,370
1933–34......		5,294	230,420

Administrators of Italian Somalia

I. *The Filonardi Company*
V. Filonardi (head of administration)   May, 1893–July, 1896

II. *Temporary Government Administration*
V. Filonardi (royal commissioner)   July, 1896–Sept., 1896
E. Dulio (royal commissioner)   Sept., 1896–Nov., 1896
E. Dulio (royal commissioner extraordinary)   Nov., 1896–Jan., 1897
E. Dulio (royal civil commissioner) ⎫
G. Sorrentino (royal commissioner ⎬   Jan., 1897–Nov., 1897
  extraordinary) ⎭
E. Dulio (royal civil commissioner)   Nov., 1897–Apr., 1898

III. *The Benadir Company*
E. Dulio (royal commissioner)   Jan., 1898–Dec., 1899
E. Dulio (provisional governor)   Dec., 1899–June, 1901
E. Dulio (governor)   July, 1901–Oct., 1903
E. Cappello ⎫
U. Ferrandi ⎬ (acting governors)   Oct., 1903–Nov., 1903
E. Cappello (acting governor)   Nov., 1903–Dec., 1903
A. Sapelli (provisional governor)   Dec., 1903–Apr., 1904
A. Sapelli (governor)   Apr., 1904–Apr., 1905

IV. *Government Administration: Southern Italian Somalia (Benadir)*
L. Mercatelli (royal commissioner general)   May, 1905–Jan., 1906
A. Sapelli (acting vice-commissioner general)   Jan., 1906–Feb., 1906
G. Cerrina Feroni (acting governor)   Feb., 1906–May, 1907
T. Carletti (royal civil commissioner)   May, 1907–Apr., 1908

V. *The Colony of Italian Somalia*
T. Carletti   Apr., 1908–Dec., 1908
G. Macchioro (acting governor)   Dec., 1908–Apr., 1910
G. De Martino   Apr., 1910–Sept., 1916
G. Cerrina Feroni   Sept., 1916–June, 1920
C. Riveri   June, 1920–Oct., 1923
C. M. De Vecchi di Val Cismon   Oct., 1923–June, 1928
G. Corni   June, 1928–July, 1931
M. Rava   July, 1931–Mar., 1935
R. Graziani   Mar., 1935–May, 1936

VI. Governo *of Somalia*
R. Santini   May, 1936–Dec., 1937
F. S. Caroselli   Dec., 1937–June, 1940

Annotated Bibliography

I. BIBLIOGRAPHICAL AIDS

The best collection of Italian literature on colonialism and Somalia is located at the Istituto Italiano per l'Africa in Rome. The Istituto's collection incorporates the library of the former colonial ministry and that of the former Istituto Coloniale. The Istituto has not yet been able to publish a list of its holdings. The Museum of the Garesa in Mogadishu contains several hundred volumes of materials on Somalia, but it, too, has not published any lists of its holdings, which include many works printed in Somalia. An extensive, but by no means complete, listing of books on Italian colonialism is given in A. Martineau, P. Roussier, and J. Tramond, *Bibliographie d'histoire coloniale, 1900–1930* (Paris: Société de l'Histoire des Colonies françaises, 1932), pp. 558–613. A partial list of works on Somalia, concentrating on agriculture, is contained in *Contributo ad una bibliografia italiana su Eritrea e Somalia* (Florence: Istituto Agronomico, 1953). Other works containing partial bibliographies of Somalia are the *Guide bibliografiche dell'Istituto Coloniale Fascista* (Rome: Istituto Coloniale Fascista, 1928); *Bibliografia dell'Italia d'Oltremare* (Spoleto: Istituto Nazionale per le Relazioni Culturali con l'Estero, 1940); *Raccolta di pubblicazioni coloniali italiane* (Rome: Tipografia della Camera dei Deputati, 1911); D. H. Varley, *A Bibliography of Italian Colonization in Africa* (London: Royal Empire Society, 1936); R. C. Woolbert, "Italian Colonial Expansion in Africa," *Journal of Modern History*, IV (1932), 430–45; and

S. Zanutto, *Pubblicazioni edite dall'amministrazione coloniale e sotto i suoi auspici, 1882–1937* (Rome: Società Anonima Italiana, 1938).

II. SOURCE MATERIAL

A. *Unpublished*

The chief source of unpublished material dealing with Italian colonialism in Somalia is the Archivio Storico dell'ex Ministero dell'Africa Italiana (ASMAI) in Rome. It would have been impossible to write this work without access to the documents contained in these archives. ASMAI contains some eighty thousand documents dealing with all phases of Italian interest and administration in Somalia. The archives are not perfectly preserved, however. During the war they were transferred from Rome to northern Italy, and losses occurred in the various moves from Rome northward. Material on the Fascist period is particularly sparse. Certain documents of the ASMAI were classified as *riservato* ("reserved," or "confidential"), *riservatissimo* ("highly confidential"), and *segreto* ("secret"). The only condition required of me in order to be granted permission to use the archives was that I not quote directly from the secret documents. As the first non-Italian and the first scholar permitted access to these documents on Somalia, I found a vast, highly important collection, including the correspondence of colonial governors and officials with the foreign and colonial ministries, confidential correspondence of the trading companies and exploratory societies with the government in Rome; reports of travelers, explorers, special government investigators, and administrators; special sections of documents on slavery, arms, boundaries, and other colonial questions; copies of diplomatic correspondence; and minutes of cabinet meetings and parliamentary debates.

One limitation was the non-availability of the colonial archives of Somalia. During the British occupation from 1941 to 1950, those documents which the Italian colonial authorities had not destroyed were methodically confiscated and shipped to London, where they are not yet available to scholars.

B. *Published*

It would serve little purpose to give a complete list of the published material on Somalia, since much of it is purely descriptive and some of it was meant as propaganda. I have therefore limited myself to mentioning only the works that were most valuable for this study.

1. Official Sources

Treaties dealing with Italian political penetration into East Africa and Somalia are to be found in E. Hertslet, *The Map of Africa by Treaty* (3d ed., 3 vols.; London: His Majesty's Stationery Office, 1909) and in the *Raccolta dei trattati, dei protocolli . . . relativi all'Africa,* edited by Giacomo Agnesa, head of the Colonial Office. The latter work is a collection of laws, treaties, and protocols for the years 1895–1905.

The official account of the extension of Italian protection over the sultanates and numerous tribes of Somalia and of the leasing of the Benadir ports was published as a *Libro Verde* ("Green Book"), *Documenti diplomatici presentati al Parlamento italiano dal Ministro degli Affari Esteri (Blanc): Somalia italiana (1885–1895)* (Rome: Tipografia della Camera dei Deputati, 1895). Useful for the diplomacy of imperialism, although no real contribution to an understanding of Italian colonialism in East Africa, are the *Documenti diplomatici italiani* (Rome: Liberia dello Stato, 1952——). The Comitato per la Documentazione dell'Opera dell'Italia in Africa has already published eighteen of an anticipated series of twenty volumes purporting to document the work of Italy in Africa, *L'Italia in Africa* (Rome: Istituto Poligrafico dello Stato, 1955——). In general the series gives much detailed information but is superficial in its analysis of Italian colonialism; it is doubtful whether the remaining volumes in the series will be much more than an apologia for Italian colonialism.

Debates on colonial legislation are found in the *Atti Parla-mentari* of the Chamber of Deputies and of the Senate. The debates on Somalia are scattered throughout the numerous volumes of the *Atti*. Debates on colonial matters occupied only a very small part of Parliament's time, except during the crisis following Adowa in 1896. In general, Parliament was not interested in pursuing expansionist policies. A résumé of parliamentary debates, proposed laws, colonial budgets, and pertinent documents is given in the useful volume, *L'Africa italiana al Parlamento nazionale, 1882–1905,* ed. Direzione Centrale degli Affari Coloniali del Ministero degli Affari Esteri (Rome: Tipografia Unione Cooperativa Editrice, 1907). Much of the legislation for the colony was by decree of the king or of the colonial governor; many of these official documents are to be found in the ASMAI. Decrees were published in the *Bollettino Ufficiale della Somalia italiana* (1906–40). Collections of decrees pertaining to Somalia may be found in Carlo Rossetti, *Manuale di legislazione della Somalia italiana* (3 vols.; Rome: Ministero delle Colonie, 1912–14); A. Parpagliolo, *Raccolta dei principali ordinamenti legislativi delle colonie italiane* (2 vols.; Rome: Ministero delle Colonie, 1930–32); and A. Bertola, *Il Regime dei culti nell'Africa italiana* (Bologna: Cappelli, 1939).

Official reports on colonial affairs were submitted to Parliament by the foreign minister, the colonial minister, or the governor of Somalia each year. Most of these annual reports were not published, since there was no government policy of publication. The following reports, which are listed in chronological order, were published:

CARLETTI, T. *Relazione sulla Somalia italiana per l'anno 1907–1908.* Rome: Tipografia della Camera dei Deputati, 1910.

MACCHIORO, G. *Relazione sulla Somalia italiana per l'anno*

1908–1909. Rome: Tipografia della Camera dei Deputati, 1910.

DE MARTINO, G. *Relazione sulla Somalia italiana per l'anno 1910.* Rome: Tipografia della Camera dei Deputati, 1911.

——. *La Somalia italiana nei tre anni del mio governo.* Rome: Tipografia della Camera dei Deputati, 1912.

COLOSIMO, G. *Relazione al Parlamento sulla situazione politica, economica, ed amministrativa delle colonie italiane.* Rome: Tipografia del Senato, 1918.

RIVERI, C. *Relazione annuale sulla situazione generale della colonia, 1920–1921.* Mogadishu: Ufficio del Governo, 1921.

DE VECCHI, C. M. *Relazione sul progetto di bilancio della Somalia italiana per l'esercizio finanziario 1925/26.* Mogadishu: Bettini, 1924.

——. *Relazione sul progetto di bilancio della Somalia italiana per l'esercizio finanziario 1926/27.* Mogadishu: Bettini, 1925.

——. *Relazione sul progetto di bilancio della Somalia italiana per l'esercizio finanziario 1927/28.* Mogadishu: Stamperia della Colonia, 1926.

CORNI, G. *Relazione sulla Somalia italiana per l'esercizio 1928/29.* Mogadishu: Stamperia della Colonia, 1929.

——. *Relazione sulla Somalia italiana per l'esercizio 1929/30.* Mogadishu: Stamperia della Colonia, 1931.

All the above reports contain a certain amount of statistical data, along with a narrative of the colony's development. They also frequently contain a sketch of administrative policy and plans for the future development of the colony.

Important sources for native policy, in addition to the annual reports and the documents in the ASMAI, are two works by E. Bono, who was the resident of Bur Acaba, *Vade Mecum del R. Residente in Somalia* (Mogadishu: Stamperia della Colonia, 1930) and *La Residenza di Bur Hacaba* (Mogadishu: Stamperia della Colonia, 1930). The first was intended as a manual of regulations for local administrators in Somalia; the second is a good description of actual local administrative practices. The occupation and administration of the Jubaland are described in Corrado Zoli, *Relazione generale dell'Alto Commissario per l'Oltre Giuba a S.E. il Principe Pietro Lanza di Scalea, Ministro delle Colonie (Riservato)* (Rome: Arti grafiche, 1926).

Of major importance for the study of the question of slavery in the Benadir are the results of the Benadir Company's investigation. The original report, found in the ASMAI, was published with government approval as *Le Questioni del Benadir: Atti e relazione della Commissione d'inchiesta della Società del Benadir* (Milan: Bellini, 1904), by G. Chiesi and E. Travelli. The report is noteworthy for its frankness and objectivity.

From time to time the foreign ministry or the colonial ministry published monographs on Somalia. Particularly useful is the work by Acting Governor G. Cerrina Feroni, *Benadir* (Rome: Tipografia del Ministero degli Affari Esteri, 1911). Too many of the monographs are purely descriptive; an extreme example is C. Zoli, *Oltre Giuba* (Rome: Arti grafiche, 1927), a work useful only for ethnographers and geographers.

The official history of the colonial accomplishments of Fascism in the first decade of Mussolini's rule is told in Angelo Piccioli, *La Nuova Italia d'Oltremare* (2d ed., 2 vols.; Verona: Mondadori, 1934). The work was commissioned by the colonial ministry.

2. Travel and Exploration

Somalia was never thoroughly explored until long after the Italians assumed control of the territory. Consequently, when the Filonardi Company entered the Benadir, it had to rely for information on the following works:

CRUTTENDEN, C. J. "Report on the Mijjertheyn tribe of Somalis inhabiting the district forming the north east point of Africa," *Transactions of the Bombay Geographical Society*, VII (1846), 111–26.

———. *Memoir of the western or Edoor Tribes inhabiting the Somali coast of north east Africa with the southern branches of the family of Darood resident on the banks of the Webbi Shebeyli, commonly called the River Webbi.* Aden: Bombay Geographical Society, 1848.

DECKEN, C. C. VON DER. *Reisen in Ost-Afrika in den Jahren 1859 bis 1861.* 6 vols. Leipzig and Heidelberg: C. F. Winter'sche Verlagshandlung, 1863.

GUILLAIN, C. *Documents sur l'histoire, la géographie et le commerce de l'Afrique Orientale.* 3 vols. Paris: Arthus Bertrand, 1856.

MILES, S. B. "On the Somali Country," *Proceedings of the Royal Geographic Society,* XVI (1872), 147–57.

RÉVOIL, G. *La Vallée du Darror.* Paris: Challamel, 1882.

The above are all basic works for the background of European penetration of the horn of Africa.

The best accounts of exploration by Italians are the following:

BÒTTEGO, V. *L'Esplorazione del Giuba: Viaggio di scoperta nel cuore d'Africa.* Rome: Società Editrice Nazionale, 1900.

CECCHI, A. *Da Zeila alle frontiere del Caffa.* 3 vols. Rome: Loescher, 1885–87.

ROBECCHI BRICCHETTI, L. *Somalia e Benadir: Viaggio di esplorazione nell'Africa Orientale.* Milan: Carlo Aliprandi, 1899.

STEFANINI, G. *In Somalia: Nite e impressioni di viaggio.* Florence: Le Monnier, 1922.

VANNUTELLI, L., and CITERNI, C. *La Seconda Spedizione Bottego: L'Omo: viaggio nell'Africa Orientale.* Milan: Hoepli, 1899.

3. Memoirs of Officials in Somalia

Many of the governors and other officials stationed in Somalia later wrote acounts of their sojourns in the colony. Unfortunately, several of the most influential officials, Filonardi, Cecchi, and Dulio, did not keep or publish memoirs. The following works were a valuable source of information for the activities and opinions of Italian functionaries in Somalia:

DE VECCHI DI VAL CISMON, C. M. *Orizzonti d'impero: Cinque anni in Somalia.* Milan: Mondadori, 1935.

PÀNTANO, G. *Nel Benadir: La Città di Merca e la regione Bimal.* Livorno: Belforte, 1910.

RAVA, M. *Parole ai Coloniali.* Milan: Mondadori, 1935.

SAPELLI, A. *Memorie d'Africa, 1883–1906.* Bologna: Zanichelli, 1935.

SORRENTINO, G. *Ricordi del Benadir.* Naples: Trani, 1912.

Also of interest is F. Martini, *Diario eritreo* (4 vols.; Florence: Vallechi, 1946).

III. SECONDARY WORKS

A. *Colonialism and the Italian Background*

There are many histories of Italy, but few are completely satisfactory. The tendency all too often has been to stress political developments with little regard for economic and social history. Those works with an economic or social interpretation usually fail to synthesize all the elements of Italian culture into a recognizable description of Italy. Pro- or anti-Fascist sentiment often appears in recent books, precluding objectivity. The best general works on Italy are the following:

1. General Works

CROCE, BENEDETTO. *A History of Italy, 1871–1915.* Trans. C. M. Ady. Oxford: Clarendon Press, 1929.

LÉMONON, ERNEST. *L'Italie économique et sociale, 1861–1912.* Paris, 1913.

MACK SMITH, DENIS. *Italy: A Modern History.* Ann Arbor: University of Michigan Press, 1959. An unequaled history of Italy, heavy on political events, with a good insight into colonialism and the economic problems of Italy.

PINGAUD, ALBERT. *L'Italie depuis 1870.* Paris: Bibliothèque d'histoire et de politique, 1915.

SALVATORELLI, LUIGI. *A Concise History of Italy.* Trans.
B. Miall. New York: Oxford University Press, 1940. A relia-
ble work with extensive bibliography and notes.

SALVATORELLI, LUIGI, and MIRA, GIOVANNI. *Storia d'Italia
nel periodo fascista.* Turin: Einaudi, 1956. An excellent
detailed history and analysis of Fascist Italy.

SPRIGGE, CECIL J. S. *The Development of Modern Italy.* New
Haven, Conn.: Yale University Press, 1944.

TOSTI, AMEDEO. *Italia del nostro tempo.* Milan: Rizzoli, 1956.
A great quantity of information on twentieth-century Italy
embedded in a wordy and dull matrix.

2. Books on Particular Aspects of Italian Colonialism

BRUNIALTI, ATTILIO. *Le Colonie degli Italiani.* Turin: Unione
Tipografico–Editrice Torinese, 1897. An imperialist argues
for political colonies as destinations for Italian emigration.

———. *L'Italia e la questione coloniale.* Milan: Brigola, 1885.
An early work by one of the most outspoken Italian expansionists of the late nineteenth century.

CAIMPENTA, UGO. *L'Italia in Africa.* Milan: Aurora, 1937. An
attempt to identify the Fascist empire with that of ancient
Rome.

CARPI, LEONE. *Delle Colonie e dell'emigrazione italiana al-
l'estero.* 4 vols. Milan, 1874. The first statistical study of
Italian emigration and the basis for the expansionists' argument for colonies as an outlet for surplus population.

DE AGOSTINI, ENRICO. *La Reale Società Geografica Italiana e
la sua opera dalla fondazione ad oggi (1887–1936).* Rome:
Reale Società Geografica Italiana, 1937. The official history
of the Italian Geographic Society.

DE MARCO, ROLAND R. *The Italianization of African Natives:
Government Native Education in the Italian Colonies,
1890–1937.* New York: Teachers College, Columbia University, 1943. A work that reveals how very little the author
knows about Italian educational policy in Somalia.

FEDERZONI, LUIGI. *L'Africa Orientale, Il "Posto al Sole."* Bologna: Zanichelli, 1936. A collection of speeches by an ardent imperialist who advocates Italy's "place in the sun" in East Africa.

GAIBI, A. *Manuale di storia politico-militare delle colonie italiane*. Rome: Ministero della Guerra, 1928. A military history of Italian colonialism, particularly concerned with battles and "martyrs."

GIGLIO, CARLO. *L'Impresa di Massaua (1884–1885)*. Rome: Istituto Italiano per l'Africa, 1955. An excellent history of the events leading to the Italian occupation of Massaua, based entirely on previously unavailable archival material.

HOLLINGSWORTH, L. W. *Zanzibar under the Foreign Office, 1890–1913*. London: Macmillan, 1953.

MACARTNEY, MAXWELL H. H., and CREMONA, PAUL. *Italy's Foreign and Colonial Policy, 1914–1937*. London: Oxford University Press, 1938. Entirely inadequate treatment of Somalia and its place in Italian colonialism.

MÜLLER-JENA, HERBERT. *Die Kolonialpolitik des faschistischen Italien*. Essen: Essener Verlagsanstalt, 1939. Mostly an account of the economic development of Italy's colonies by the Fascist regime.

PESENTI, GUSTAVO. *Le Guerre coloniali*. Bologna: Zanichelli, 1947. A military history of European colonialism with emphasis on Italian military operations in Libya and northeast Africa. Pesenti was in command of the Colonial Troops in Somalia until the invasion of Ethiopia.

SANGIORGIO, G. *Le Colonie italiane in Africa nel passato e nel presente*. Milan: Società d'Esplorazione Commerciale in Africa, 1881.

ZAGHI, CARLO. *P. S. Mancini, l'Africa e il problema del Mediterraneo, 1884–1885*. Rome: Gherardo Casini, 1955. An admirable work that complements the Giglio book mentioned above in this section; also contains new archival material.

B. *Books on Somalia*

Several hundred books have been written about Somalia, but most of them are thin, superficial, merely descriptive, or government propaganda. Although this study was based generally on primary and not secondary sources, the following books were useful in various degrees:

BARILE, R. *Colonizzazione fascista nella Somalia meridionale.* Rome, 1935.

CAROSELLI, FRANCESCO S. *Catalogo del Museo nella Garesa a Mogadiscio.* Mogadishu: Stamperia della Colonia, 1934. A descriptive list of Arabic inscriptions found in Somalia and of documents pertaining to the Filonardi Company.

———. *Ferro e fuoco nella Somalia.* Rome: Arti grafiche, 1931. A monograph on the activities of Muhammad Abdullah Hassan, based on Italian sources and on a critical study of a work by Douglas Jardine (see below).

CASTAGNO, ALPHONSO A. *Somalia.* New York: Carnegie Endowment for International Peace, 1959. A study of the problems of the Italian trusteeship administration in preparing Somalia for independence.

CERULLI, ENRICO. *Somalia: Scritti vari editi ed inediti.* 3 vols. Rome: Istituto Poligrafico dello Stato, 1957–64. A collection of articles by the leading Italian linguist and ethnographer of the Somali.

COLUCCI, M. *Principî di diritto consuetudinario della Somalia italiana meridionale.* Florence: La Voce, 1924. A study of native law in the Benadir.

CORNI, GUIDO. *Somalia italiana.* 2 vols. Milan: Arte e Storia, 1937. A comprehensive survey of Somalia prepared by a former governor; extremely weak historically.

GRAZIANI, RODOLFO. *Il Fronte Sud.* Milan: Mondadori, 1938. A governor and military commander of Somalia gives his account of preparations for the war in Ethiopia, with frequent references to material in the closed archives.

JARDINE, DOUGLAS. *The Mad Mullah of Somaliland.* London: Herbert Jenkins, 1923. An inaccurate semiofficial account of British dealings with Muhammad Abdullah Hassan; valuable in that it presents much of the correspondence between the dervish leader and the British authorities.

KARP, MARK. *The Economics of Trusteeship in Somalia.* Boston: Boston University Press, 1960.

LEFÈVRE, RENATO. *Politica somala.* Bologna: Cappelli, 1933. An acount of how Fascism allegedly settled the problems of Somalia and gave it the promise of a bright future.

LEWIS, I. M. *The Modern History of Somaliland: From Nation to State.* London: Weidenfeld & Nicolson, 1965. An excellent presentation of the Somali background but little attention to Italian colonialism.

———. *A Pastoral Democracy: A Study of Pastoralism and Politics among the Northern Somali of the Horn of Africa.* London: Oxford University Press, 1961.

———. *Peoples of the Horn of Africa: Somali, Afar and Saho.* London: International African Institute, 1955. An excellent ethnographic study of the Somali.

MONDAINI, GENNARO. *La Legislazione coloniale italiana nel suo sviluppo storico e nel suo stato attuale (1881–1940).* 2 vols. Milan: Istituto per gli Studi di Politica Internazionale, 1941. A dry analysis of colonial legislation.

ONOR, ROMOLO. *La Somalia italiana.* Ed. Irene Onor. Turin: Bocca, 1925.

PANKHURST, E. SYLVIA. *Ex-Italian Somaliland.* London: Watts & Co., 1951. A garbled account, violently anti-Italian and indignantly pro-Ethiopian, based on a somewhat untrustworthy use of published sources and on the author's crusading biases.

PESENTI, G. *Le Origini, i primordi, gli sviluppi della Somalia italiana.* Mogadishu: Stamperia della Colonia, 1939.

PIAZZA, GIUSEPPE. *Il Benadir.* Rome: Bontempelli & Invernizzi, 1913.

RIBERA, ALMERICO. *Vita di Antonio Cecchi.* Florence: Vallecchi, 1940. A Fascist glorification of Cecchi, written under the auspices of the Ministry of Italian Africa.

ROBECCHI BRICCHETTI, L. *Dal Benadir: Lettere illustrate alla Società Antischiavista d'Italia.* Milan: La Poligrafica, 1904.

SCASSELLATI-SFORZOLINI, GIUSEPPE. *La Società Agricola Italo-*

Somala in Somalia. Florence: Istituto Agricolo Coloniale Italiano, 1926.

SCHRAMM, P. E. *Deutschland und Uebersee*. Braunschweig: Georg Westermann, 1950. A work containing some information on the activities of German agents in the Juba valley and in the Mijjertein.

TOUVAL, SAADIA. *Somali Nationalism: International Politics in the Drive for Unity in the Horn of Africa*. Cambridge, Mass.: Harvard University Press, 1963.

C. *Articles on Somalia*

ASKEW, WILLIAM C. "The Secret Agreement between France and Italy on Ethiopia, January, 1935," *Journal of Modern History*, XXV (1953), 47–48. An account of the free hand given Italy by France in Ethiopia after the Walwal incident; based on *Francia: Situazione politica nel 1935*, a secret publication of the Italian foreign ministry which is among the captured Italian documents in the National Archives in Washington.

BALDINI, A. "Somalia italiana," *Enciclopedia italiana*, XXXII (1936).

CLIFFORD, H. M. "British Somaliland-Ethiopian Boundary," *Geographic Journal*, XLVII (1936), 289–307.

EX-DIPLOMATICO. "La Politica coloniale dell'Italia," *Nuova Antologia* (November 15, 1884), pp. 316–29.

HESS, R. L. "Italy and Africa: Colonial Ambitions in the First World War," *Journal of African History*, IV (1963), 105–26.

———. "The 'Mad Mullah' and Northern Somalia," *Journal of African History*, V (1964), 415–33.

LEWIS, I. M. "The Somali Conquest of the Horn of Africa," *Journal of African History*, I (1960), 213–30.

MESFIN WOLDE MARIAM. "Background to the Ethio-Somalian Boundary Dispute," *Journal of Modern African Studies*, II (1964), 189–219.

ROSSETTO, CARLO. "La Colonizzazione italiana agricola del Benadir," *L'Italia Coloniale*, I (December, 1900).

ZAGHI, CARLO. "Gli Albori del giornalismo coloniale italiano," *L'Oltremare,* VI (1932), 509–11.

D. *Periodicals*

Annali dell'Africa Italiana. 1938–43. A Fascist propaganda vehicle, important for determining official attitudes.

Atti del Primo Congresso Antischiavista Italiano. Rome: Polo, 1903. The records of a do-good organization, ingenuous and factually inaccurate.

Atti del Primo Congresso di Studi Coloniali. 6 vols. Florence: Centro di Studi Coloniali, 1931. Contains some good reporting on the problems of Somalia.

Oltremare. Rarely objective, usually reflecting official policy.

Rivista delle Colonie. The oldest magazine on colonial affairs. The years before 1923 often contain interesting articles by colonial pioneers.

Somalia d'Oggi. Sponsored by the Italian Trusteeship Administration; stresses Somali history and culture.

E. *Newspapers*

The ASMAI contain a generous sprinkling of newspaper clippings. Among the papers represented and consulted in further detail are the following:

Il Commercio di Milano
Corriere di Napoli
Corriere della Sera (Milan)
Corriere della Somalia (Mogadishu)
Giornale d'Italia (Rome)
Kölnischer Zeitung
Kreuz Zeitung (Berlin)
London Post
London Times
La Nazione (Florence)
La Perseveranza (Milan)
Somali Chronicle (Mogadishu)
La Tribuna di Roma

Index

227